Field Guide to Mushrooms
of Britain and Europe

D0299673

Field Guide to Mushrooms of Britain and Europe

HELMUT AND RENATE GRÜNERT

Consultant Editor: Dr Derek Reid

The publishers would like to thank Mr Michael R. Tennant for translating the original German text, and Dr Derek Reid for adapting the text for the English language.

Illustrations by Fritz Wendler

Front cover photograph: *Lycoperdon* (Peter Wilson, Natural Image)
Back cover photograph: Fly Agaric (Ron Croucher, Nature Photographers)

This edition first published in 1991 by
The Crowood Press Ltd
Ramsbury, Marlborough
Wiltshire SN8 2HR

This impression 1992

© 1984 Mosaik Verlag GmbH, Neumarkter Strasse 18
  8000 München 80, West Germany
© 1991 Revised English Edition, The Crowood Press Ltd.

British Library Cataloguing in Publication Data

Grunert, Helmut
  Field guide to mushrooms of Britain and Europe.
  1. Europe. Mushrooms
  I. Title II. Grunert, Renate III. Pilze. *English*
  589.222094

ISBN 1 85223 592 6

Original title: *Steinbachs Naturführer: Pilze* by Helmut and Renate Grünert

Typeset by Chippendale Type Ltd., Otley, West Yorkshire
Printed and bound by
Times Publishing Group, Singapore.

Contents

Introduction

The problems in identifying fungi, which are familiar to all collectors, lie in the nature of these strange organisms:

(1)   There are so many species of fungi in so many groups that even a trained expert cannot identify on the spot each and every find that may be made.
(2)   The appearance of fungi is extremely variable. Differences caused by the age of the fungus within the same species can appear greater than the differences between various species themselves. In addition, there are variations in habitat and climate which can lead to uncertainty when making an identification.
(3)   The appearance of fruit bodies is heavily dependent on the weather, on seasonal fluctuations, on other environmental influences and on the presence of particular plants. With fungi, no one year is the same as any other. Forecasts concerning the timing and quantity of fungus finds are inherently unreliable.

Most mushroom hunters do not merely have a passion for collecting, they have a quite definite aim: they want to eat what they take home from the woods. This desire is catered for in this book. The most important edible mushrooms have been depicted and native poisonous fungi have been given as thorough a treatment as the useful species.

Damage to the environment caused by man is not only leading to the disappearance of butterflies and wild flowers and the death of trees and forests but is also harming the habitats of many fungi. Whole areas of forests are being stripped near towns by collectors on the continent especially, and the still widespread senseless destruction of poisonous or unknown fungi has contributed to the loss of what were once districts rich in fungi. Our primary interest in mushrooms should go beyond their culinary attractions and become a broader and less selfish understanding.

This book seeks to provide a good starting point for the study of fungi. In the section devoted to identification, numerous species are described, some of them rare, which are neither poisonous nor suitable for the table. It has only been possible to give examples of such fungi, since a comprehensive coverage of all species is not possible in a handy field guide of this kind.

Few species can be identified from a picture alone; a good photograph is, however, indispensible for initial recognition. To do justice to the variable appearance or particular details of a species in many cases two illustrations have been provided alongside the relevant text. When identifying a fungus, however, the beginner in particular should read the descriptive text thoroughly and should look carefully for the various features on the mushroom found.

The division of the species into ten groups follows, and is essentially, the scientific system of classification. The symbols utilized are intended to assist the layman in particular in using the book. The nomenclature, which in the case of fungi is often complex and subject to change, is up to date at the time of publication.

Guide to Symbols

Gill fungi
page 16

Fungi with very
decurrent gills;
gill-type fungi
page 180

Hedgehog
fungi
page 198

Boletes
page 200

Bracket fungi
page 230

Fairy clubs and
coral fungi
page 242

Puff-balls
page 252

Phalloids
page 262

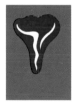

Jelly fungi
page 266

Cup fungi, morels
and others
page 268

 edible

 inedible

 poisonous
or
doubtful

7

Biology of Fungi

Fungi are plants without chlorophyll, organisms which consist of few or many elongated, branching threads (hyphae) with a single nucleus or several nuclei. The hyphal walls are composed chiefly of chitin and cellulose. Chitin is not a constituent of green plants but is an important component of the hard outer exoskeleton of insects.

The fruit bodies of higher fungi, which are the subject of this book, arise from a vegetative mycelium which is mainly underground, in detritus on the soil, in dead or living wood, or under tree bark, in animal droppings, feathers, or insect larvae.

The vegetative hyphae of the fungus, together constitute the mycelium. Generally they grow in the form of threads or webs, but can be found in thick ropes or as lumps of hard material (sclerotium); see also *Grifola umbellata* page 238.

What we recognize and collect as mushrooms are the fruit bodies of the fungi. Classification is based largely on an examination of these fruit bodies. In or on these fruit bodies the spores develop which are the means by which the fungus reproduces.

Many taxonomists are inclined to place fungi alongside the animal and vegetable kingdoms in a kingdom of their own, justified on the basis of their structure, make-up and life cycle (the absence of chlorophyll, for example). In recent times a huge variety of fungi and fungus-like organisms have been classified in a 'natural' system. However, many aspects still await scientific clarification, with the result that this system is subject to constant alteration. Again and again new species are being discovered and described, while others are being shown to be merely varieties of species already described.

New discoveries and classifications therefore also demand a change in the nomenclature. Different scientific names for the same fungus in different works on the subject can baffle the mushroom enthusiast and require constant adaptation.

In this book only those larger fungi with obvious visible fruit bodies are described and depicted. These are the higher fungi or macromycetes. Various claims are made in literature regarding how many such fungi there are, but 3,000–5,000 is a rough guideline for Europe. The macromycetes can be subdivided into three major classes:

(1) *Basidiomycetes*;
(2) *Ascomycetes*;
(3) the slime moulds or *Myxomycetes*.

If *Ascomycetes* or, more rarely, *Basidiomycetes* enter into a symbiotic relationship with algae, then these 'new' organisms are termed 'lichens'.

Many scientists do not consider slime moulds to be fungi but fungus-like animals referred to as *mycetozoa*. Their development differs from that of true fungi. They first form swarm spores, single cells which are propelled by a flagellum. These develop into the swarm cells. Many of these coalesce into a slimy mass which is also able to move slowly, but later congeals. By plasma division the spores appear; they are dust-like when ripe and are then released. *Fuligo septica* (Flowers of Tan)) is included in this book (see page 268) as a representative of numerous species belonging to this class.

In the case of *Ascomycetes* eight spores generally develop inside tube-like sacs called asci which open at the free end or decay completely and release the ripe spores.

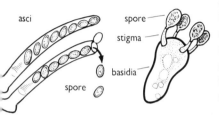

In the case of the *Basidiomycetes*, the spores are borne on spine-like structures at the apex of the club-shaped basidium. The basidium normally displays four such apical spines or sterigmata, on which the spores are formed and from which they are later released. Asci and basidia are only visible under the microscope. The most reliable way of classifying many fruit bodies is therefore by means of a microscopic examination of the spore-producing structures.

The fungi described in this book under groups 1–9 are *Basidiomycetes*, those in group 10 are *Ascomycetes*. *Fuligo septica* (Flowers of Tan) has been placed at the beginning of this section as the only representative of the *Myxomycetes*.

The basidia are situated, in the case of gill and hedgehog fungi, for example, on the sides of the gills or spines; in boletes they line the inside of the tubes and in puff-balls are inside the fruit body in the gleba. The asci of the morels and cup fungi develop on the inside surface of the 'honeycomb' or line the inside of the cup-shaped fruit bodies.

The spores of fungi are vital for the dispersal of the species. The number of spores produced by a fruit body is dependent on the species, but is often many billions. With the naked eye these can be seen only as a dust or powder and not as individual bodies. If pressure is applied to a ripe puff-ball, the spores are released as a powdery cloud. Wind, rain and animals combine in helping to spread the spores. When it is necessary to determine their colour, a microscope slide can be prepared using collected fallen spores. Identifying spore powder colour on the gills is difficult and often impossible, since the gills often have a different colour from that of the spores.

The size of spores is on average between 5 and 15mu (thousandth of a millimetre) and form, colour and structure vary from species to species.

Making spore prints

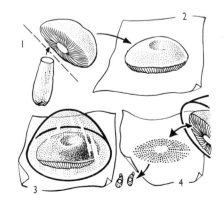

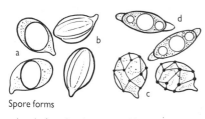

Spore forms

a, b and c from *basidiomycetes*; d from an *ascomycete*

For the taxonomist, spores are a very important aid to identification and they also play a major role in classification of fungi. Even without microscopic examination, the spore powder can assist identification, for example, in distinguishing the white-spored *Amanita* species from the dark purple-brown spored *Agaricus* species.

Reproduction of Basidiomycetes

Some species have spores of differing strains – either positive or negative. A positive or a negative spore germinates and forms a tube which divides forming a collection of segments each with one nucleus. Further division and branching produces a tangled mass of hyphae, spreading in all directions, and is the so-called primary mycelium. To produce new fruit bodies, a positive and a negative system of threads from the same fungus species must meet and fuse to form a so-called secondary mycelium.

In a highly complex process the protoplasm of two segments of opposite strain merge, though remarkably their nuclei do not unite. In other words, after merging, a single segment contains two nuclei. If growth continues by division, then each individual resulting segment contains two nuclei.

Under favourable environmental conditions (substrate, mycorrhizal partner present, nutrients, moisture, warmth) fruit bodies can form on such a mycelium. Only in the special reproductive structures of the fruit body, the basidia, do the nuclei combine and then immediately divide again, generally each passing into one of the four spores, giving two positive and two negative.

Fungal reproduction has only been sketched in a very simplified form here. The individual processes can vary from species to species and from genus to genus.

The Fruit Body

In the case of gill fungi, a small cap first appears which expands in the course of growth, and this can be astonishingly fast. It consists of more or less firm flesh, surrounded by a skin. On this surface skin there can still be remnants of the veil, the *velum universale*, which when present, initially completely encloses the developing fruit body, for example, in species of the genus *Amanita*.

Under the protective cover of the cap is the fertile surface. It takes many forms, for example, gills, ribs, tubes, pores or spines. The cap is borne on a stem, which in some species and genera bears a ring, which may be transitory. This is the remains of a protective membrane, the inner veil or *velum partiale*, which stretches over and protects the fertile layer during growth. As the cap

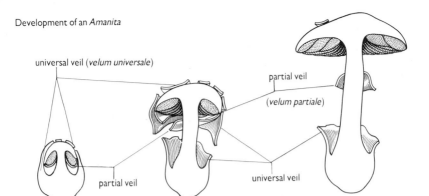

universal veil (*velum universale*)

partial veil

(*velum partiale*)

partial veil

universal veil

expands and flattens, this membrane is ruptured at the edge of the cap and remains hanging from the stem as a ring. In other species, the membrane detaches completely from the stem and remains hanging in fragments on the edge of the cap. In others, it disintegrates completely and vanishes. This inner veil is not, however, always membranous. In the genus *Cortinarius*, a cobweb-like veil is formed, which is later recognizable only as a more or less obvious fibrillose zone on the stem.

In some species the stem emerges from an open, cup-like sac, the volva. Sometimes, though, it is visible just as a collar, or as a ring of warts, marking the remains of the universal veil. Carefully noting such details of structure can help, for example, in the avoidance of fatal poisoning by the Death Cap and others. Only the examination of all the individual features of a fungus can prevent mistakes being made in identification. In many fungi the embryonic fruit body is present enclosed within this universal veil, and when the veil ruptures, the fungus emerges within a few hours, without 'growing' in the true sense of the

word. Rather it simply unfolds its compressed form. The Stinkhorn is a good example of this process. If the 'egg' is cut lengthways, careful examination reveals the perfect fruit body.

Types of Fungus

Mycorrhizal fungi enter into symbiotic associations with particular plants, often trees. In symbiosis, both partners derive benefit from the association and indeed, sometimes they are entirely mutually dependent. In stark contrast is the more or less marked exploitative relationship between the parasite and its host, which can sometimes lead to the death of the host.

Unlike plants containing chlorophyll, fungi do not require light. The forest floor offers many organic nutrients and usually enough moisture to be a favoured habitat of most edible species. Every sort of woodland has its fungi, even dense conifer stands on acid subsoil where few, if any, green plants will grow. Stands of firs, spruces, pines, larches, birches, beeches, oaks or poplars on their own as well as deciduous

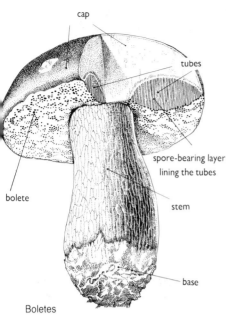

cap

tubes

spore-bearing layer
lining the tubes

bolete

stem

base

Boletes

Fairy Rings

In woods and meadows one occasionally comes across circular groups of fruit bodies. The explanation for this is simple: the fungal mycelium generally grows evenly in all directions. Inside the circle the substrate becomes exhausted, the mycelium finds no nutrients and dies. What remains is a ring of mycelium from which, given good environmental conditions, fruit bodies are produced. Very evenly formed rings often result, which superstition has linked with witches and fairies.

or mixed woodland, all have their own fungal flora. Clearings, woodland margins, trees in open fields, hedges, meadows, pastures, dung, burned areas, rubbish tips, damp, mossy and boggy places, as well as dry lawns and heathland all offer a habitat to fungi. Fungi can even be found in dunes and in the salt-laden, sandy soils of the coast.

As a rule these places have their own communities of above-ground (epigeal) and below-ground (hypogeal) mycorrhizal fungi, saprophytes (which live on decaying matter) and parasitic fungi.

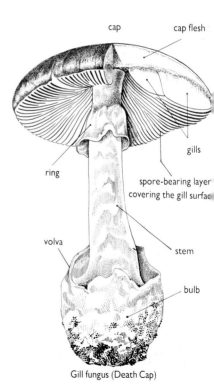

cap

cap flesh

gills

ring

spore-bearing layer
covering the gill surface

volva

stem

bulb

Gill fungus (Death Cap)

On this, and the next two pages the most important terms used in the species descriptions are explained by means of line drawings.

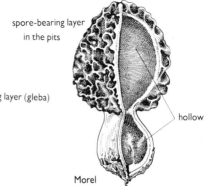

spore-bearing layer in the pits

hollow

Morel

coarse, outer layer (peridium)

spore-bearing layer (gleba)

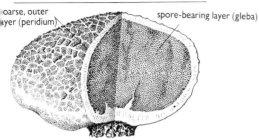

Puff-ball

Stem surface

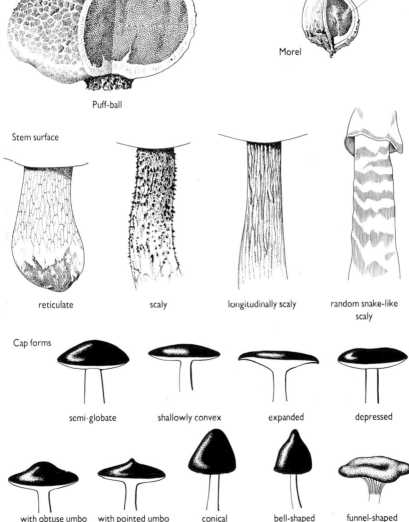

reticulate

scaly

longitudinally scaly

random snake-like scaly

Cap forms

semi-globate

shallowly convex

expanded

depressed

with obtuse umbo

with pointed umbo

conical

bell-shaped

funnel-shaped

CAP SURFACE	CAP EDGE	GILLS

tessellated

undulating

crowded gills

with fibrous scales

lobed

distant gills

imbricate, with scales overlapped like roof tiles

grooved, plicate

forked gills

with warts or remnants of the veil

split

pseudo-gills with transverse veins

GILLS

remote, free

narrowly attached,
adnexed

broadly attached,
adnate

sinuate

attached to
a collar

decurrent

broad gills

narrow gills

gill edge
saw-toothed/undulating

gills easily detached

gills complete

intermediate gills

15

Amanita phalloides   Death Cap

The **cap** up to 15 cm across is initially semi-globular, later flattened. It is slightly greasy, olive-green or yellowish-green with a radially streaky appearance and devoid of patchy scales. There is also a white variety with a matt silky sheen. The **gills** are of variable length, crowded and free, white in colour. The **stem** can be 12–15 cm tall and up to 2.5 cm thick. It is yellowish or greenish with a zig-zag ornament and is sheathed at the base by a white sac-like volva. The pendulous ring is slightly striate and membranous. The **flesh** smells foetid and unpleasant.

Spore print: White.

Distribution: Widespread and locally common. It is usually found beneath oak, but also under beech, rarely in pure coniferous woodland. It prefers richer soils. Grows July–October

Possible confusion: *Tricholoma sejunctum*, page 74, has similar cap surface and colour but lacks both a ring and volva. *A. citrina* (False Death Cap) differs in pale lemon-coloured cap with whitish membranous patches, and by the lack of a freestanding volva. The white form of the Death Cap could be confused with some of the true mushrooms (*Agaricus spp.*), but mushrooms have whitish-grey to pinkish gills when young, later turning dark brown to blackish and their spore-powder is a purple-brown colour.

Edibility: The Death Cap is deadly poisonous, containing more than twenty different poisonous compounds. The chances of survival depends on the amount consumed. 50 g of raw mushroom can be fatal. Medical attention essential!

Amanita citrina   False Death Cap

The 5–10 cm broad **cap** is pale lemon-yellow, more rarely a yellowish-green, semi-globular at first, then flattened; ornamented with large, flat, creamy-white remnants of the veil, which may turn brownish with age. The cap surface is moist to slightly tacky and the cap margin lacks striations. The **gills** are free and white or pale yellowish, soft, crowded, their edges fluffy. The **stem** 10–12 cm high, is 1–1.5 cm thick and the same colour as the cap, bearing a pale yellow, pendulous, smooth ring. The base of the stem is bulbous to globular with an obvious free lip (see illustration). The **flesh** is soft and white and smells of potatoes – an important feature distinguishing it from *A. phalloides*

(Death Cap) and *A. virosa* (Destroying Angel).

Spore print: White.

Distribution: Widespread and common throughout the British Isles. It lives in symbiosis with various decidous trees and conifers. Generally appears August–November.

Possible confusion: The white form, *A. citrina var. alba*, could be mistaken for the white forms of the Death Cap but there are obvious differences in the base of the stem, the Death Cap having an open membranous volva, whereas the False Death Cap has a globular bulb with a small free lip.

Edibility: The mushroom is not poisonous, but is unpalatable.

17

Amanita virosa   Destroying Angel ☠

The **cap** 3–7 (10) cm across, is typically conical to conico-campanulate and usually retains that shape, although older specimens may be broadly convex or expanded, white with a hint of cream becoming instantly yellow with potassium hydroxide (KOH). When moist, sticky; when dry with a dull sheen. **Gills** are free, crowded, and white. The **stem** is up to 15 cm tall, 1–1.5 cm thick, white, slender, fragile, with a floccose–fibrous surface. It bears a pendulous, often imperfect ring, and is sheathed at the base by free saccate volva, which is often deep in the ground. **Flesh** is white, delicate and smells slightly unpleasant.

Spore print: White.

Distribution: Under deciduous trees on acid soils. Rare in the south of Britain, more common and widespread in Scotland where it often grows with birch. Appears June–September/October.

Possible confusion: There is another white species *A. verna* with convex cap and similar to the white form of the Death Cap but unlike both it and *A. virosa* (Destroying Angel) shows no reaction to strong bases (KOH, NaOH). Likes warmth, sometimes appears in spring. It favours oaks and chestnuts and is more common in southern Europe. It, too, is deadly poisonous. Careless collectors might confuse *A. virosa* with young mushrooms (*Agaricus spp.*). The characteristic 'jaunty' cap, the pure white gills, the stem base with the volva usually to one side and the colour of the spore powder are, however, clear distinguishing features.

Edibility: Like the Death Cap it is deadly poisonous.

Amanita echinocephala

The **cap**, initially snow-white, 5–15 cm across, bears numerous small, whitish spines, concentrated mainly at the centre. With age the mushroom begins slowly to take on a mouse-grey or yellowish colour with a slight greenish tinge. When young the edge of the cap has an irregularly fringed appearance. The crowded **gills** of varying length are a good distinguishing feature because of their unusual colour: it ranges from turquoise to sea-green, later from a greyish-yellow to a yellowish green-grey. Just beneath the cap the **stem** bears a conspicuous, striate, pendulous ring, and in old specimens may be up to 16(20) cm tall with a swollen rooting base banded with warts. The colour of the stem is whitish with a hint of yellow or olive-green. The **flesh** is of a similar colour to the gills, but paler. It smells and tastes unpleasant.

Spore print: Greenish.

Distribution: It favours south-facing chalk downland with birch scrub, also beech woods. Appears July–September.

Possible confusion: Often occurs with *A. strobiliformis* which is distinguished by the large thick flat greyish patches on the cap, and the stem covered by snow-like flocci.

Notes: The scientific name comes from the Greek *echinocephalus* meaning 'with a head like a hedgehog'.

18

Amanita muscaria Fly Agaric ☠

The Fly Agaric is certainly one of the best known mushrooms. It can be recognized from afar by its beautiful red or orange-yellow **cap** covered with white pyramidal warts. When young it appears as a small whitish sphere, but soon the cap expands and the veil disrupts, into the characteristic warts, which usually adhere to the surface. The edge of the cap is slightly grooved. The **gills** are always white, crowded and free from the stem. The **stem** is white and bears a conspicuous pendulous ring. Like all the *Amanita* species the Fly Agaric develops within a universal veil, but in this instance it is reduced to a ring of warts on the bulbous base of the stem and does not form a free saccate volva. The **flesh** is odourless and tasteless, with yellowish areas beaneath the cap surface.

Spore print: White.

Distribution: Common under birch on acid soils, rarely with conifers or other deciduous trees. The fruit bodies are formed from July until October.

Possible confusion: *Amanita regalis*, with its umber-coloured cap and contrasting white warts is extremely rare in Britain. It is more common in the northern and eastern spruce forests of Europe. It is equally poisonous.

Edibility: The Fly Agaric is poisonous. Consuming it is rarely fatal, but it can cause serious illness and should be avoided. It has an intoxicating effect.

Notes: The poison is called muscarin after the species name, but it occurs in the mushroom in only very small amounts.

Amanita caesarea Caesar's Mushroom

To many the name *Amanita* conjures up thoughts of the deadly poisonous members of the group, but there are very desirable edible mushrooms, among them this one, unknown in Britain, which is mainly found in southern climes. The **cap** 6–18 cm across, is quickly recognizable from the glowing red or orange colour. In its early stages it is ovoid or convex but soon becomes flattened with distinctly striate margin. The **gills** are crowded, free and of a beautiful golden yellow. The almost cylindrical **stem** is also of this colour and bears a pendulous yellow ring toward the apex, while at its base there is a well-developed white saccate volva. The **flesh** smells and tastes pleasant, although lacking in any particular character.

Spore print: White.

Distribution: Not known in Britain although it does occur in parts of Europe. It prefers acid soils in old deciduous woodland, where it is most likely to be found under oaks and sweet chestnuts. Occasionally it can also be found in coniferous woods. It appears between summer and autumn.

Possible confusion: One might mistake Caesar's Mushroom for the Fly Agaric (*A. muscaria*). The yellow gills and the yellowish stem are the distinctive features; in the Fly Agaric both are white.

Edibility: In countries where it is common it is eagerly sought for its edible qualities.

Notes: Caesar's Mushroom was much sought after in the Ancient World.

Amanita pantherina Panther Cap

The **cap** is up to 10(12) cm across, ochre to brown in colour with many evenly distributed white warts. In old specimens these white veil remnants may be washed off by rain leaving the cap almost naked. The edge is conspicuously striate which is an important feature for identification. The closely crowded **gills** remain white even in age, feel soft, and are free. The **stem** is up to 15 cm tall and white, with a fairly narrow, smooth ring. It is cylindrical with a basal bulb surrounded by a free-standing collar or lip. Occasionally, several bands can be seen above the bulb. The **flesh** has a weak radish-like flavour.

Spore print: White.

Distribution: Widespread throughout the North Temperate Zone. In Britain it can be found in both deciduous and coniferous woods on acid soils but is uncommon. Fruit bodies are formed from July to October.

Possible confusion: There is the *var. abietinum*, which is also poisonous. This is a more compact fungus, virtually lacking the striate edge to the cap and with the warts more diffuse and greyish. It grows in coniferous woods in mountainous regions and in the Alpine foothills. Under some circumstances the Panther Cap might be confused with *A. spissa* or *A. rubescens* (The Blusher). If one takes note of the grey or pinkish-brown veil remnants, the type of volva and colour of the flesh in the base of the stem, confusion should be avoided.

Edibility: The Panther Cap is very poisonous.

Amanita rubescens The Blusher

The **cap** is up to 15 cm across, when it appears broadly convex and displays numerous mealy, dirty white or yellowish patches on a flesh-coloured or reddish background. If the cap surface is peeled the flesh beneath is pink. The white **gills** are crowded and free. With age they often acquire pink flecks. The **stem** is up to 15(18) cm tall, 1–4 cm thick and fleshy. At first it shows only a vague reddish colouration on a white background, but finally it becomes a clear wine-red. Towards the base it is bulbous, with unobtrusive rows of warts. The membranous ring, is white or whitish-pink and striate. If the **flesh** of the Blusher is cut a reddish colour is always visible, especially in the tunnels of insect larvae and at the base of the stem.

Spore print: White.

Distribution: Widespread and common from June/July until October in deciduous and coniferous woodland.

Possible confusion: The cap colour and appearance of the mushroom vary considerably (see photographs). The most important diagnostic features are reddening of the flesh at the base of the stem. It is frequently confused with *A. pantherina* (Panther Cap), which has a smooth ring and a free collar at the base of the stem; and with *A. spissa*, which is greyish under the skin of the cap and does not show any reddening in the flesh. Beginners should in all cases exercise great caution before eating this species.

Edibility: Connoisseurs who eat mushrooms value the Blusher not only because it appears early, but also because it is a good tasty species but after a long period of damp weather it can acquire an unpleasant, earthy taste. It should not be eaten raw.

Amanita spissa

The **cap** of this robust fungus can reach 15 cm in diameter. The grey to brownish surface is covered by many mealy white or greyish patches. Beneath the cap are the crowded white free **gills**, which do not change colour even at maturity. The **stem**, white above and greyish below, can grow to between 10 and 12 cm tall and has a thickened, bulbous base. Around the basal bulb is a row of small warts. The ring placed high on the stem, is persistent and striate. The **flesh** is white, in some forms slightly brown. As a rule it has a mild taste and keeps its firmness even when the mushroom is over-mature, although the smell and taste are sometimes unpleasantly musty and earthy.

Spore print: White.

Distribution: Widespread. It can be found between summer and autumn in coniferous woods, more rarely under deciduous trees.

Possible confusion: Could be confused with young *A. rubescens* (Blusher), although the flesh, stem and cap of the latter show a pinkish-flesh colour; also with the *A. pantherina* (Panther Cap), which has regular remnants of the veil, a free collar at the base of the stem, and striate margin to the cap. However, the last named feature is not always a reliable characteristic.

Edibility: *A. spissa* is edible, but poisonous when raw. When cooked, it often tastes very earthy. If in doubt, it should be avoided because of the danger of confusion.

Notes: *Spissa* means 'thickened squat'.

Amanita porphyria

The **cap** is 4–8(11) cm across, thin-fleshed, purple-brown to greyish-violet in colour, campanulate when young but soon expanded and is occasionally ornamented with membranous grey patches of the veil. The cap surface is dry and silky, the edge non-striate, smooth. The **gills** are free or slightly adnexed, whitish, soft, rather narrow and crowded. The **stem** up to 9 cm tall and 1 cm thick, is whitish or the colour of the cap, sometimes with a patchy zigzag pattern. It bears a pendulous, transient, smooth, whitish or greyish-violet ring. The stem base (see drawing) is round and bulbous with a distinct but poorly developed free volva, sometimes reduced to a rim similar to *A. citrina* (False Death Cap).

The **flesh** is white with a violet hue beneath the cap and soon becomes hollow in the stem. It smells, as does *A. citrina* strongly of sprouting potatoes and tastes of radish.

Spore print: White.

Distribution: *A. porphyria* is uncommon to rare in Britain where it is found in coniferous and deciduous woodland on poor, acid soils. In Europe it appears to have no north-south limit and is found at altitudes of over 1,600m. *A. porphyria* needs moister conditions than its relatives. Fruit bodies appear from July until the end of October.

Possible confusion: If one pays close attention to the colour, distinct free volva or volval rim, the smooth membranous ring, the random pattern on the stem and the potato smell, then confusion is not possible.

Edibility: When raw the fungus is poisonous, and because of its unpleasant smell and taste it is not suitable for eating.

From the limp white volva the fungus rapidly develops to a height of about 10 cm. The light to dark grey **cap** is at first conical or acorn-shaped and gradually broadens out until it is almost flat with a central umbo. The deep striations at the edge of the cap are immediately striking. The **gills** are crowded, free, white and unchanging. The **stem**, which lacks a ring, is up to 12(15) cm tall, tapering upward, gives the impression of a fairly thin and fragile fungus. Its surface has a zigzag pattern and it varies between white and various shades of a dull light grey. The white, **flesh** has a mild taste and no real smell.

Spore print: White.

Distribution: It is found in coniferous and deciduous woodland. It is widespread but much less frequent than *A. fulva* (Tawny Grisette). It fruits from July to October.

Possible confusion: The Grisette is externally similar to both *A. phalloides* (Death Cap) and *A. citrina* (False Death Cap) when inside the universal veil, but is easy to recognize from the base of the stem. In addition the edge of the cap generally bears marked radial grooves. It has no ring and in only a few cases does it bear remnants of the veil on the surface of the cap. Confusion with *A. mairei* or *A. argentea* is not dangerous. The latter is, however, more robust and often bears remnants of the veil on the cap. In any case, it is very rare.

Edibility: Edible, but it is not popular because of its fragility.

The **cap** grows to 3–7 cm across, fleshy, dark reddish-brown or fox-coloured with a paler, deeply grooved edge. At first it is acorn-shaped then expanded and flattened with a low umbo and generally without remnants of the veil. The **gills** are free, whitish, and crowded. The **stem** is 7(12) cm tall and 0.8–1.2 cm thick; whitish or a delicate reddish-brown, with pallid zigzag markings; ring absent. The base of the stem is sheathed by a free sac-like volva which is white outside and red-brown within. The **flesh** is white and later hollow in the stem. It has no particular taste or smell.

Spore print: White.

Distribution: Common and widespread in both coniferous and deciduous woods, favouring acid soils, often in moist, swampy districts. The fruit bodies are formed from June until October.

Possible confusion: The edible *A. crocea* is very similar, but it is more massive and the cap is brighter orange-yellow sometimes covered with remnants of the veil. The stem is pale orange-yellow with a zigzag pattern. It grows in deciduous woodland, especially under birches.

Edibility: Edible. Its fragility means that it has limited value.

Notes: Mycologists recognize about thirteen similar taxa. These are white, grey and various shades of brown, all having approximately the same appearance. In former times almost all of them were classified as variants of *A. vaginata* (Grisette). They have no partial veil and therefore no ring. The universal veil is easily visible at the base of the stem as an open, limp volva. The edge of the cap generally bears very obvious radial grooves. *Fulva* means 'reddish or brownish-yellow'.

Macrolepiota procera   Parasol Mushroom

When young resembles drumsticks, but when fully expanded the **cap** becomes flattened with a small central umbo and may reach a diameter of 25(30) cm. The cap of the Parasol Mushroom bears large conspicuous brown to grey-brown scales on a pale fibrous background. Only the small umbo in the centre remains uniformly brown. The broad **gills** are of varying lengths, crowded, free, and attached to a collar around the stem apex. Initially they are white or pale yellow, becoming brownish when old. The **stem** can be up to 40 cm tall, and have a diameter 1–2(4) cm. It is hollow, fibrous and hard. Towards the base it thickens into an obvious bulb covered with white mycelium. When young the surface is uniformly brown, but later disrupts into snake-like zigzag markings. There is a conspicuous double ring, white on the upper surface and brown below. This can be moved up and down the stem – an important diagnostic feature. The **flesh** is soft, white and has a nutty smell.

Spore print: White.

Distribution: Occasional and widespread from summer into the autumn, at the edge of clearings, woods and paths. It prefers grassy places. Likelihood of confusion: Could be mistaken for *M. rhacodes* (Shaggy Parasol), but the flesh of the latter turns red.

Edibility: The Parasol Mushroom is one of the most delicious edible fungi. Young mushrooms should be left to mature, since they are at their best only when fully expanded.

Notes: Since the stem is so firm, it is advisable to take only the caps. *Procera* means 'slender and tall'.

Macrolepiota rhacodes   Shaggy Parasol

The **cap** up to 15 cm across, is covered by many shaggy and rather coarse brown scales on a paler fibrous background. When young, the mushrooms resemble small drumsticks and even when mature they do not expand as much as the Parasol. The cap also retains its almost hemispherical if not somewhat expanded shape, with an inconspicuous umbo. The **gills** are of varying lengths, crowded and free, and when bruised take on a distinct reddish hue. Initially they are white but they become increasingly brown with age and sometimes develop a darker edge. The **stem** may be up to 15 cm tall and has a large basal bulb. It is almost smooth, whitish to ochre-coloured when older, and lacks markings. It bears a white double ring which is movable. At the slightest bruising, the **flesh** turns a vivid reddish-saffron after about 30 seconds.

Spore print: White.

Distribution: Common and widespread in coniferous and deciduous woods as well as in shrubberies.

Possible confusion: There is also a large, fleshy parasol-type fungus which occurs on humus-rich, well-manured soils in parks and gardens. It has a stem with a massive, roundish, darker marginate bulb. The flesh of this taxon: *M. rhacodes var. hortensis* becomes rapidly salmon-coloured. The identity of this taxon has not been definitely established. It is said to be poisonous.

Edibility: Edible.

Notes: *Rhacodes* means 'with a ragged appearance'.

29

Lepiota aspera

When young, the **cap** is bell-shaped, but expands and is finally flat. It reaches 12(15) cm across, is rust or clay-brown and covered with striking ochre to dark brown sharp conical warts. The **gills** are free, white, often forked, fairly thin and crowded, with an eroded edge. The **stem** reaches 12 cm in height, 1–2cm in thickness and is whitish. Below the pendulous, membranous, fibrous ring the stem is generally covered with warts of the same colour as those on the cap. The stem is cylindrical, the lower part somewhat bulbous. The **flesh** is white and has a very unpleasant taste and smell which is reminiscent of the Earth Balls (*Scleroderma spp.*)

Spore print: White.

Distribution: This beautiful fungus is found in deciduous woodland, favouring thick undergrowth on the edge of paths. It appears from August until October.

Possible confusion: There are a number of species with obvious conical warts or pointed scales with a more or less similar appearance such as *L. hystrix* and *L. echinacea*. These fungi are, however, generally smaller. Identification requires experience, and reference to specialist literature and a microscope.

Edibility: Because of its revolting smell and taste, *L. aspera* is considered inedible.

Notes: *L. aspera*, together with other species having warts formed of rounded cells, is now often placed in the genus *Cystolepiota*.

Lepiota clypeolaria

The initially ovoid **cap** reaches a diameter of 4–8 cm, but becomes shallowly bell-shaped, retaining an obvious umbo in the centre of the cap. The whitish surface is covered by innumerable minute yellow-brown to brown granular scales, contrasting with the whitish background. The centre is darker and smooth. Remnants of the veil hang from the margin of the cap even when mature. The white to cream-coloured **gills** are free, distant and of variable length. The **stem** up to 8 cm long and only 0.4–1 cm thick, is white and floccose beneath the fluffy ring, which is not always distinguishable although its position is generally obvious. The **flesh** is white, soft, with a fruity smell and a sweetish taste.

Spore print: White.

Distribution: Uncommon, chiefly in southeast England. Late summer and autumn in deciduous and coniferous woodland.

Possible confusion: *L. clypeolaria* can be confused with the following species: *L. ventriosospora* is more brightly coloured in shades of yellow-brown; *L. ignivolvata* turns a fiery saffron-orange colour at the base of the stem slowly as it dries, quickly when bruised. Neither species is common.

Edibility: The fungus is not poisonous, but it is not edible.

Notes: *Clypeus* means 'round shield', and the cap with its blunt umbo is reminiscent of just that.

Lepiota cristata

The **cap**, which reaches a diameter of only 3–4 cm, is initially conical but becomes flattened with a prominent boss or umbo at the centre. This is an intense reddish-brown or dark ochre colour, causing it to contrast with the white surface flecked with light ochre scales. The whitish **gills** are free from the stem, and crowded. The slender, cylindrical, hollow **stem** reaches a height of 4–6 cm and a diameter of 0.8 cm and its white surface may show a slight pink colouration towards the base. In younger specimens there is a well developed membranous ring but this is transitory and is often quickly lost. When the white **flesh** is cut it gives off a strong, unpleasant smell, reminiscent of Earth Balls (*Scleroderma spp.*).

Spore print: White.

Distribution: Common and widespread. It is found alongside grassy paths often amongst nettles, etc, in gardens, in thickets and all types of woodland. It usually grows in groups, summer and autumn.

Possible confusion: It could be taken for *L. clypeolaria*, but this is more robust, paler and lacks the dark central disc, the stem is also conspicuously woolly. *L. helveola*, which can cause serious poisoning, is rare. It has reddish flesh, and darker vinaceous-brown concentrically arranged scales on a whitish background.

Edibility: Poisonous.

Notes: *Cristata* means 'having a crest'.

Melanophyllum echinatum

The **cap** is 10–30 mm across, hemispherical or bell-shaped, and when old expanded with a blunt umbo. The upper surface is dry, mealy-granular, appearing powdery when older, fringed at the edge with remnants of the veil. Colour varies from brownish wine-red through dirty grey-brown to very dark brown with olive-coloured coating. The **stem** is of a similar colour, evenly tubular, 20–40 mm long and 2–4 mm thick, carmine-red at the top and dark brown with a mealy-granular covering below. It has a transient, flaky, membranous ring. The **gills** are free, at first dark pink, later blood-red to brownish wine-red. The thin **flesh** appears whitish in the cap, reddish in the stem, darker towards the base. It smells fruity or strongly of raddishes and has a mild taste.

Spore print: Initially olive-grey, later reddish.

Distribution: Widespread but rare in Britain. In Europe from Spain and Italy to Sweden, but the species is widely scattered and localized, appearing sporadically. Fruits from late June until early October. It has a preference for damp woodland, for sodden clayey soils, and likes to grow under nettles and rank vegetation and in moist places where there has been fire, by the edge of paths, and in greenhouses.

Edibility: The fungus is inedible.

Notes: *M. echinatum* has a relative, *M. eyrei*, which is even less frequent. It has blue-green gills, while cap and stem are olive-brown to creamy-brown. *Echinatum* means 'prickly like a hedgehog'. This fungus is now often cited under the name *Melanophyllum haematospermum*.

Cystoderma amianthinum

The **cap** 2–4(5) cm in diameter, is at first campanulate then broadly campanulate with a central umbo. The edge remains slightly inrolled and is fringed with remnants of the veil. The bright ochreous-yellow cap, darker in the centre, is powdery or thickly coated with tiny mealy-granular scales. The **gills** are of varying length, crowded and adnexed to the stem. Their colour varies from milky-white to cream. The fragile-looking **stem** up to 6 cm tall is cylindrical, hollow and coloured like the cap. On the upper portion there is a small, transient ring, below which the surface is granular-scaly. The **flesh** is yellowish, soft in the cap, coarser in the stem, and smells unpleasantly earthy.
Spore print: White.
Distribution: Not uncommon on acid soils in heathy places, and coniferous woods. It appears from late summer to autumn.

Possible confusion: There is a group of similar, more or less obviously ochre-coloured species of *Cystoderma*.
Edibility: These fungi are all inedible. They are not, however, known to be poisonous.
Notes: The photographs show the rich variation of the species, including the form *rugoso-reticulatum*, with its radially wrinkled cap. The scientific name *amianthinus* means 'immaculate' and comes from *amiantos*, 'which can be separated into the finest of fibres'.

Cystoderma carcharias

The **cap**, 2–6 cm across, is broadly convex or conical with an umbo, flesh-coloured, buff, or whitish with granular or mealy surface. The edge of the cap is fringed with velar remnants. The white to pallid **gills** are adnexed, almost crowded, interspersed with shorter intermediate gills. The **stem**, which grows to 7 cm in length and 0.8 cm in diameter, is smooth and white above the ring, but below it is coloured like the cap and has a granular, scaly surface. The membranous ring is funnel-shaped, smooth and white above, greyish below. The **flesh** is pale and has an unpleasant earthy smell. It has a very unpleasant taste.
Spore print: White.
Distribution: Rare in the south, less so in the Scottish Highlands where it is found on acid soil. This fungus is widespread in the northern hemisphere in heathy places, often with conifers, and especially spruce.

The fruit bodies are formed from September to November.
Possible confusion: Distinguishable from most allied species by colour.
Edibility: Its smell and taste make it totally inedible.
Notes: Currently the genus *Cystoderma* has around a dozen or so species. They are mostly *saprophytes*, living on decaying matter, but some of them appear to enter into a symbiosis with particular species of tree. They are mostly fairly small fungi with a cap diameter of 2–6 cm, rarely up to 15 cm. Cap and stem have a mealy-granular surface and the latter often bears an erect ring. The gills are adnexed. *Carcharias* means 'coarse, with a rough surface'.

Gill Fungi

35

Agaricus spissicaulis ←●

The **cap** is 5–8 cm across, initially hemispherical but quickly expands to become almost flat with an inrolled margin. The colour is whitish flecked with yellow and ornamented with yellow-grey scales. When touched it bruises yellow. The irregular **gills** are initially wine-red or flesh-red, later chocolate to dark brown, with a white edge. The **stem** is clavate and squat and bears an apical membranous white ring, which can be peeled upwards. The whitish **flesh**, thick in the cap, has a vague smell of bitter almonds and when cut it changes to a pale greyish-red.

Spore print: Dark brown.
Distribution: Rare. From July in meadows, parks and pastures, on chalky soils and in dry grass and especially near the coast.
Possible confusion: This mushroom can be confused with many *Agaricus* species and their precise identification requires specialist literature and use of a microscope. *A. spissicaulis* is probably identical with *A. maskae*.
Edibility: Edible, but of poor quality.
Notes: With all white or pale mushrooms the similarity with *Amanita virosa* (Destroying Angel) must always be borne in mind. The latter has a different stature, a sac-like volva at the base of the stem and a white spore powder. *Spissicaulis* means 'thick, squat'.

Agaricus campestris   Field Mushroom ←●

The **cap** up to 10 cm in diameter is at first hemispherical but soon expands to become almost flat. The surface is strikingly white, sometimes disrupted into white or brown, fibrous scales. **Gill** colour changes from an initial pale pink to the characteristic chocolate-brown and finally becomes almost black. This feature is important to ensure that there is no confusion with *Amanita phalloides* (Death Cap). The **stem**, with a diameter of at most 2 cm, tapers downwards and bears a poorly developed apical ring which may be reduced to a mere frill. The **flesh** is white, but turns slightly reddish when cut.

Spore print: Purple-brown.
Distribution: Less common than formerly, it prefers meadows and pastures, particularly those which are manured by horses. Usually appears in groups or rings from early summer until autumn, especially when rain follows a dry period.

Possible confusion: The highly poisonous *Amanita phalloides* (Death Cap) has gills of a pure white, never pink to dark brown! In addition, true mushrooms lack a sac-like volva at the base of the stem. Confusion with other mushrooms is less serious, since apart from *A. xanthodermus* (Yellow Stainer) and its allies with characteristic smell of carbolic or ink and intense yellow staining when bruised, they are all edible.
Edibility: Edible.
Notes: Recently there have been a number of reports that the heavy metal content (lead and cadmium) has increased in some varieties of mushroom. In some countries there is a recommended limit to the amount to wild mushrooms consumed per head per week.

Agaricus xanthoderma Yellow Stainer

The **cap**, up to 15 cm across, which is initially hemispherical, becomes flattened, has thin flesh and a similar white colour to that of the *A. campestris* (Field Mushroom). It is usually smooth, and only occasionally develops a slightly scaly surface. Some specimens may have a greyish or brownish tint. When rubbed the surface bruises a vivid egg-yellow. The **gills** start pink, and then become chocolate-brown. The slender **stem** up to 15 cm tall, with its well-developed spreading white, membranous ring, has a bulbous base, which likewise turns chrome-yellow when bruised. The **flesh** smells unpleasantly of ink, sweat or carbolic, though it can be unobtrusive.

Spore print: Purple-brown.

Distribution: Very common in garden shrubberies, under trees in parks and cemeteries, and in woodland. From early summer to autumn.

Possible confusion: It is very similar in appearance to both the Field Mushroom and especially the Horse Mushroom. However, when the base of the Yellow Stainer is cut, the chrome-yellow colour which gives it its name is immediately evident.

Edibility: The Yellow Stainer causes severe stomach upsets and is regarded as poisonous.

Notes: It is best to avoid all mushrooms which stain yellow and smell of carbolic, many of these have caps ornamented with fine black or brown scales. *Xanthoderma* means 'yellow-skinned'.

Agaricus arvensis Horse Mushroom

The white, silky **cap**, which becomes yellowish, can reach a diameter of almost 20 cm. When young it is hemispherical, but expands to broadly convex. The colour of the **gills** passes through a series of changes: initially greyish, then pink or flesh-coloured and finally dark brown. The slender **stem**, up to 10 cm tall, has an apical membranous two-layered ring of which the lower splits radially like spokes of a wheel. The white **flesh** has a marked smell of aniseed.

Spore print: Purple-brown.

Distribution: This mushroom prefers open sunny situations such as downland, meadows, pastures, parks, etc. where it often grows in large fairy rings. It fruits from early summer to autumn.

Possible confusion: Formerly *A. arvensis* was much confused with the very similar *A. nivescens* from which it can only be distinguished after an examination of its spores under the micrcoscope. It can be confused with the poisonous *Amanita virosa* (Destroying Angel) which always, however, has pure white gills and a sac-like volva at the base of the stem.

Edibility: Many gourmets prize this mushroom even more than the Field Mushroom for its pleasant flavour of aniseed. Some of this characteristic flavour is lost in cooking.

Notes: *Arvensis* means 'growing in fields'.

The pure white **cap**, at first hemispherical, later campanulate or convex and up to 12(14) cm across, may have a slight blunt umbo. The surface is smooth, and bruises yellowish when roughly handled. The **gills** are free and very crowded, initially pale they become flesh grey, then dark red-brown to dark brown or blackish. The **stem** grows to 12 cm and is 0.8–2 cm thick, cylindrical, becomes somewhat narrower towards the apex and has an abruptly bulbous base; it is silky-fibrous above the ring, which is thin, pendulous and fringed on the underside with warts. The white **flesh** is very thin in the cap, often hollow in the stem. It smells pleasantly of aniseed.

Spore print: Purple-brown.

Distribution: *A. abruptibulbus* is very widespread and common and grows in deciduous woodland or among spruces, preferring grassy patches among fallen needles, from summer to late autumn.

Possible confusion: When the fungus is still young, closed and dome-shaped, there is a strong similarity with *A. virosa* (Destroying Angel). This latter is, however, pure white with a sheen, usually feels slippery, and its cap does not turn yellow when rubbed as does that of *A. abruptibulbus*. The Destroying Angel has a sac-like volva at the base of the stem. The edible *A. silvicola* (Wood Mushroom) is very similar, but confusion with this mushroom would present no risk, since it, too, is edible.

Edibility: A good table mushroom, the aniseed smell is not to everyone's liking.

Notes: *Abruptibulbus* means 'abruptly bulbous'.

Agaricus silvicola   **Wood Mushroom**

The **cap** barely reaches a diameter of 6–8(12) cm and has very thin flesh. When young, it has the shape of a drumstick. Later, the cap becomes flattened. The surface is smooth and creamy-white but yellowish patches are not uncommon especially if the fungus is roughly handled. The free **gills** are initially pink or flesh-coloured, gradually becoming deep chocolate-brown. The hollow **stem** is strikingly slender and grows to 8 cm at most; it is cylindrical with a slightly bulbous base, similar to *A. abruptibulbus*. It cannot, however, be confused with the true sheathing volva of *Amanita virosa* (Destroying Angel). The membranous apical ring is large and pendulous and often collapses onto the stem. The **flesh** smells even more strongly of aniseed than does that of *A. arvensis* (Horse Mushroom).

Spore print: Purple-brown.

Distribution: Occasional in both deciduous and coniferous woodland from summer into autumn.

Possible confusion: The only confusion which could have fatal results is that with *Amanita phalloides* (Death Cap) or *A. virosa* (Destroying Angel), but these never have pink or choclate brown gills. Confusion with *A. xanthodermus* Yellow Stainer is improbable, because the latter has such a striking colour change when bruised and it also possesses a different smell.

Edibility: The Wood Mushroom is a really spicy edible mushroom with a pleasant taste of aniseed.

Notes: *Silvicola* means 'living in woods'.

Agaricus silvaticus

The **cap** to 10 cm in diameter is at first hemispherical but becomes flattened with age. The surface is densely covered with prominent ochre to dark brown, fibrous scales. The free **gills** are initially pale, but not pure white, and they gradually redden until they finally become chocolate-brown. The slender **stem** to 12 cm tall, is whitish, occasionally slightly scaly, but turns red when touched, as does the **flesh** of the cap. The base of the stem is clavate or slightly bulbous, and bears a pendulous apical-membranous ring which is actually white but often appears dark brown from the falling spores.

Spore print: Purple-brown.

Distribution: Widespread and common in deciduous and coniferous woodland. From summer to autumn.

Possible confusion: There is one unpleasant mushroom, the poisonous *A. placomyces*, with which confusion really should not arise. Its cap appears as if sprinkled with blackish powder and unlike *A. silvaticus* it bruises yellow when handled. Confusion with such similar-looking mushrooms as *A. haemorrhoidarius* and *A. langei* present no danger; separation depends on a study of their micro-characteristics.

Edibility: A good edible mushroom.

Notes: *A. silvaticus* is one of a group of mushrooms which stain red, grow in woodland and are sometimes hard to tell apart. *A. silvaticus var. pallens*, has a paler cap with less distinct scales, and rather larger spores. It also turns a less intense red. *Silvaticus* means 'belonging to the forest'.

Agaricus langei

Initially hemispherical the **cap** can occasionally reach a diameter of 15 cm but is usually much smaller. The surface is entirely covered by broad fibrous rust-brown scales. Its flesh reddens when cut, especially at the interphase between flesh and surface and between flesh and gills. The **gills** are free, pink at first and then become chocolate-brown and finally brownish-black. The **stem**, too, can be quite massive, sometimes reaching a height of 12 cm, with an apical pendulous ring. The white **flesh** of the stem immediately turns blood-red when cut, and has a 'typical mushroom' smell.

Spore print: Purple-brown.

Distribution: Occasional and wide-spread. The fruit bodies are most often found among conifers on lime-rich soils between August and October. It also occurs less frequently among deciduous trees. Here it tends to be replaced by *A. haemorrhoidarius*.

Possible confusion: Because of its distinctive fibrous scales and its size, it can hardly be confused with *A. silvaticus*, which has smaller spores. Such confusion would anyway present no danger.

Edibility: *A. langei* is considered to be a good edible mushroom.

Notes: Experts distinguish a number of reddening mushrooms, white to brown in colour with more or less fibrous scales, including their variants, which grow in various habitats. None are poisonous. The species name *langei* is in honour of the Danish mycologist J. E. Lange.

43

Hygrocybe punicea Crimson Wax Cap ✦

The **cap**, which grows to 14 cm across, is bell-shaped with inrolled margin and a blunt umbo. It is initially scarlet or blood-red, fading to orange-red and has a moist greasy surface. The **gills**, narrowly adnexed or almost free, swollen, thick and widely spaced, are yellow-orange, and often red at the base. The **stem** is 6–10 cm tall and 0.8–2.5 cm thick, cylindrical, but sometimes flattened with vertical furrows, narrowed at the base, dry, hollow and coloured like the cap or paler. The **flesh** is whitish, otherwise the colour of the stem.

Spore print: White.

Distribution: Uncommon but widespread. This fungus grows mainly in autumn in damp meadows.

Possible confusion: Possibly with *H. coccinea* (Scarlet Wax Cap), but the latter is smaller and has broadly adnate and toothed gills.

Edibility: Edible.

Notes: The *hygrocybes*, of which there are many species, are mostly small, thin-fleshed and very colourful grassland fungi. Some species are poisonous. The Crimson Wax Cap is the largest species of the genus. The scientific name *punicea* means 'Punic, Phoenician' and thus 'purple, scarlet'.

Hygrocybe coccinea Scarlet Wax Cap ✦

This fungus has an initially hemispherical **cap** with a diameter of 2–6 cm but it gradually becomes campanulate. The surface feels slightly greasy when moist but in dry conditions this is less noticeable. It is cherry-red to blood-red and even when the mature fungus fades, the edge of the cap remains an intense red. The **gills**, broadly adnate, sometimes toothed are distant, orange to blood-red, with the edge often yellowish. The surface of the **stem** is also a vivid red colour, but later may fade to a paler orange. The stem itself often appears slightly compressed and is hollow and smooth. Towards the base it becomes increasingly yellowish. Even the **flesh** has the glowing colouration of the cap and stem. It is watery and fragile.

Spore print: White.

Distribution: Widespread, occasional. Principally in damp grassland. Fruit bodies can be found from September to October.

Possible confusion: *H. punicea* (Crimson Wax Cap) is very similar, but grows considerably larger.

Edibility: Edible.

Notes: *Coccinea* means 'scarlet-coloured'.

Hygrocybe conica   Conical Blackening Wax Cap

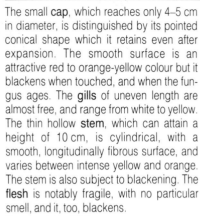

The small **cap**, which reaches only 4–5 cm in diameter, is distinguished by its pointed conical shape which it retains even after expansion. The smooth surface is an attractive red to orange-yellow colour but it blackens when touched, and when the fungus ages. The **gills** of uneven length are almost free, and range from white to yellow. The thin hollow **stem**, which can attain a height of 10 cm, is cylindrical, with a smooth, longitudinally fibrous surface, and varies between intense yellow and orange. The stem is also subject to blackening. The **flesh** is notably fragile, with no particular smell, and it, too, blackens.

Spore print: White.

Distribution: Widespread and common in meadows, damp pastures and downland. It fruits from summer to autumn.

Possible confusion: The brilliant colouration makes this fungus easy to recognize.

It is very similar to *H. nigrescens*, though the latter has a bluntly conical cap and a rather thicker stem, as well as being larger, but final identification must be made with the microscope: the basidia of Conical Blackening Wax Cap bear two to four spores, those of *H. nigrescens* only four.

Edibility: It is not known exactly how poisonous it is, but it causes digestive disorders. Under no circumstances should it find its way into the collector's basket.

Notes: *Conica* means 'cone-shaped'.

Hygrocybe psittacina   Parrot Wax Cap

The **cap**, 1–4 cm across, is initially bell-shaped then expanded, with a central umbo, finally often with upturned margin. When young and in damp weather it is very slimy or glutinous, translucent, striate, but shiny when dry. The colour varies greatly. When young it is either entirely or in part dark or olive-green becoming yellow to orange or even flesh-red, but eventually fading. The **gills** are adnate, thick, distant, yellowish-green, becoming more yellowish toward the edge. The smooth, slippery, slender **stem**, 3–7 cm long, is hollow, generally of even thickness (2–4 mm), sometimes compressed at the base varying from blue-green at the apex, to yellow or orange below. The greenish **flesh** is watery, fragile and both odourless and tasteless.

Spore print: White.

Distribution: Widespread and common.

The Parrot Wax Cap grows from August until October, often in large numbers in short turf or grassland, such as lawns.

Possible confusion: Usually the Parrot Wax Cap is easy to recognize from the green colour and glutinous nature of both cap and stem. However, specimens with only slight green colouration can be mistaken for *H. laeta*, but this has clearly decurrent gills. Old, faded fruit bodies cannot always be distinguished in the field from other similarly coloured *Hygrocybes*.

Edibility: Not poisonous.

Notes: *Psittacina* means 'pertaining to parrots'.

Hygrophorus pudorinus

One of the largest and most beautiful of the *Hygrophoraceae*. The **cap** up to 20 cm diameter is extremely fleshy, at first almost spherical it quickly expands and on maturity is flattened with a slight central depression. The smooth surface feels moist or greasy to the touch, and varies from pale to intense pinkish-orange, with the centre usually darker. The slightly paler cap margin is inrolled. The **gills** are adnate or slightly decurrent, with a salmon-pink tint especially towards the edge of the cap. The **stem** reaches a height of 12 cm and a diameter of 3 cm, and when moist is slightly slimy and the same colour as the cap, yellow and narrowed at the base. The **flesh** is a delicate orange in the cap, white in the stem and yellow at the base.

Spore print: White.

Distribution: Very rare and little known in the British Isles. It is found under conifers from August to November.

Possible confusion: Confusion with *H. poetarum* is possible but this is another very rare and little known fungus in Britain. Is rare in Germany. Both fungi look very similar, but *H. poetarum* grows in beech woods and smells pleasantly fruity. It is said to be edible.

Edibility: *H. pudorinus* should be avoided not only because of its turpentine flavour, but also because of its rarity.

Notes: *Pudorinus* means 'blushing with shame'.

Hygrophorus russula

The robust fleshy **cap**, 7–14 cm in diameter, is at first semi-globate, but becomes flattened with age. The background colour is pale pinkish or flesh-coloured to purple-red finely spotted with intense colouration in places. The **gills** are sinuate and slightly decurrent. Initially white, they become pinkish and speckled with vinaceous brown or rosy-purple with age. The **stem**, more or less cylindrical and 1–2 cm thick, reaches a height of 6–8(12) cm, is white and mealy above, but bears many small, reddish patches in the lower portion. The **flesh** is white, vaguely reddish in places, odourless and mild.

Spore print: White.

Distribution: Very rare and little known in Britain. It is found only under deciduous trees, especially oak. It appears from summer to autumn. In Europe it would seem to be a warmth-loving species, which becomes increasingly rare to the north.

Possible confusion: Confusion with the similar-looking *H. erubescens*, which grows in spruce woods on limestone, and has a whitish cap washed with, or spotted with a purple-pink colour. Very rare in Britain. *H. purpurascens* has a transitory ring and its gills are edged with red. It is unknown in Britain.

Edibility: An edible fungus.

Notes: *Russula* means 'reddish'.

Gill Fungi

49

Hygrophorus chrysodon

The moist, viscid **cap**, up to 7 cm across, is whitish with bright yellow woolly scales at the margin. The **gills** are adnate to decurrent, white, often with a yellow tinge at their edge. The **stem**, up to 6 cm tall and 1.5 cm thick, is white with the apex dotted with small yellow scales. The **flesh** is white beneath the cap cuticle, yellowing in places, juicy, mild and odourless.

Spore print: White.

Distribution: A lime-loving species found in deciduous woodland with oak and beech, from August to November. It is occasional, but widespread in southern England and especially in suitable woods on the chalk downs of the south-east.

Possible confusion: Unlikely to be confused with other fungi. The characteristic yellow dotting at the apex of the stem and on the edge of the cap make for easy identification.

Edibility: *H. chrysodon* is an edible fungus, but unfortunately often infested with maggots.

Notes: In literature two further variants are named, *var. leucodon* with white dots on the stem and also *var. incarnatum* with partly flesh-coloured gills and flesh which turns pink. There are close family resemblances between the genus *Hygrophorus* and the genus *Tricholoma*. Species belonging to the former have a slimy cap and stem although the stem can be dry. The gills are generally decurrent and are soft and waxy. *Chrysodon* comes from *chrysos* meaning 'gold' and *odontos* meaning 'tooth'.

Hygrophorus nemoreus

Initially somewhat bell-shaped the **cap** soon expands and becomes flattened with a diameter of 5–8 cm, sometimes 10 cm. The conical umbo and the inrolled edge are striking. The cuticle has a greasy but never viscid texture, and in dry conditions appears almost tomentose and minutely streaked with radiating innate fibrils. The fox-brown to orange colour becomes more intense towards the centre. The thick, broadly adnate to decurrent **gills** are wax-like, and of a pale cream colour, later becoming reddish or ochre. The solid **stem** seldom exceeds a height of 6–8 cm and is cylindrical tapering slightly towards the base. The surface is fibrillose with the apex mealy-granular and overall colour is a pale ochre. The thin white **flesh** tastes and smells mealy.

Spore print: White.

Distribution: This fungus is found in deciduous woods, particularly on chalk or limestone. It is decidedly uncommon to rare in south-east England although there are years when it appears more frequently.

Possible confusion: *Camarophyllus pratensis* (Meadow Wax Cap) is similar but lacks the mealy smell and the innately fibrillose surface to the cap. Poorly developed specimens might be confused with *H. chrysodon*, but the latter has the cap margin and apex of the stem dotted with yellow scales.

Edibility: The fungus is edible.

Notes: In the above section comparison is made with *H. pratensis*. This may seem surprising since the latter is a typical species of grassland while *H. nemoreus* occurs in woodland. However, *H. pratensis* also occurs occasionally in more open woodland sites. *Nemoreus* means 'pertaining to deciduous woods'.

Hygrophorus agathosmus

The viscid **cap**, up to 8 cm across, is initially convex, later flat with umbo, grey, olive-grey, yellowish-grey, and rarely even white; but usually paler toward the margin which is slow to unroll. The thick, distant and occasionally forked soft **gills** are adnate to decurrent, when young white, becoming pale grey later. The dry **stem** reaches 7 cm in length and is thickened at the base; it is white with white or yellowish flocci especially at the apex. The **flesh** is whitish, watery and very soft, with a strong characteristic smell of bitter almonds reminiscent of marzipan.

Spore print: White.

Distribution: Chiefly in the Scottish Highlands under pine where it occurs occasionally. Elsewhere in the British Isles it is very rare. It may be found in autumn.

Possible confusion: The grey colour, strong smell of bitter almonds and occurrence with conifers are diagnostic and confusion is unlikely.

Edibility: This species is considered edible, but is unlikely to be met with owing to its restricted distribution and rarity.

Notes: *Agathosmus* means 'sweet smelling'.

Hygrophorus marzuolus

The non-viscid **cap** of this fungus can reach a diameter of 10 cm. When young it is white, but as it matures it changes through grey to an almost blackish colour. Initially more or less convex it becomes very irregular in shape and no two specimens look the same as the thick cap curves upwards in many places to such an extent that the gills are exposed. The **gills** are strikingly thick, of various lengths, waxy and fairly distant, scarcely decurrent and often interveined. The **stem** tends to be squat although it may reach 6 cm or even occasionally 8 cm in length, and gives the impression of plumpness. Initially white, it becomes grey and is rather scurfy towards the apex. Beneath the surface of the cap the **flesh** is grey, elsewhere white. It has no definite smell.

Spore print: White.

Distribution: Emerges just after the snow has melted, and has even been found in January after a particularly mild winter, although it may continue fruiting into May. However, specimens often remain covered by vegetation and debris so that once detected the surrounding area should be carefully searched for more fruit bodies. It occurs in small colonies in mixed woodland, or with conifers and although not yet known in Britain it should be looked for in the early part of the year in the Scottish Highlands.

Possible confusion: *H. camarophyllus* looks similar, but does not appear until autumn, so confusion is highly improbable. However, one should always bear in mind that fungi may on occasion fruit out of season. Both fungi are edible.

Edibility: An excellent edible species.

Notes: *Marzuolus* means 'pertaining to the month of March'.

53

Camarophyllus pratensis Meadow Wax Cap

The **cap** is initially campanulate or bell-shaped but soon becomes more or less flattened with a prominent central boss. The uniformly smooth surface is orange, apricot or tawny buff. The thick, wax-like **gills** are markedly decurrent and more or less the same colour as the cap although paler. The bare, smooth **stem** reaches a length of approximately 7 cm, tapers towards the base, and is up to 1.5 cm thick expanding upward. The colour is noticeably paler than that of the cap, with a silky sheen. The **flesh** is similar in colour to the stem, though paler inside, and odourless.

Spore print: White.

Distribution: From September until well into November. It is characteristic of grassland, occurring in meadows and pastures. However, it may occasionally occur in open woodland or in grassy clearings. This fungus is common and widespread throughout the British Isles. In Alpine regions it is found at heights of up to 2,200m.

Possible confusion: With its peculiar top-shape this fungus can only be confused with allied species of *Camarophyllus*. Mycologists distinguish three similar species; apart from *C. pratensis*, there are *C. angustifolius*, a completely white variety, and *C. berkeleyanus*, which has a paler cap with a greyish-yellow to ochre centre and a whitish edge. *C. pratensis* is therefore more uniformly orange-coloured.

Edibility: Edible, and only rarely riddled by insect larvae.

Notes: *Pratensis* means 'growing in meadows'.

Volvariella bombycina

The **cap** grows to 8–20 cm across and is white, but yellowish in *var. flaviceps*. It is oval to bell-shaped when young, later expanded with an umbo. The surface of the cap has a dense, uniform covering of silky hair-like fibres which hang down from the margin. The **gills** are free, white at first, then a delicate pink, finally flesh-pink, crowded and deep. The **stem**, 8–15 cm long, 1–1.5 cm thick, is smooth, and tapers towards the apex. There is no ring, but the stem emerges from a basal leathery sac-like volva. The white **flesh** is soft and smells slightly of radishes.

Spore print: Pink.

Distribution: Uncommon to rare, but widespread. Along with the yellow-capped *var. flaviceps*, it grows either saprophytically or parasitically on roots, trunks and in hollows of various deciduous trees especially elm, often several metres above ground level, from June until October.

Possible confusion: This medium to large-sized fungus is very easy to recognize by its silky and hairy white cap, its tough, dingy-brown cup-like volva and its occurrence on trees, often in hollow elms.

Edibility: It is a good edible species.

Notes: The fruit body in the photograph was about 2m from the ground in a split fork of a 'Boskop' apple tree in a park. The scientific name *bombycina* derives from *bombyx*, meaning 'silkworm' and its cocoon which is silky or woolly.

The **cap** is up to 8(12) cm across and top-shaped but when mature may become depressed at the centre, often with a wavy edge, and has a greyish-white frosted suede-like surface. The very thin **gills** are crowded and decurrent, at first white, and later pale pink. The short **stem** 2–5 cm high, is the same colour as the cap and has a pruinose covering and a cottony base. It is strong smelling.

Spore print: Pink.

Distribution: The Miller can be found from summer into autumn. It prefers deciduous woodland.

Possible confusion: This mushroom should be very carefully examined to avoid confusion with *Clitocybe phyllophila* or *Clitocybe dealbata* and other white *Clitocybe spp.* These are poisonous or inedible. They lack the definite mealy smell which distinguishes the Miller; the latter also has a more decidedly pink spore print.

Edibility: Many collectors appreciate this mushroom, which is good in mixtures with other fungi. Not to be eaten raw!

Notes: *Prunulus* means 'little plum'. The Italian, A. Cesalpino (1519–1603) found the mushroom under a plum tree.

Rhodocybe mundula

The greyish **cap**, 3–7 cm across, has a marked depression when old, and the edge is inrolled; sometimes it is concentrically marked; the flesh of the cap is thin and tough. An important diagnostic feature is that when touched, especially at the margin, the fungus turns patchy smoke-black. The greyish **gills** are narrow, decurrent, crowded, thin and also turn black when bruised. The **stem** is similarly greyish, short and relatively slender, and at the base there is a cottony tomentum. The **flesh** is pale yellowish and slowly blackens, especially in the stem. It has a strong mealy smell and a very bitter taste.

Spore print: Pale pink.

Distribution: A rare but widespread species in Britain, and likewise rare in Europe where it has occasionally been found in Denmark, France, Germany and northern Italy. It grows singly or in colonies among leaves, needles and woody detritus from the end of August until late autumn in very lime-rich damp meadows and beech woods, rarely in spruce forests. It is often overlooked because of its dull colouration.

Possible confusion: Because parts of the fungus turn black when bruised, there is the likelihood of confusion with blackening species of the genus *Lyophyllum*.

Edibility: Inedible because of its very bitter taste.

Notes: The genus *Rhodocybe* comprises about eleven species. They are small to medium-sized fungi, coloured flesh-brown, orange-brown, yellow-brown, grey-brown or grey. The gills are sinuate, adnate or decurrent. The spore print is pink or, rarely, grey-brown.

Pluteus atricapillus (P. cervinus)

Bell-shaped **cap**, expanding to 15 cm and becoming flattened with a low umbo, sepia to dark umber brown often with innate radiating streaky fibrils, especially in older specimens. The **flesh** is fragile and thin except at the umbo, the surface smooth. Initially the crowded free **gills** appear almost white, but they gradually take on a pink shade until, at maturity, they are dark pink. The **stem** can be up to 15 cm long but only 1–2 cm thick, and is basically whitish, ornamented with longitudinal brown fibrils especially towards the base.

Spore print: Pink.

Distribution: Very common and widespread on stumps of deciduous and coniferous trees, or at times on buried wood or on heaps of rotting sawdust, chiefly during autumn but less often at other times of the year.

Possible confusion: This fungus is unlikely to be confused with any similar-looking species of a dangerous nature. *P. atromarginatus* looks most like *P. atricapillus*, but has a black edge to its gills.

Edibility: European collectors do not rate this fungus very highly, since its taste is not particularly exciting.

Notes: The older Latin name was *P. cervinus. Cervinus* means 'like a stag' and indicates the colour of the fungus well.

Pluteus roseipes

The young, more or less bell-shaped **cap** expands with age to 8(10) cm in diameter. It is brown or dark umber, becoming more brownish-grey at maturity, with the centre slightly darker. The fine velvety cuticle is noteworthy and appears as if covered by delicate, fine, white particles. The edge of the cap is slightly striated. The beautiful pink **gills** are free, crowded, and rounded where they meet the edge of the cap. The slender **stem** grows to 9 cm high and is slightly thickened below. It is longitudinally fibrillose and often slightly twisted, whitish with a strong hint of pink, mauve or lilac towards the base. The whitish **flesh** is pink at the base of the stem and often greyish and water-soaked and very tender.

Spore print: Pink.

Distribution: On fallen wood and stumps of conifers, mainly in mountainous situations but as yet unknown in Britain. In the highlands of south Germany it is not common, but fairly widespread. The fungus is usually solitary. The photographer found the fungus on buried spruce logs in his garden.

Possible confusion: Hardly exists because of the dominance of the pink colouration.

Edibility: Edible, but unlikely to be met with.

Notes: Distinguishing the numerous species of the genus *Pluteus* is impossible without specialist literature and a microscope. *P. roseipes*, for instance, has long fibrillose elements in the cuticle of the cap, and there are bulbous *cystidia* (sterile cells) with elongated cylindrical tips on the gill edge. These features can only be seen with the aid of the microscope. *P. atricapillus* also has striations on the cap surface, but the cystidia are thick walled and have one to three apical hooks. *Roseipes* means 'pink-footed'.

59

Entoloma nitidum

The **cap**, 2–5 cm across, is of a character-istic dark blue to steel-blue and only becomes pale in senescence. When young it is bell-shaped, then convex with a slight umbo, smooth, silky, and thin-fleshed. The crowded **gills** are almost free, whitish at first, becoming pink on maturity. The **stem** grows to 8 cm in length and is the same colour as the cap with a white woolly base. The suface is longitudinally fibrillose striate. The white **flesh** is soft, becoming hollow in the stem with age, odourless and mild.
Spore print: Pink.
Distribution: Rare but widespread in Britain; almost absent in northern Europe. It is very rare in the North German Plain whereas in south Germany with its highlands it is quite widespread and common. It grows in very acid soils in coniferous woods, on the edge of boggy places, among mosses and bilberries. July to October.

Possible confusion: With the much less common and more robust *E. madidum*. This, however, is more grey-blue, with an ochreous centre when older. Its cap is often wrinkled. The base of the stem is more yellowish, and its flesh smells of meal. In Europe this species is scattered over a large area and is much less common in Germany than *E. nitidum*. It is found in meadowland, heaths and dunes. There have been a few reported finds in the Jura limestone areas.
Edibility: The fungus is probably edible, but not recommended. Far better to enjoy its beautiful colour and shape.
Notes: The genus *Entoloma/Rhodophyllus* comprises about 153 species, some of which are edible, but their use demands exact knowledge of the particular species.

Entoloma clypeatum   Roman Shield

The **cap** 3–10 cm across, initially campa-nulate, later expands and becomes more flattened with a central umbo, often with deep undulations in its edge. The surface is sooty-brown to grey-brown in colour when wet, but since it is hygrophanous, the colour of the cap changes and becomes paler on drying, often with darker, watery streaks. The broad **gills** are fairly distant, and when young are white, but gradually assume a beautiful pink shade. They are adnate, with a little tooth where they join the stem. The **stem**, up to 10 cm tall and 1–1.5 cm thick, is hollow in older specimens, and some-times also twisted, varying in colour from white to light grey. The fungus has a mealy smell especially when crushed.
Spore print: Pink.
Distribution: The Roman Shield is associ-ated with trees and shrubs of the *Rosaceae*, such as apple, pear, cherry, rose,

hawthorn, etc., often in gardens or under hedges. It appears early April to June, and its season has usually past by the time its poisonous relatives appear.
Possible confusion: It resembles a whole series of related species, among them the very poisonous *E. sinuatum* (Livid Entoloma). The smaller *E. vernum* also shows some similarities, but lacks the mealy smell.
Edibility: Connoisseurs consider the Roman Shield one of the finest edible mushrooms, but because of the very real risk of confusion with allied species which are poisonous it is best avoided. Some authorities even consider the Roman Shield itself to be suspect in regard to edibility.
Notes: *Clypeatus* means 'shield-like'.

Entoloma sinuatum   Livid Entoloma

The fleshy **cap** can reach 18 cm in diameter. At first convex-campanulate it expands but seldom becomes entirely flat. The distinctly inrolled cap margin adds to the impression of compactness. The cap is ivory to light ochre with a silky sheen, sometimes varying to grey-brown. A fine white frosty pruina is evident on the edge. The **gills** are crowded. Initially white, then pale ochre and finally flesh-pink or salmon colour. The robust **stem**, white to yellowish, is frequently 2.5 cm wide and up to 12 cm high, often thicker towards the base, while at the apex the surface has a frosty pruina similar to that on the margin of the cap. The **flesh** has a mealy smell.

Spore print: Pink.

Distribution: Uncommon but widespread in southern England. In Europe its distribution is insufficiently known. It prefers clayey soils with a lime content among beeches, oaks and in mixed woodland.

Possible confusion: Possible with *Calocybe gambosa* (Saint George's Mushroom), *Clitopilus prunulus* (The Miller) and *Lepista nebularis* (Clouded Funnel Cap). In spring among *Rosaceae* there also grows the edible *E. sepium*, a smaller version of the Livid Entoloma.

Edibility: Poisonous.

Notes: The poison, still unknown, has a rapid effect. *Sinuatum* means 'wavy'.

Entoloma nidorosum   Nitrous-smelling Entoloma

The thin-fleshed **cap** reaches 9 cm in diameter. It is convex, later with an umbilicate depression at the centre. It is sometimes indistinctly umbonate, grey-brown or olive-grey becoming paler to almost white and shiny on drying. When moist the pale shiny grey changes to a vaguely foxy shade. The edge of the cap when moist, is translucent and striate, and often split. The sinuate **gills**, sometimes adnate, are broad, apart and tend to have wavy edges. The initial white colour changes gradually to the flesh-pink which characterizes all *Entolomas*. The tall, slender, white **stem**, which when old is rather shiny grey and silky, reaches a height of 10 cm, with a diameter of only 3–6(10) mm.   It is cylindrical, and at the apex has a whitish or ochre frosty pruina. The **flesh** is whitish and moist throughout, smelling more or less strongly nitrous.

Spore print: Pink.

Distribution: Very common from summer into autumn on heaths, lawns and deciduous woodland.

Possible confusion: Very similar to many other *Entolomas*, but in this instance the nitrous smell is diagnostic.

Edibility: The unpleasantly strong smell makes culinary use impossible, and furthermore the species may be poisonous.

Notes: *Nidorosus* means 'strong-smelling'.

Melanoleuca grammopodia

The **cap** reaches a diameter of 13 cm. When young it is a more or less bell-shaped with a broad umbo and inrolled edge. Later it becomes flattened with a blunt umbo at the depressed centre, the edge being slightly turned down, but not inrolled. The cap surface is greyish-ochre, with grey shades predominating, when older mixed with shades of dirty ochre, matt or with a slight sheen. The very crowded **gills** are sinuate or slightly decurrent, and sometimes forked, whitish and easily separable from the cap. The **stem**, up to 12 cm tall and 2.5 cm thick is coarsely longitudinally fibrillose, appearing almost striate. It is tough and often club-shaped, greyish-brown, largely coloured as the cap. The **flesh** is white and has an unpleasant smell.

Spore print: White.

Distribution: The fungus is widespread and occasional, growing singly or in groups. It is found from August to October in grassy woodland.

Possible confusion: With other *Melanoleuca* species. Precise identification of species of this genus is difficult and requires the use of a microscope.

Edibility: *M. grammopodia* is edible.

Notes: The genus includes a number of species, none of which are known to be poisonous. They are mostly fleshy, white, ochre or grey-brown fungi with rather crowded sinuate white gills and a stem ornamented with longitudinal fibrils, and with the flesh of the stem either white throughout or distinctly brown toward the base. The spore print is whitish. Some species appear in spring. *Grammopodia* is Greek for 'with longitudinally striped stem'.

Melanoleuca cognata

The **cap** may reach 10 cm across and when young is somewhat convex but becomes flattened with age with a small central umbo. The surface is smooth and greasy. The colour is strikingly ochre or yellowish-ochre, a darker brown when moist but paler when dry. Shades of grey are usually absent. The **gills** are whitish when young, later yellowish-ochre. They are sinuate and crowded. The **stem** is about 4–12 cm tall and up to 2 cm thick. It is cylindrical and only slightly expanded at the white cottony base, otherwise ochreous and longitudinally striate. The **flesh** is vaguely yellowish and fibrous in the stem with an acid smell.

Spore print: Not pure white, but with a hint of yellow.

Distribution: This fungus appears in April and May, more rarely there is a second flush from September to November. It is found on the grassy edges of coniferous woods and in the twiggy debris alongside forest roads. It is also often found with stinging nettles.

Possible confusion: *M. phaeopodia* is very similar being distinguished from the species under discussion only by its dark chestnut-brown stem. The identification of species within the genus *Melanoleuca* is very difficult and requires microscopic study.

Edibility: *M. cognata* is edible, but not highly rated by mushroom hunters. Its taste is not particularly distinctive.

Notes: *Cognata* means 'related'.

Lyophyllum connatum

The **cap** may be up to 5–7 cm across, rarely 10 cm, initially bell-shaped, then convex, and finally expanded, with the thin margin inrolled in young specimens, while in mature caps is often undulating. The cap is pure white, although when watersoaked may appear somewhat greyish-white. The **gills** are crowded and slightly decurrent. Initially they are white, later cream, and slightly yellowish in old specimens. The **stem** is at first pure white but later slightly yellowish with a diameter of 1–2 cm and a height of 4–10 cm. Stems are generally clustered. The **flesh** is white with a waxy-cartilaginous texture. It has a mild taste and a slight mealy smell, which is masked, however, by a scent reminiscent of larkspur.

Spore print: White.

Distribution: Rare. It is found in deciduous and mixed woodland from August to October, almost always in dense clusters.

Possible confusion: There are similar-looking white Funnel Caps (*Clitocybes*) which are very poisonous, but if attention is paid to the clustered growth and the scent of larkspur, a mix-up is hardly possible. A further distinction is the slow blue-violet colouration of the flesh when treated with ferrous sulphate (FeSO4). The change in colour is especially clear in the gills.

Edibility: Edible.

Notes: *Connatum* means 'grown together'.

Lyophyllum loricatum

The **cap** has a diameter of 5–10 cm, and is initially convex, but later expands and becomes bell-shaped or flattened often with a central umbo, with the colour ranging from mid to olive-brown. It is thick and cartilaginous, and when dry has a sheen, although when moist it is rather greasy in texture. The **gills** are adnexed, often with a tooth, sometimes decurrent. They are white or slightly yellowish in colour and of a tough consistency. The tough **stem** reaches 5–10 cm in height, with a diameter of 1–1.5 cm, and is whitish or pale brown in colour. At the lower end, which tapers slightly, several stems often grow together in clusters. The **flesh** is white, firm and cartilaginous. It gives off a strange smell and has a sweetish taste, though sometimes with a burning or bitter after-taste.

Spore print: White.

Distribution: *L. loricatum* is a rare species which can be found from late summer to autumn, in deciduous and mixed woodland. It grows in small clusters in grassy spots and also by the edge of paths.

Possible confusion: In habit *L. loricatum* is reminiscent of its near relatives *L. fumosum* and *L. decastes*. Identifying these species is very difficult. *L. fumosum* has greyish gills while *L. decastes* tends to grow in larger clusters.

Edibility: These species are edible.

Notes: *Loricatum* means 'armoured'.

Catathelasma imperiale

The **cap** grows to 5–16(20) cm in diameter and is initially convex or hemispherical, but later expands and becomes more flattened. The surface is dry, deer-brown to hazel and frequently flecked with remnants of the veil, while the margin remains characteristically inrolled for a considerable time. The narrow, crowded **gills** are decurrent, whitish at first, later pale brown with a blackish edge. The **stem** is pointed, deeply rooted and somewhat banded by scales. It grows to 15 cm tall and 3–5 cm thick and has two rings, the upper one coming from the partial veil (*velum partiale*) and the lower one from the universal veil (*velum universale*). The white **flesh** is compact, firm and smells slightly mealy or of cucumber.

Spore print: White.

Distribution: As yet unknown in Britain. In Europe this species seems to be widespread in mountainous locations in the north and in sub-alpine regions. It can be found more especially in Scandinavia, in the northern and southern Alps, in the Jura, and in the highland areas. In Germany it is only rarely found north of the Main. It grows in summer and autumn on limy soils in coniferous forests in the mountains and in the bushier alpine meadows.

Possible confusion: Unlikely. The double ring and the pointed stem rooting deep into the ground are sufficient to identify this species.

Edibility: *C. imperiale* is edible, but should not be gathered because of its relative rarity.

Notes: The genus *Catathelasma* comprises this single species. The name *imperiale* was probably given to it because of its size.

Tricholoma colossum

This fungus thoroughly deserves its name not only because of the size of its **cap**, which reaches 20(25) cm in diameter!, but also because of the overall impression it gives is one of massiveness. Even young specimens, with their thick-fleshed, hemispherical caps and inrolled margin, are robust. Later the cap flattens, but the edge remains hugging the upper, white part of the stem for some time. The surface, a foxy-red or reddish-brown colour, is a little greasy, and can easily be peeled. The **gills** are very crowded, fairly narrow, and rounded where they join the stem. Even when old they remain pale, and often show reddish flecks. This *Tricholoma* looks extraordinarily massive especially because the **stem**, up to 4 cm thick, is short, squat and bulbous, reaching a height of only 6 cm, or rarely 10 cm. Where the cap, in expanding, separates from the stem there is a zone left around the base which resembles a ring but should not be confused with one. Below it, the colour is similar to that of the cap surface. The **flesh**, which is white, reddens gradually when cut.

Spore print: White.

Distribution: This rare fungus is found in pine woods in the Scottish Highlands, during autumn.

Possible confusion: No other fungus of the genus has such a massive form. The ring-like band on the stem is a good diagnostic feature. *T. aurantium* looks similar at first sight but grows under spruce on limestone soils and tastes and smells of meal.

Edibility: It is considered edible, but its firm flesh makes it difficult to digest and it does not agree with everyone, so that digestive problems may result. Because of its rarity it should not be collected.

Notes: *Colossum* means 'enormous'.

Tricholoma pardinum

Specimens up to 15 cm across are in no way exceptional. With the edge of the **cap** initially inrolled, this fungus gives an impression of stockiness. Even in fully-grown specimens, which are relatively flat, a slight umbo at the centre of the cap is still discernible. The mouse-grey, silver-grey or grey-brown surface consists of more or less large imbricate, fibrillose scales on a paler background. The **gills**, of uneven length, are rather thick, and sinuate or rounded where they join the stem. They are whitish, sometimes with a hint of yellow. The massive **stem** reaches a height of 8–10 cm and may be up to 2.5 cm thick. The surface, finely fibrous or with fluffy areas, ranges from white to ochre. The **flesh** is always whitish or greyish with a mealy smell. An important diagnostic feature is at the edge of the gills and the apex of the stem where watery droplets are exuded.

Spore print: White.
Distribution: Not yet recorded in Britain. The European distribution of this fungus is not yet sufficiently well-known. In Germany it is found mainly in the south, becoming rarer towards the north and seems to prefer beech woods on very limy soils. In France and America it grows under conifers.
Possible confusion: With *T. portentosum*, *T. scalpturatum*, *T. terreum*, and *T. virgatum*. In Europe anyone wishing to collect these similar species for eating must take great care to ensure correct identification.
Edibility: The fungus is poisonous, causing severe stomach and digestive problems.
Notes: *Pardinum* means 'marked like a panther'.

Tricholoma virgatum

The **cap** of *T. virgatum* is initially conical and ash-grey or lilac-grey, but then expands to 4–8 cm, retaining a broadly conical shape or becoming campanulate with an umbo. The surface is smooth, dry, and initially fibrillose. The white or grey **gills**, whose colour approaches that of the cap, are sinuate and generally have small dark grey patches. The **stem** grows to a height of 9 cm and is about 1.5 cm thick, with cylindrical shape. The upper third may appear minutely granular or flecked, otherwise the stem is smooth or finely fibrillose, white and tends to have pale pink patches towards the base. The **flesh**, which is white when cut, shows a greyish zone beneath the surface of the cap. It sometimes smells earthy and immediately tastes more or less peppery.
Spore print: White.
Distribution: Occasional in summer and autumn in coniferous and deciduous woodland, favouring mossy places.
Possible confusion: *T. portentosum* is very similar in colour, but is different in shape and the flesh has a mealy taste; *T. pardinum* has a cap with fibrillose scales and flesh which does not taste so hot as does that of *T. virgatum*.
Edibility: Quite apart from the hot, burning taste, the fungus is probably poisonous.
Notes: *T. virgatum* can be recognized easily from the shape of its cap, but specimens should be studied carefully to avoid misidentification. There are about nineteen similar *Tricholomas*, of which some are yellowish, others reddish, some mild, others hot. *Virgatum* means 'striped, plaited'.

71

Tricholoma flavovirens

The **cap** of this medium-sized *Tricholoma* reaches a diameter of about 8 cm. When young it is broadly campanulate with a blunt umbo, but it gradually expands and has a slightly turned-down margin. The colour of the cap is a vivid yellow covered with minute fleck-like, more or less olive-brown, fox-coloured or brownish-yellow scales. Even when moist it is only slightly sticky and soon dries. The **gills**, of uneven length, are deeply sinuate, lemon to sulphur-yellow, and crowded. The thin **stem**, up to 1 cm thick, may reach about 5 cm in length, or exceptionally up to 10 cm and is coloured like the cap with a covering of isolated brownish flecks. The **flesh** is bright yellow to ochre-yellow. It has a slightly mealy smell.

Spore print: White.

Distribution: Rare in the south of Britain, less so in Scotland, found mainly in coniferous woods, and less commonly in deciduous woodland, in autumn.

Possible confusion: With *T. auratum*, also edible, and grows under pines, but is more massive and squat, with a surface which is slimy when wet and sticky even when dry. Its flesh is paler and often whitish. It could also be mistaken from a distance for the inedible *T. sulphureum* (Gasworks Tricholoma), but the smell of the latter is diagnostic.

Edibility: Both *T. auratum* and *T. flavovirens* are considered good edible fungi

Notes: Neither species has yet been fully researched. In the case of *T. flavovirens*, the question of habitat requires further investigation. In literature, finds have been mentioned from both coniferous and deciduous woods on limestone and on acid, poor soils. *T. auratum* appears limited to sandy soils under pines. *Flavovirens* means 'yellow-green'.

Tricholoma sulphureum   Gasworks Tricholoma

The Gasworks Tricholoma has a campanulate **cap** with a central umbo reaching a maximum diameter of about 7 cm. The surface is sulphur-yellow, and remains unchanged even in maturity but it may be more intense at the centre, and can also tend towards greenish. The **gills** are adnate with a small notch where they join the stem. They, too, are bright sulphur-yellow, thickish, and distant. The **stem**, the same colour as the cap and gills, can grow to 8 cm and has a fibrillose surface. The **flesh**, like the remainder of this fungus, is also sulphur-yellow and does not change when exposed to air. The very strong smell is reminiscent of gasworks or coal gas and is very unpleasant.

Spore print: White.

Distribution: The Gasworks Tricholoma is common and widespread in coniferous and deciduous woodland, in summer and autumn.

Possible confusion: It is very similar to the edible *T. flavovirens* and *T. auratum*, but the characteristic smell at once serves to distinguish it. There is another variety of the Gasworks Tricholoma (*T. bufonium*) which is currently regarded as a species in its own right. This fungus which grows in coniferous woods and pastures also has the gas-like smell, but the cap is umber or tawny with a red-brown centre.

Edibility: There is a suspicion that the Gasworks Tricholoma is poisonous, but the poison is as yet unknown. Eating it could cause digestive problems.

Notes: *Sulphureum* means 'sulphur-yellow'.

Tricholoma sejunctum

This is one of the larger members of the genus, for its **cap** can reach a diameter of up to 12 cm. Initially conico-campanulate it flattens with age, and is not always umbonate at the centre. The surface is slightly moist and shiny in damp conditions but matt when dry. It is ornamented with dense innate radial brown, olive-brown or black fibrils on an otherwise greenish-yellow or pale yellow background. The fairly crowded **gills** are sinuate, their edges notched, their colour varying from white to a yellowish shade which is noticeable especially in older specimens. The **stem** reaches 8 cm in length and is cylindrical, firm and solid. The surface bears small, granular flecks at the apex, and is white, or often patchy yellow. The bitter-tasting **flesh** remains white even when cut and exposed to the air, though beneath the cap surface it shows a slight yellowish colouration. It has a definite mealy smell.

Spore print: White.

Distribution: Widespread and occasional from summer to autumn, it grows in both deciduous and coniferous woods, particularly under oaks and sweet chestnuts.

Possible confusion: This fungus is similar to other members of the genus. It would be fatal to confuse it with *Amanita phalloides* (Death Cap), with which it has a superficial similarity. *T. sejunctum*, however, lacks both the volva and the ring on the stem.

Edibility: Possibly poisonous.

Notes: Another very similar-looking fungus is *T. subsejunctum*. In this species the gill edge has a striking saw-tooth appearance and toward the margin of the cap the gills are often yellow. The spores are rather larger. *Var. coryphaeum* has a more yellowish-brown cap with brownish scales. *Sejunctum* means 'cut off, different'.

Tricholoma saponaceum   Soap-scented Tricholoma

The **cap** grows to about 8–10 cm across and has thin flesh. Initially dome-shaped it expands and becomes somewhat campanulate, often with an irregularly lobed margin, which remains visibly inrolled for a long time. The colour of the cap is very variable: greenish, yellowish, brownish or brownish-grey, white to slightly reddish, and many shades inbetween make identification difficult. The **gills** are distant and sinuate. They are pale coloured sometimes with a greenish tint, and often with rust-brown patches. The **stem** is up to 10 cm in height and 1.5–3 cm thick, and may be either somewhat bulbous or cylindrical. Its colour is roughly the same as that of the cap, though often slightly paler. The surface is sometimes ornamented with fine black scales, but completely smooth specimens are also found. The white **flesh** when cut displays reddish patches. The fungus has a very distinct smell of scented soap. The taste is mild to slightly sweet, but is also often bitter.

Spore print: White.

Distribution: Common and widespread in deciduous and coniferous woods between late summer and autumn. It often grows gregariously.

Possible confusion: As can be seen from the description, this is a very variable species and many varieties have been described. The author, however, has found in the same place and in the same group of fruit bodies specimens which could fit into several of these varieties.

Edibility: Because of its smell and taste the fungus is inedible.

Notes: *Saponaceum* means 'smelling of soap'.

Tricholoma scalpturatum

The **cap**, up to 6 or 8 cm in diameter, is initially conical, then shallowly campanulate with a blunt central umbo. The surface, covered by radial fibrils or very fine scales, is silvery grey-brown, and often shows lemon-yellow patches when old. The white sinuate **gills** become yellow in the course of maturity. The whitish **stem** which reaches 6–8 cm in height, has a silky fibrillose surface. The **flesh** is white and has a mealy smell.

Spore print: White.

Distribution: Common and widespread in both coniferous and deciduous woods, and even in gardens and parks during late summer and autumn.

Possible confusion: *T. terreum* looks similar, but usually occurs with pines, has grey gills and lacks a mealy smell. *T. atrosquamosum*, is also similar but has a cap covered with blackish-grey tinted scales.

Edibility: The fungus is edible.

Notes: *T. scalpturatum* is distinguished by its mealy smell, and silvery-grey cap marked with radial fibrils or fibrillose scales. There are about eighteen similar grey to grey-brown, dry, fibrillose scaly species of *Tricholoma*. Some of these are poisonous, for example, *T. pardinum*, which is more robust and has a silvery cap ornamented with imbricate scales. All these grey *Tricholomas* are best avoided. *Scalpturatum* means 'felty, with a scaly cap'.

Tricholoma vaccinum

The **cap**, up to 7(10) cm across, may be reddish flesh-brown, or brownish coppery-red and is flattened, sometimes with a small umbo. It has a dry surface, which is generally very scaly, particularly at the inrolled edge, woolly and felt-like. The broad **gills** are sinuate, initially white, then brownish flesh-colour. The **stem** can reach 10 cm in height and is 1–2 cm thick, of a pale reddish-brown colour and even paler near the apex. The **flesh** is whitish or rosy, becoming reddish-brown especially in the stem. It has a mealy smell and a bitter taste.

Spore print: White.

Distribution: *T. vaccinum* often grows in colonies in coniferous woods, favouring grassy locations. In Britain it is rare, perhaps less so in the Scottish Highlands and the fruit bodies are formed from August to October.

Possible confusion: *T. imbricatum* is similar but the fine scaly cap lacks the woolly margin of *T. vaccinum* and its gills become red-brown when bruised.

Edibility: Inedible because of its bitter taste.

Notes: The genus *Tricholoma* comprises over sixty-five species ranging from medium to large, fleshy mycorrhizal fungi with sinuate white gills. The stem is mostly without, more rarely with, a cottony veil, termed a cortina. The spore print is white. Some of the brown and grey species are poisonous. *T. vaccinum* is one of a group of about nineteen brown species, of which two are poisonous. *Vaccinum* means 'pertaining to the cow' (brown).

Tricholoma aurantium

The **cap** reaches a diameter of about 8–12 cm. Initially convex, it expands and becomes convex-campanulate with an inrolled margin and firm but thin flesh. The surface is viscid and usually bears small, dark scales. The colour is a very striking yellow-orange to orange-red with the centre being more brownish. The broad **gills** are crowded, sinuate, and white, though they do develop rusty patches. The **stem**, about 8 cm high with a diameter of 1.5–2 cm, gives the fungus a robust look. The surface is orange with numerous bands of darker scales, but the apex is abruptly white, almost as though there were a ring zone. This is often ornamented with orange droplets. The **flesh** is white with a mealy smell and a slightly bitter taste.

Spore print: White.

Distribution: This beautiful mushroom is exceedingly rare in Britain but may be found in the Scottish Highlands. Known in many European countries, but its distribution is uneven. It favours conifers, almost always spruce and is a mushroom of the northern mountains, appearing far more frequently in Scandinavia, in the south of Germany and in the limestone Alps, from August to November.

Possible confusion: If attention is paid to the combination of colour, scaly stem and white spore print, confusion is unlikely.

Edibility: The fungus is inedible.

Notes: *Aurantium* means 'orange-coloured'.

Tricholomopsis rutilans Plums and Custard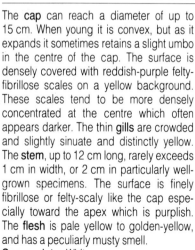

The **cap** can reach a diameter of up to 15 cm. When young it is convex, but as it expands it sometimes retains a slight umbo in the centre of the cap. The surface is densely covered with reddish-purple felty-fibrillose scales on a yellow background. These scales tend to be more densely concentrated at the centre which often appears darker. The thin **gills** are crowded and slightly sinuate and distinctly yellow. The **stem**, up to 12 cm long, rarely exceeds 1 cm in width, or 2 cm in particularly well-grown specimens. The surface is finely fibrillose or felty-scaly like the cap especially toward the apex which is purplish. The **flesh** is pale yellow to golden-yellow, and has a peculiarly musty smell.

Spore print: White.

Distribution: Widespread and very common, growing exclusively on or near the roots or stumps of conifers. It can be found during late summer and autumn.

Possible confusion: *T. rutilans* is easy to recognize by its purple-coloured cap, yellow gills and habitat. Another similar species is *T. decora*, a rare species of the Scottish Highlands which grows in similar places, but is characterized by brown or blackish scales on the cap.

Edibility: Not recommended. It is said to cause minor digestive problems.

Notes: The genus *Tricholomopsis* consists of four species, distinguished from the true *Tricholomas* by their occurrence on, or association with wood and by microscopic features. *Rutilans* means 'yellowish-red'.

79

The old species name *viridis* conveyed something of the colour of the **cap** of *C. odora*: the word is Latin and means green. The blue-green colour, however, is not always intense. At most 8 cm across, the cap is initially campanulate, later flattened and sometimes even saucer-shaped with the edge initially slightly inrolled. The colour becomes paler with age. The broad, irregular **gills** are tinted with the colour of the cap, but paler, and are sometimes adnate to slightly decurrent. The **stem** 3–7 cm high is somewhat paler than the cap, and the base appears white and cottony. The **flesh**, too, is slightly greenish, and has a particularly characteristic and intensely fragrant smell of aniseed.

Spore print: White with a greenish tinge.

Distribution: The fungus is widespread and frequent in both Britain and in the North Temperate Zone of Europe. It requires con-siderable amounts of lime in the soil. It fruits from summer until late autumn in mixed woodland especially those with beeches.

Possible confusion: Collectors should always be careful not to confuse this fungus with the white Funnel Caps, which are all inedible, and some poisonous. The fading of the green colour with age sometimes makes identification by sight quite difficult. On the other hand, the intense smell of aniseed helps to avoid confusion.

Edibility: It should only be used as a garnish, since the strong smell of aniseed does not disappear during cooking.

Notes: *Odora* means 'smelling'.

Clitocybe geotropa

The **cap** reaches a diameter of 5–20 cm, more rarely 30 cm. It is initially convex, then becomes flattened with a central depression in which is a small but prominent umbo. The surface feels moist and smooth to the touch. The colour is creamy-white varying to pallid yellow-ochre or greyish-yellow. The surface has a silky frosting, the margin is clearly inrolled. The **gills** are strongly decurrent, and are initially white, but become slightly yellowish with age. The **stem**, characteristically tall and club-shaped below reaching a height of 15 cm, is the same colour as the cap. All parts of the fungus have a noticeable sweetish smell rather like lavender. The **flesh** is very dry and always rather tough.

Spore print: White.

Distribution: *C. geotropa* usually occurs in fairy rings, in autumn, in deciduous woodland. In Britain it is widespread but occasional.

Possible confusion: Provided attention is paid to its size, shape, elongated tough stem, colour and occurrence in fairy rings in woodland, confusion should be avoided.

Edibility: *C. geotropa* is one of the most prized edible mushrooms. Anyone who comes across a large number should select only the young specimens as the fungus becomes increasingly tough with age.

Notes: *Geotropa* (Greek) means 'turned towards the earth'.

Clitocybe gibba (*C. infundibuliformis*) Common Funnel Cap

The **cap** seldom exceeds 5–8 cm in width. It is initially convex with an umbo, and with increasing maturity becomes more and more funnel-shaped. The umbo at the centre is always present. The surface feels silky or felt-like and is pale pinkish-buff or pale ochre. The flesh becomes thinner towards the margin which is initially tightly inrolled. The **gills** are closely crowded, very decurrent, and white. The **stem** is slender, flexible, solid, cartilaginous and the same colour as the cap. The tough whitish **flesh** has a sweet smell rather like almonds.

Spore print: White.

Distribution: The Common Funnel Cap is a very frequent and widespread species, generally growing in groups in deciduous or coniferous woodland often along grassy glades. It appears in early summer until late autumn.

Possible confusion: A whole series of Funnel Caps closely resemble this species, and confusion with some of the white Funnel Caps could be very dangerous since some are very poisonous.

Edibility: Edible, with reservation. It is said to cause stomach upsets. Best avoided.

Notes: The Funnel Caps (*Clitocybe*) are a very extensive group of about ninety species, of which at least ten are poisonous. They are, to a greater or lesser extent, fleshy and usually have funnel-shaped or umbilicate caps. Their gills are thin, adnate, and often decurrent. The spore powder is white, cream or pink. *Gibba* means 'with a hump'.

Lepista inversa (Clitocybe flaccida) Tawny Funnel Cap

This species can reach 4–8 cm in diameter at maturity. It is initially convex, then depressed, and finally distinctly funnel-shaped. The surface of the **cap** is usually yellowish or ochreous buff, darkening with age to tawny, though it may show irregular blotches. The margin of the cap is inrolled. The **gills** are closely crowded and obviously decurrent. Initially they are pale ivory, but with increasing maturity they become more deeply coloured. Slight pressure with the fingers quickly separates the gills from the cap. The **stem** is generally cylindrical but is sometimes thickened towards the base. Its surface is the same colour as the cap.

Spore print: Whitish.

Distribution: The Tawny Funnel Cap is a very common and widespread species without preference for either deciduous or coniferous woods, being equally at home in both and frequently occurring along tracks. It can be found from early summer until late autumn.

Possible confusion: *C. flaccida* is a thin-fleshed form of the Tawny Funnel Cap found in deciduous woodland, regarded by some authors as a species in its own right. *L. gilva* is also similar, but has clear watery marks on the cap. *L. lentiginosa* is again similar, its cap appearing almost divided into zones by rust-brown scales.

Edibility: The Tawny Funnel Cap is not recommended.

Notes: *Inversa* means 'rolled inwards'.

Clitocybe clavipes   Club Foot Funnel Cap

The **cap** can be up to 6 cm in diameter, only rarely larger, and is top shaped, sometimes with a slight umbo. The surface is brown to grey-brown or occasionally off-white at the margin, which is sometimes irregularly wrinkled. The **gills** are pale creamy-yellow, rather distant and deeply decurrent. The **stem** is up to 7 cm high, rarely to 10 cm, and up to 2 cm wide, reaching to 4 cm at the club-shaped base. In young specimens the long, club-shaped stem and initially small cap seem out of proportion. The whitish **flesh** is very thin at the margin of the cap and soft, spongy and occasionally fibrous in the stem. It has a sweetish smell and a mild flavour.

Spore print: White.

Distribution: A common fungus in Britain found in all types of woodland from July to November. It is also widespread in Europe, especially throughout the North Temperate zone.

Possible confusion: Unlikely to be confused with any other fungus, except *Lepista nebularis*, (Clouded Funnel Cap) from which it is distinguished by its swollen, club-shaped stem, less robust and more brownish cap, yellowish-cream gills, and less gregarious habit.

Edibility: The Club Foot Funnel Cap is edible, with reservation: in combination with alcohol it is said to have a poisonous effect similar to that of *Coprinus atramentarius* (Common Ink Cap).

Notes: *Clavipes* means 'club-footed'.

Lepista nebularis   Clouded Funnel Cap

The **cap** can reach a diameter of up to 20 cm. Its flesh is firm, and the fungus is long lasting. The cap is at first shallowly convex, but later becomes flattened and top-shaped or may even have a slight depression in the centre. The edge of the cap is initially slightly inrolled, and the colour varies between brown, ash-grey, brownish-grey and off-white, and when dry is noticeably paler. The surface has a fine frosty pruinose bloom. The **gills** at first whitish, and later pale yellowish are crowded, narrow and decurrent. The **stem** is swollen below and tapers upward, and varies from whitish to pale grey, its surface having a slightly fibrillose appearance. The **flesh** is white with a slightly unpleasant smell.

Spore print: Whitish-cream.

Distribution: A very common and widespread species found from early summer until very late in the year in all types of woodland, or in gardens on or around compost heaps. It frequently grows in large fairy-rings. It is one of the commoner mushrooms of central and southern Europe.

Possible confusion: At first sight it could be confused with similarly coloured Funnel Caps. But its late occurrence often in fairy rings, together with its colour, characteristic smell and considerable size distinguish it quite clearly. However, it does have to be carefully compared with *C. clavipes* (Club Foot Funnel Cap) and the distinctions are discussed under that species.

Edibility: To be avoided, since not everyone can tolerate this mushroom. Young fruit bodies in particular can cause quite serious digestive problems.

Notes: In earlier times it was bought and sold at markets, referred to as *Clitocybe nebularis*. Nebularis means 'clouded'.

Lepista nuda   Wood Blewit ⬤

The **cap** initially campanulate, expands and becomes shallowly convex with a central boss, and may eventually become saucer-shaped and upturned with a wavy edge. Initially bluish-lilac to mauve the greasy surface becomes brownish with age. The cap may reach 12 cm in diameter on maturity. The crowded, sinuate **gills** are mauve at first, but gradually fade to buff. The **stem** may reach a height of up to 8–10 cm and a diameter of 1.5–2.5 cm, and is bluish-lilac, sometimes greyish-lilac, with a longitudinally fibrillose surface. The **flesh** also has a lilac tinge. It smells and tastes perfumed.

Spore print: Pale flesh-pink.

Distribution: Wood Blewits may occur in hedgerows, in gardens, near compost heaps, or in humus-rich deciduous woodland. It appears from summer until late autumn, even into the New Year.

Possible confusion: The closest resemblance is with *L. glaucocana*, which is little more than a paler variant of the Wood Blewit. Inexperienced collectors sometimes confuse it with the mauve *Cortinarius violaceus* or with *C. hercynicus*. However in the *Cortinarius* species the cobwebby veil on the stem, and the brown spore print should prevent misidentification.

Edibility: The Wood Blewit is a very good edible mushroom, particularly recommended in mixtures. Its abundance and the fact that it comes when there are few other fungi to be had make it much sought-after.

Notes: This mushroom can be cultivated. *Nuda* means 'naked'.

Calocybe gambosa   Saint George's Mushroom ⬤

The genus name *Calocybe* means 'beautiful heads'. This species can be recognized from a distance by its white to cream or very pale ochre **cap**. It can reach 10 cm across, and is initially convex with strongly inrolled margin but expands gradually until almost flat. The whitish **gills** are very crowded and only indistinctly sinuate. The **stem** is cylindrical or club-shaped reaching a length of 8 cm and is whitish or pallid. The white **flesh** smells and tastes of meal.

Spore print: White.

Distribution: It appears towards the end of April around St George's Day (23 April), or during May, typically in fairy rings, in grassy roadside verges, pastures, open shrubby heathland or edges of woodland.

Possible confusion: *Inocybe patouillardii* appears at about the same time of year and is very dangerous. It looks simiilar, but its cap is more conical and its flesh reddens when bruised, often quite markedly, even in old specimens.

Edibility: It is a good edible mushroom, but there are collectors who are not keen on its strong mealy smell and taste.

Notes: The genus *Calocybe* comprises about thirteen species.

Leucopaxillus candidus   Giant Funnel Cap

The **cap** can reach a diameter of up to 25 cm. Initially the fungus is hemispherical but expands and flattens finally becoming funnel-shaped or depressed at the centre. It is milky-white and only when fully mature does it develop yellowish marks. The margin is slightly inrolled, smooth, downy, and sometimes undulating. The **gills** are somewhat decurrent, white, and easily removed from the cap with the finger. The thickish **stem**, the same colour, reaches a maximum height of 8 cm, and the fairly imposing diameter of 2–3.5 cm. Many specimens have a definite cylindrical form, others have a slight thickening about the middle, and the apical portion is covered by an obvious frosting or pruina. The **flesh**, which is also white, smells of meal or may be radish-like.
Spore print: White.
Distribution: Not recorded in Britain. According to many authors, the Giant Funnel Cap occurs gregariously only in Alpine pastures, but it can also be found in grassy places in highland areas. Finds in the plains are rare. It tends to form fairy rings, appearing during summer and autumn.
Possible confusion: There is a very similar species, *L. giganteus*, whose gills become cream to pale leather-coloured on maturity, however, confusion of the two would present no danger.
Edibility: A good edible mushroom, but it should not be collected for reasons of conservation.
Notes: Where extensive fairy rings occur, the grass in the centre dies. *Candidus* means 'pure white'.

Leucopaxillus gentianeus

The **cap** of this fungus, 5–10(15) cm across, is initially convex, but flattens with age sometimes becoming depressed at the centre. This species has a rather squat appearance, with the cap surface in young specimens appearing minutely velvety but this is soon lost and the leather-colour of young fruit bodies gives way to a cinnamon-brown or very dark brown colour. Only the inrolled margin remains a little paler, or even whitish, and has a slightly frosty pruinose cover and fine striations. The **gills** are crowded and sinuate, or sometimes decurrent with a tooth, while their colour is white to ivory. The thick **stem** is rather squat reaching to about 6 cm, and is often club-shaped. The surface is finely streaked and almost felt-like at the apex, at first white but bruises brown on handling. The **flesh** is white, rubbery with an immediate very bitter taste. The smell is mealy, and sometimes rather rancid.
Spore print: White.
Distribution: It is very rare but in recent years has been found several times in south-east England. It occurs in groups in autumn under deciduous or coniferous trees.
Possible confusion: It bears a similarity to some *Tricholoma* species. A good diagnostic feature is the extremely bitter taste.
Edibility: The bitter taste makes it inedible.
Notes: Formerly, the fungus was known as *L. amarus*. *Amarus* means 'bitter'.

Armillaria mellea Honey Fungus or Boot-lace Fungus

The Honey Fungus grows in dense clusters. In individual fully-grown specimens, the **cap** which may be shallowly depressed with a low umbo, reaches a diameter of about 15 cm. When young, the brownish to yellow sometimes olive-tinted surface is covered with darker filamentous scales, which can disappear with age. The initially whitish **gills** assume a yellowish or pale brownish colour and become slightly decurrent. The slender **stem** can grow to 15 cm in length, and bears a thick cottony, whitish or pale brownish ring. If the **flesh** is chewed raw, the initially pleasantly mild taste becomes unpleasant and catches the throat.

Spore print: White.

Distribution: A very common species in all types of woodland, parks and gardens during autumn. The Honey Fungus occurs at the base of living and dead trees and specimens apparently growing out of soil in reality are attached to roots or buried wood. On rare occasions it may be found on trunks some height above the ground. The Honey Fungus is parasitic on a wide variety of woody plants including privet and is responsible for the death of many trees each year.

Possible confusion: Some authors now distinguish five different species of Honey Fungus. *Pholiota squarrosa* (Shaggy Pholiota), another tufted fungus with conspicuously scaly caps is also parasitic on deciduous trees, has yellow flesh and brown spore print.

Edibility: Only the younger caps of this prolific fungus should be collected. It should be eaten with caution, since some people find it does not agree with them and causes digestive problems. It is advisable to cook them thoroughly and throw away the liquid.

Notes: *Mellea* pertains to honey and in this instance refers to the cap colour.

Flammulina velutipes Velvet Shank or Winter Fungus

The sticky **cap**, 2–10 cm across, is flat or slightly convex and is bright yellow with a darker tawny centre. The **gills** are somewhat distant, are sinuate and with a colour range from white (when young) to cream. The densely velvety **stem** is cylindrical, pale yellowish above, but dark brown to almost black in the lower half. The **flesh** is white or pale yellow with a pleasant smell.

Spore print: Cream or whitish.

Distribution: This very common and widespread fungus may be found any time during autumn and spring. It can be found in deciduous woodland, on fallen trunks particularly elm, on shrubs such as gorse and elder, and on exotic trees, in parks and gardens. It grows gregariously, sometimes in small clusters, even during snowy conditions and can survive severe frosts.

Possible confusion: The colour and sticky surface of the cap, the dark velvety stem and time of appearance are diagnostic for the Velvet Shank. The genus *Flammulina* also includes a smaller species restricted to the roots of Rest-harrow (*Ononis arvensis*).

Edibility: The fungus is edible, and particularly valuable in winter. Those wishing to eat it should take only the caps.

Notes: Velvet Shank is a popular edible fungus in Japan where it is commercially grown. It can also be cultivated in the garden on beech wood where it produces abundant fruit bodies. *Velutipes* means 'with a velvet foot'.

Collybia maculata   Foxy Spot or Spotted Tough Shank

This fungus seldom exceeds 8–10(12) cm in diameter. The **cap** is initially shallowly convex, and with age becomes slightly more flattened. It is fleshy, and at first white but gradually acquires rust-brown spots and patches. The margin of the cap is strikingly thin and inrolled. The **gills**, crowded, narrow, sinuate and attached with a tooth, are initially white and with age they too acquire rust-brown spots. The **stem** reaches a height of 6–10 cm, and in young specimens is solid, but later becomes increasingly hollow. It has a hard, fibrous texture. The stem, often twisted and indistinctly longitudinally striate may be slightly club-shaped or tapered and rooting below. Like the rest of the fruit body the white surface gradually develops rust-brown patches. The **flesh** is white and has a bitter taste, which is an additional diagnostic feature.

Spore print: Whitish-cream.

Distribution: Common and widespread from early autumn onwards. Can be found in coniferous, and less often deciduous woodland, usually in fairy rings. Also under bracken on heath ground.

Possible confusion: The white, convex cap with rusty patches, is distinctive and should ensure correct identification.

Edibility: Because of its tough fibrous texture and bitter taste it is inedible.

Notes: It is one of the large genus *Collybia* which comprises more than thirty species. They are small to medium-sized fungi with smooth caps, cartilaginous or flexible stems, and adnate or sinuate gills. In young specimens the margin of the cap is often inrolled. They all live on soil or wood. The spore print varies from white to cream or pale ochre.

Collybia fusipes   Spindle Shank

The tough brownish-red **cap** is initially campanulate but with increasing maturity it expands and flattens, although retaining a blunt umbo. The **gills** are distant, almost free but sometimes connected by veins, and are whitish then flesh-coloured but develop rusty patches. The 8–12 cm long **stem** is solid only when young, later hollow, often twisted, with longitudinal grooves, spindle-shaped and with a tapering root. The colour is the same as the cap. The **flesh** is whitish or tinged with red-brown, and very tough.

Spore print: White.

Distribution: Common and widespread from early summer in clusters at the base of trees especially oak. In Europe it is mainly found in the south, but occasionally as far north as southern Sweden. In Germany it occurs in oak and hornbeam woods and grows at an altitude of up to 650m. South of the Alps it is also found with sweet chestnuts.

Possible confusion: The fungus is readily identified by the spindle-shaped, rooting stem and the distant, non-white gills.

Edibility: It is edible, but with reservations. It is not really considered as a worthwhile edible mushroom, since neither the taste nor the smell are noteworthy.

Notes: The species name *fusipes* means 'spindle-footed'.

Collybia dryophila   Russet Shank

The **cap** reaches a maximum diameter of 3–6 cm. When young it is shallowly convex but on maturity it becomes flattened and slightly depressed at the centre, with a smooth surface varying in colour from pale yellowish or buff to almost white, being paler when dry and more intensely coloured when moist. The **gills** are crowded, very narrow and sinuate with a notch at the stem and colour which varies between whitish and buff. The **stem** is cylindrical, occasionally showing a thickened base. The whole fungus has a frail look, mainly brought about by the thin, hollow and fairly tough stem, which is orange-yellow to tan. The **flesh** is very thin, pale and watery.

Spore print: White.

Distribution: The Russet Shank is common and widespread and appears throughout the season from spring into autumn in all types of woodland, and grass verges.

Possible confusion: Identification is not easy since there are a whole series of relatives which are externally very similar. For example, the poisonous *C. hariolorum*, causing stomach complaints, which has a smell rather like Camembert.

Edibility: The Russet Shank is said to be slightly poisonous when eaten in large quantities, or at the very least difficult to digest.

Notes: Identification of the various *Collybia* species is often very difficult and requires careful study. The features of the genus will be found under *C. maculata* (Spotted Tough Shank). *Dryophila* is made up from Greek *dryu* meaning 'oak', and *philos* meaning 'loving'.

Collybia butyracea   Greasy Tough Shank or Buttery Tough Shank

The **cap** reaches a diameter of up to 8 cm, initially slightly domed, it soon flattens markedly, while retaining a rather prominent central umbo. With age the edges may become upturned to reveal the gills. The fleshy cap when moist is a greasy reddish brown to dark brown, more intensely coloured and darker towards the centre, but becoming pale buff on drying. The **gills** are broad, crowded, sinuate and rounded where they meet the stem, sometimes even free, and of a chalky white colour. The tough elastic **stem** has a white cottony base but is otherwise the same colour as the cap to the extreme apex contrasting markedly with the white gills. The **flesh** has a mushroomy smell.

Spore print: White to very pale pink.

Distribution: Very common and widespread, from summer into autumn the Greasy Tough Shank occurs in both deciduous and coniferous woods especially on acid soils. It often occurs in very large numbers.

Possible confusion: The characteristic buttery texture of the cap surface and the marked contrast between the white gills and dark colour of the stem ensure accurate identification.

Edibility: The Greasy Tough Shank is perfectly edible, though connoisseurs do not prize it highly because it has an insipid taste.

Notes: Some authors distinguish between *C. butyracea* (Greasy Tough Shank) and *C. asema*, which is pale ash-grey but otherwise hardly distinguishable from the typical species. *Butyracea* means 'buttery'.

Collybia confluens   Clustered or Tufted Tough Shank

The tough thin-fleshed **cap**, 2–4 cm across, is shallowly campanulate when young, but later becomes flattened with a slightly raised centre. The colour is a brownish-flesh colour when moist, drying out rapidly to almost white or pale yellow. The **gills**, almost free, narrow and exceptionally closely crowded, initially white, and later cream to flesh-coloured. The **stem** is up to 12 cm long, tough, cylindrical and the same colour as the cap, although densely covered over the entire length with minute hairs giving a whitish granular or felted appearance, especially in dry specimens. The tough **flesh** is whitish, thin, and smells initially of bitter almonds.

Spore print: White.

Distribution: *C. confluens* (Clustered Tough Shank) is widespread, very common and found in both deciduous and coniferous woodland, growing in dense clusters.

Possible confusion: It could be confused with *C. acervata*, which also grows in clusters. Its stem is, however, naked at least over the upper part. It grows on conifer trunks. If the cap of *C. confluens* (Clustered Tough Shank) is pulled off with an upward jerk, a knob-like swelling remains attached to the stem.

Edibility: The fungus would be edible but is not recommended.

Notes: There are still more *Collybia* species with a clustered habit and scaly or felted stems, but none worthy of consideration as edible mushrooms. *Confluens* means 'flowing together', and the name is derived because of the clustered growth form.

Collybia peronata   Wood Woolly-foot

The **cap** of the Wood Woolly-foot can reach 3–7 cm in diameter. Initially shallowly campanulate it gradually flattens and when mature it is smooth and leathery, with thin flesh and slightly wrinkled margin. The colour varies from tan to pale reddish-brown when moist, but is more often found in semi-dried condition when it is buff-coloured. The **gills** initially sinuate, pull away from the stem, and are interconnected by veins, with colour ranging from yellowish to a brownish-ochre. The **stem** can reach a height of 5–7 cm, is cylindrical, with only slight thickening at the base where it is densely covered with buff-coloured woolly hairs which is a good diagnostic feature, otherwise the tough, leathery stem is the same colour as the cap. The **flesh** is wood-coloured and the taste peppery.

Spore print: White.

Distribution: This very common and widespread fungus is found on leaf litter in deciduous woodland and less often with conifers during summer and autumn.

Possible confusion: Even if one were to confuse it with other species of *Collybia*, the taste would correct the error immediately: at first it seems mild, but after a few moments it becomes hot and peppery.

Edibility: Needless to say, the fungus is inedible.

Notes: There is no evidence that it is poisonous. Presumably the Wood Woolly-foot does no harm, apart from its taste, which lingers for a long time on tongue and palate. *Peronata* means 'wearing boots of felt'.

97

Marasmius scorodonius

The **cap** of this little fungus, is at most 1–2 cm in diameter, and initially hemispherical but becomes flattened and shallowly campanulate in older, expanded specimens and may eventually develop a slight depression at the centre. The surface is smooth and the margin slightly striated. When moist the cap has a reddish-flesh colour, but on drying becomes pallid. The **gills**, with an undulating edge, are fairly well-spaced, of uneven length and white, occasionally with a slight reddish tinge. The slender **stem** reaches 4–6 cm in height, tapering towards the base, and is smooth and slightly shiny, varying in colour between fox-red and dark brown. The exceedingly thin **flesh** smells strongly of garlic as does that of *M. alliaceus* which has a longer black stem. The latter fungus grows in beech woods on chalky soils.
Spore print: White.

Distribution: Occasionally on needles in coniferous woods, from summer into autumn, often in very large groups.
Possible confusion: One similar species is mentioned above. It can also be confused with *Micromphale perforans*, which also grows on conifer needles and has a very thin black hair-line stem.
Edibility: When dried, this tiny mushroom is very useful since it can often be harvested in large quantities, and used for flavouring as a garlic substitute.
Notes: *Scorodonius* comes from the Greek and means 'pertaining to garlic'.

Marasmius alliaceus

The **cap** has a diameter of 1–4 cm, and is at first campanulate, later expanded and shallowly campanulate with the margin vaguely striate or wrinkled. The colour can be pallid dirty buff, but is generally clay to grey-brown. The dirty-white **gills** are in striking contrast with the black **stem**. The latter, 8–10 cm tall (exceptionally to 20 cm) and 1–3 mm thick, is dark brown or completely black with only the very apex of a paler brown colour. It has a velvety surface and a tough, rigid texture. The very thin **flesh** is whitish in the cap, brownish in the stem, and has a strong unmistakable smell of garlic.
Spore print: White to pale cream.
Distribution: Chiefly in southern Britain and especially in the south-east where it may be found in beech woods on chalky soils, growing in leaf litter and amongst fallen twigs during autumn. It occurs regularly in some localities but in general must be regarded as uncommon and local.
Possible confusion: This fungus gives off such a strong and lasting smell of garlic that it is almost impossible to confuse it with any other. Even the smell of a single fruit body is very obvious. *M. prasiosmus* is uniformly brown except for the apex of the stem, tastes strong and grows on leaves.
Edibility: Edible, but not to everyone's taste.
Notes: *Alliaceus* means 'pertaining to garlic'.

Marasmius epiphyllus

The **cap** scarcely exceeds 5–10 mm and has a delicate appearance suggesting a minute umbrella, although older specimens gradually become flatter. The surface is slightly wrinkled and remains milky-white at all times. The few **gills** are very widely spaced, branched and interveined and may appear slightly decurrent. Like the cap they remain white. The **stem** up to 2.5 cm high is very narrow, thread-like, but tough. It is white, becoming brown below and under a lens is seen to have a minutely velvety surface.

Spore print: White.

Distribution: A very common and widespread fungus but no doubt often overlooked because of its small size and occurrence on fallen leaves and twigs during autumn, often in very large numbers in deciduous woodland.

Possible confusion: Because of the habitat, the white colour and the very distant, almost vein-like gills, it cannot be mistaken for anything else.

Edibility: No-one would think of collecting this minute species for the pot! It does not, however, appear to be poisonous.

Notes: *Epiphyllus* from the Greek *epi* meaning 'on' and *phyllon* meaning 'leaf'.

Marasmius bulliardii

This is a particularly pretty little fungus, whose radially grooved **cap** reaches a diameter of only 0.3–1 cm. Fully expanded specimens are more or less convex with a navel-like depression in the centre and vary in colour from pale ochre to wood-brown. Occasionally much paler specimens are also found, appearing almost white. The **gills** are whitish, distant and attached to a collar surrounding the apex of the stem. The tough **stem** is very narrow, thread-like, almost black with only the extreme apex remaining pallid. The **flesh** is very thin, without obvious smell.

Spore print: White.

Distribution: Probably both common and widespread but often overlooked on account of its small size. It grows *en masse* on fallen needles or leaves among moss, and can be found between summer and autumn.

Possible confusion: The following species look similar to *M. bulliardii*: *M. epiphyllus* grows on dead branches, twigs and leaf petioles. The larger *M. ramealis* grows abundantly on fallen twigs but has a pallid brownish-flesh colour. *M. perforans* prefers rotting needles, especially of spruce, and has a whitish stem which is brown towards the base and has a strong smell of cabbage water.

Edibility: Totally worthless species because of its small size.

Notes: *Bulliardii* in honour of the French mycologist Pierre Bulliard.

Marasmius oreades Fairy Ring Champignon

The **cap** is initially convex but when mature it is campanulate with a prominent central boss and can reach a diameter of up to 5 cm. The surface is smooth, and when moist the colour ranges from ochre with a pink tinge to pale reddish-brown, but on drying soon becomes pale buff. The **gills** are distant, at first white, but soon assume a pale brown or buff colour. The tough **stem** reaches a height of 4–7 cm, and varies from whitish to buff with a white felty cover at the base. The **flesh** is thin, pale ochre and smells slightly of cyanide.

Spore print: Whitish.

Distribution: The Fairy Ring Champignon, as its name suggests, usually grows in rings or rows in short turf or on lawns in gardens and parks, from spring to autumn. A very common and widespread species.

Possible confusion: It bears a similarity to *M. lupuletorum*, which has an almost black stem, and also to *M. wynnei*, which has a cap with pale violet tint and stem which is reddish or chocolate-brown below. The Fairy Ring Champignon can be confused with poisonous *Clitocybe* species, but these are never so tough, lack thick distant gills and do not have the characteristic humped centre to the cap.

Edibility: A very popular edible mushroom, especially as it can often be found early in the year, and because it can be dried for future use.

Notes: *Oreades* is Greek and means 'mountain nymph', a reference to the appearance in fairy rings.

Mycena pura Lilac Mycena

The thin **cap** of this medium-sized fungus reaches a diameter of 3–6 cm. Initially bell-shaped, it expands with age but usually retains a blunt umbo. The surface has quite varied colouration according to the degree of hydration, from dirty pink through pale lilac to white with a hint of greyish-pink but is usually rosy-pink or lilac. The cap margin is striate when moist. The **gills** are sinuate, widely spaced, and interveined with the same colour as the cap but usually slightly paler. The **stem** is up to 7 cm long and the same colour as the cap, or sometimes a little darker. The **flesh** is watery and will smell and taste of radish.

Spore print: White.

Distribution: It is widespread and common usually in deciduous woodland during summer and autumn, and often quite late in the season.

Possible confusion: *M. pelianthina* is very similar to the Lilac Mycena but has a dark dotted gill edge and grows mainly in deciduous woods in the vicinity of beech. *M. rosea* is generally more massive than the Lilac Mycena and has a beautiful whitish-pink cap and a pink stem, it too grows under deciduous trees. *M. diosma* is a recently-described species growing in late autumn on rotting beech leaves but has not been found in Britain.

Edibility: The Lilac Mycena was previously considered edible, but a number of cases of poisoning have now been recorded.

Notes: *Pura* means 'pure'.

Mycena alcalina

The conical or bell-shaped **cap** retains its form into maturity, scarcely flattening with age and reaches a diameter of about 1–3 cm. The centre of the cap is grey-brown or honey-brown, sometimes darker, while the long striations running from the centre to the whitish margin become more and more grey. The membranous flesh of the cap is fragile. The **gills** often protrude from the cap margin and are distant, and pale grey with a white edge. The slender **stem** can reach 6 or even 7 cm in length, and is the same colour as the cap, also shading from grey to yellowish-brown. The fungus has a thin **flesh** which smells strongly of ammonia, although this smell is sometimes entirely absent.

Spore print: White.

Distribution: *M. alcalina* is widespread but occasional and grows in clusters on the mossy trunks of conifers, though also on fallen needles. It may appear in the spring, but the main fruiting period is during the autumn.

Possible confusion: Possibly with other *Mycena* species, for example, *M. leptocephala*, which occurs in deciduous and coniferous woodland among detritus and moss. Apart from this, the strong smell of ammonia makes confusion unlikely.

Edibility: The fungus is inedible, mainly because of the highly unpleasant smell and taste. It is not known to be poisonous.

Notes: Collectors should not collect *M. alcalina* in the interest of conservation. *Alcalina* comes from Arabic and means 'alkaline'.

Mycena renati

Within the genus, this fungus ranks as medium-sized. The **cap**, which is pinkish brown, expands to a diameter of 2 cm, and when young is bell-shaped with obvious frosting at the margin. The **gills** are sinuate and initially white, later with a pinkish tinge. The **stem** can reach 3–5 cm in length, and is initially golden-yellow, later yellowish-brown or leather-brown. The whitish **flesh** has a similar smell to that of *M. alcalina*, both smelling strongly and unpleasantly of ammonia.

Spore print: Whitish.

Distribution: A rare species in southern England, although it can be considered a characteristic species of the central and southern European highland beech woods, preferring chalky soils. It fruits, often in quantity, in autumn on moist, rotten wood, principally of beech and other deciduous trees.

Possible confusion: There are similarities with *M. viridimarginata* which is not described further here but which also has a clear smell of ammonia. Both belong to a group of about eighteen species which are often difficult to distinguish even for experienced mycologists.

Edibility: *M. renati* is totally inedible because of its unpleasant smell. Its small size also ensures that no one would think of collecting it to eat.

Notes: None of the *Mycena* species described has much value as an edible mushroom, owing to their small size.

Mycena galericulata Bonnet Mycena

The somewhat radially wrinkled **cap** can have a diameter of 4–6 cm. Initially it is shallowly campanulate or bell-shaped, but soon expands while retaining a prominent obtuse central boss. It is grey to grey-brown when moist but can dry to almost white with a hint of pink. There are vein-like connections between the **gills**, which are initially whitish but gradually become pale flesh pink. The **stem** reaches a height of 8–10 cm, but with a diameter of only 5 mm and has a tough texture. It is hollow, smooth and shiny, with a slightly white woolly base but otherwise the same colour as the cap. The **flesh** has a mealy smell when crushed.

Spore print: White.

Distribution: The Bonnet Mycena, one of the commonest members of the genus, is found on the stumps of deciduous and coniferous trees. It grows in small tufts, less commonly singly, and appears at almost any time of year, although most frequently in autumn.

Possible confusion: This smallish but tough fungus is unlikely to be confused with any other, at least as long as the gills have not turned pink. It is by far the most common tufted species of *Mycena* fruiting on dead wood.

Edibility: It is not known to be poisonous, but should not be collected, because it is worthless as an edible mushroom.

Notes: *Galericulata* means 'having a small hood'.

Mycena inclinata

Like most *Mycena* species, it is small. Its **cap** reaches 2–4 cm in diameter. Initially bell-shaped it retains this shape to maturity, with the cap margin, which is striate, and crenulate, over-reaching the gills. The colour is a dark grey-brown and the surface often has a moist greasy sheen. The narrow **gills**, which are adnate, have a pale, sometimes pinkish colour. Mature specimens may have greyish gills. The tough **stem**, 6–10 cm long and 2–4 mm thick, initially steely blue-grey, soon becomes dark red-brown with a paler apex. It is elastic, leathery and tough, longitudinally striated, and rather fibrous with a white woolly base. The **flesh** is whitish in the cap and pale ochre in the stem, turning golden-yellow when bruised. It has a rancid taste and smell.

Spore print: White.

Distribution: This very common species is, in Britain, almost restricted to growing on the rotting stumps of oak, appearing in dense clusters from late summer until late autumn.

Possible confusion: Because of the striated cuticle and the grey colour of the cap, it might be taken for *M. galericulata* (Bonnet Mycena). This latter, however, is easily distinguished by its uniformly dull-coloured stem and the gills being pink when mature.

Edibility: The tiny cap is of no value to the collector who is only interested in edible fungi. They are not known to be poisonous.

Notes: *Inclinata* means 'leaning', a reference to the frequently curved stems.

106

Mycena epipterygia Slimy Yellow-stemmed Mycena

The **cap** is at most 1–1.5 cm across, and either conical or campanulate even at maturity when it resembles a small helmet in shape. The pale greyish or fawn cap is striate almost to the centre, and covered by a transparent, completely separable, elastic layer of mucilage. The **gills** are decurrent with a tooth, at first white, later with a hint of pink and a detachable elastic gill edge. The thin **stem** can grow to 8 cm. It, too, is covered by a layer of mucilage. The colour is pallid except for its pale yellow or lemon-yellow base and apex. The fungus is thin-fleshed without any particular taste or smell.

Spore print: White.

Distribution: The fungus is both very common and widespread growing gregariously amongst grass, especially along tracks over heathland during summer and autumn.

Possible confusion: *M. viscosa* is another similar species with darker sticky cap and yellow mucilage. It grows on conifer stumps and has a rancid taste and more robust habit.

Edibility: Worthless as an edible fungus.

Notes: *Epipterygia* is Greek and means 'covered with a skin'.

Mycena crocata Orange-milking Mycena

Initially conical, the **cap** later becomes bell-shaped, with a diameter of 1–3 cm, and is striate at the margin. The colour varies from olive-grey to greyish-brown, and when roughly handled bruises a vivid orange-red. Similar production of latex results when the adnexed, whitish **gills** are bruised. The **stem** grows to 4–8 cm in length and 2–3 mm in diameter, and is hollow with the base covered in a white woolliness. The colour varies from sulphur-yellow near the apex to saffron-yellow below and when the stem is broken it exudes a copious orange-yellow milky fluid. The thin **flesh** is also yellow and exudes the same brightly coloured fluid, which stains the fingers.

Spore print: White.

Distribution: This uncommon fungus is of local occurrence in south-east England in beech woods on chalk, where it usually

grows singly. It grows in the same kind of habitat as *Marasmius alliaceus*, from September to November.

Possible confusion: Because of the exudation of orange-yellow milk this fungus is unmistakable. Growing in clusters on wood, the closely related *M. haematopoda* has a dark blood-red juice, whereas the scattered but gregarious fruit bodies of *M. sanguinolenta* which grows on the ground in grassy places such as lawns and woodland rides, exudes a watery, blood-red juice.

Edibility: Not poisonous, but worthless for eating.

Notes: *Crocata* is Greek meaning 'saffron-coloured' (like a crocus).

Laccaria amethystea Amethyst Deceiver

The diameter of the **cap** reaches 1–6 cm, with larger specimens being the exception. Initially the cap has an inrolled margin and convex shape, but it later expands and can be irregularly shaped often with a shallow saucer-like appearance with upturned edge. When moist the surface is deep purplish-violet to amethyst, but soon dries to a beige colour when the felty texture is more apparent. The margin is slightly striate. The **gills** are distant, adnate, and of the same attractive colour as the cap and they too pale as the fungus dries. The **stem** has a maximum height of 10 cm, usually less, and a diameter of 4–10 mm. The upper part has a mealy, pruinose surface, while the base is woolly and of a bright lilac colour. The **flesh** is thin, hygrophanous, elastic and mauve-coloured with a slightly fruity smell and a mild taste.

Spore print: White.

Distribution: This completely amethyst-coloured fungus grows from early summer until late autumn, often somewhat gregariously in all types of woodland. It is very common and widespread with no particular soil requirements.

Possible confusion: With *Mycena pura* (Lilac Mycena), although the habit, colour and texture are different.

Edibility: Some connoisseurs prize this mushroom, although only in mixtures, since it does not have a very marked flavour. It can be safely collected without risk of mis-identification.

Notes: *Amethystina* means 'dark lilac-blue'.

Laccaria laccata Deceiver

The **cap** reaches 5 cm in diameter, initially convex, it later becomes more flattened and often shows a navel-like depression at the centre. When young the edge is inrolled but soon becomes undulating. When moist the fungus is brick-red with a striate edge, but when dry it appears more or less pale ochre but with a felt-like surface. The pink to flesh-pink **gills** are broadly attached with a decurrent tooth, and are broad, thickish, and distant. The **stem** reaches a height of 10 cm and is thin, coloured like the cap, tough, fibrous and covered at the base with white mycelium. The **flesh** is thin, flesh-red or paler, fairly tough in the stem, and has a pleasant smell.

Spore print: White.

Distribution: A very common and widespread species, which can be found from June until November in deciduous and coniferous woodland, as well as in bogs and other damp and wet places.

Possible confusion: There are numerous varieties of this species, which can only be identified with the use of a microscope. The much more robust, and taller *L. proxima* has a more orange-brown scaly cap. Like *L. laccata* (The Deceiver) it is also hygrophanous, and is found in boggy or swampy areas. Some authors mention the possibility of confusion with *Cortinarius orellanus*, which has, apart from other diagnostic features such as the filamentous covering and orange-brown gills, a rust-brown spore print. Only very inexperienced collectors could make such an erroneous misidentification. Nevertheless such collectors should note that *L. laccata* (The Deceiver) is very variable in appearance, and looks quite different in the moist and dry state.

Edibility: The fungus is edible.

Notes: *Laccata* means 'painted'.

The **cap** of this large thin-fleshed fungus appears initially convex, about 5 cm in diameter, but becomes shallowly campanulate or flattened at maturity reaching a diameter of about 15 cm. The tough surface is entirely ornamented with tiny radiating fibrils, and the colour varies between brown and grey. The whitish **gills** are soft, sinuate and very deep. The tough **stem** can reach about 12 cm in height and about 1–1.5 cm in diameter, and is cylindrical with only slight thickening towards the base. The surface is longitudinally striate and fibrillose, its colour similar to that of the cap but paler and passing at the base into white string-like strands of mycelium. The **flesh** is white and odourless, sometimes with a bitter taste.

Spore print: White.

Distribution: This is a widespread and common species found both on rotting tree stumps and in humus-rich soils arising from buried wood, from early summer into autumn. By following the white stringy chords back from the fruit bodies its origin can be traced.

Possible confusion: There is no similar fungus which is poisonous. Because the edge of the cap is often split radially, really inexperienced collectors might take it for a species of *Inocybe*, but the habitat, the broad, pale gills and the mycelial strands at the base of the stem are quite different.

Edibility: Edible, but with reservations. It is only suitable in mixtures with other mushrooms.

Notes: *Platyphylla* means 'broad-leaved', and refers to the gills.

Oudemansiella mucida Slimy Beech Tuft, Poached Egg Mushroom or Porcelain Fungus

The very thin-fleshed **cap**, almost hemispherical when young, becomes shallowly convex and may reach a diameter of up to 8 cm at maturity, although 5–6 cm is a more usual size. Moist caps have a thick covering of mucilage which gives the fungus its specific name. The colour, usually white, can be slightly greyish, less commonly brownish-grey, while the surface is slightly transparent. The broad, white **gills** are distant and either adnate or adnexed with a small tooth. The thin **stem** grows to 7 or 8 cm and is tough with the apical portion appearing striate. Also on the upper portion of the stem there is a membranous, white, striate ring, which may disappear as the fruit body ages. The base is often thickened into a bulbous shape. The thin **flesh** is white.

Spore print: White.

Distribution: In Britain this very common and widespread fungus is almost exclusively confined to dead branches of beech trees which may be either still attached high in the crown of the tree or lying on the ground. Only very rarely is it found on oak. It normally grows in clusters, but solitary fruit bodies are also found. In Europe it occurs wherever beeches grow, from summer through to autumn.

Possible confusion: It is the only white species of the genus in Europe with a ring, and therefore easy to identify, apart from its marked preference for growing on beech.

Edibility: The slimy texture and thin flesh makes this species gastronomically worthless.

Notes: The species name *mucida* comes from the Latin *mucus*, a reference to the slimy surface of the fungus.

Xerula radicata (Syn. Oudemansiella radicata) Rooting Shank

The **cap** has a diameter of between 5 and 7 cm, initially conical, it expands and becomes shallowly campanulate or flattened with a central umbo. The surface is usually coarsely radially wrinkled or grooved from the centre, and when moist is somewhat slimy, pallid, ochre-brown or olivaceous. The deep **gills** are distant, adnexed or adnate with a decurrent tooth, and they are white, sometimes with a brown edge especially after frost. The **stem** can reach considerable lengths, up to 15 or 20 cm, and is usually less than 1 cm thick. The surface is smooth, or longitudinally striate and white with a flush of the cap colour toward the slightly thickened base which is prolonged into a deeply rooting portion. The thin white **flesh** is tasteless and odourless.

Spore print: White.
Distribution: Often one of the first species to fruit in early summer from June into autumn. The Rooting Shank grows apparently on the ground in deciduous woodland but if the long fungus root is traced back it will be seen that it is associated with decaying roots or buried wood, especially of beech. It is even said sometimes to colonize coniferous wood.

Possible confusion: Some other species of the genus e.g. *X. longipes* (Velvety Stemmed Rooting Shank) look similar but it has a velvety stem.

Edibility: The Rooting Shank is edible and could be used in mixtures, but on its own its culinary value is small.

Notes: *Radicata* means 'rooting'.

Xerula longipes (Syn. Oudemansiella longipes) Velvety Stemmed Rooting Shank

The **cap** is initially conical but expands to a bell-shape or becomes flattened reaching 3–6 cm in diameter, but a small central umbo is always discernible. The dry, slightly velvety surface varies from milky-brown to almost chestnut-brown in colour, and the margin of the cap is somewhat striate. The broad, distant **gills** are either adnexed or adnate and white to yellowish. The elongated form of the **stem** is the basis for the Latin name – *longipes* means 'long foot', and it can grow to a length of 20 cm. In colour it is similar to the cap and has a velvety surface. In many specimens the stem is slightly striate. The **flesh** is white and often rather bitter-tasting.

Spore print: White.
Distribution: In Britain the Velvety Stemmed Rooting Shank is widespread but uncommon growing in deciduous woodland and from dead roots near oak, chestnut or beech. It appears in summer and continues into autumn.

Possible confusion: There are two varieties which can be distinguished by, among other factors, the differing hair colour on the stem. The enlarged photograph opposite illustrates the hairy stem.

Edibility: In literature there are diverging claims regarding edibility of this fungus; some reporting it to be edible while other indicating that it is inedible.

Agrocybe praecox

The **cap** reaches a diameter of 7 cm, and is initially hemispherical but it expands and becomes convex then flattened. The colour is mainly pale ochreous-cream or dirty white when dry but when older it can show light tan patches at the centre. The adnate **gills** are initially pale clay-coloured, but with maturity they become pale red-brown. The **stem** may reach 6 cm in height, and a diameter of 4–8 mm; it is creamy-white but often streaked and discoloured brownish, and toward the apex there is a membranous, striate ring, ragged remnants of which are often found on the edge of the cap. Many authors emphasize the mealy smell of the **flesh**, but this should never be relied upon, since it is not always pronounced. Many specimens taste unpleasantly bitter.

Spore print: Greyish-brown or cigar-brown.

Distribution: A. praecox is a common and widespread vernal species which often appears in May, and can be found throughout the summer months. It is a grassland species which occurs on roadside verges, in meadows and pastures, gardens and parks.

Possible confusion: This is a somewhat variable species, and distinguishing it from others of the same genus can often be difficult. A. dura is generally more massive, with firmer flesh, and cap often cracked in places. It grows in dry, warm and chalky places.

Edibility: Although reported as edible by some authorities, others consider it to be inedible.

Notes: Identification of the similar members of this genus requires the use of a microscope. Praecox means 'premature' and refers to its fruiting rather early in the season.

Agrocybe cylindracea (Syn. A. aegerita)

The small convex and later flat **cap** reaches a maximum diameter of 10 cm. It is pale buff to almost white, usually with a foxy-brown flush at the centre. The surface of the cap is often uneven and irregularly wrinkled or pitted toward the margin, and may be somewhat cracked exposing the white flesh. The **gills** are crowded and either adnate or decurrent with a tooth, and initially whitish, but on maturing they become cinnamon-brown. The **stem**, up to 15 cm long, and 1–1.5 cm wide, is often curved and may taper towards the base; it is creamy-white but sometimes becomes brown below. There is on the upper third of the stem a persistent white, membranous dependent ring. The **flesh** is hard, white, sometimes slightly brownish especially in the base of the stem. The fungus has a slightly unpleasant rancid or cheese-like smell.

Spore print: Brown.

Distribution: A. cylindracea is rather uncommon in Britain and tends to be a southerly species since it is widespread throughout the Mediterranean region, becoming increasingly rare in central and northern Europe. The fruit bodies are generally found in clusters on the stumps and trunks of various broad-leaved trees, particularly poplar and willow, and even on elder from spring into autumn.

Possible confusion: Scarcely possible.

Edibility: This mushroom was already well known and popular with the Greeks and Romans and indeed was cultivated by them.

Notes: In the Mediterranean region, and particularly in southern France, this mushroom is cultivated on thick planks of poplar which are rubbed with the gills of ripe fruit bodies and covered with turf.

Pholiota aurivella

The fleshy **cap** has a diameter of 6–12(16) cm and is convex or somewhat flattened at the centre when mature with an inrolled margin. The surface of the cap varies from a lemon-yellow to a rusty-yellow, with very obvious concentrically arranged chestnut-brown scales. In damp weather the cap is very slimy and the scales which are then gelatinous, float in the gluten and are easily washed off. The **gills**, broadly sinuate or adnate, are initially yellowish, then rusty and finally chestnut-coloured. The **stem** reaches 5–8 cm in height with a diameter of 1–1.5 cm. It is yellowish with a rust-brown base and is ornamented below the ring with bands of squarrose brown scales. In younger specimens the upper part of the stem bears a yellow, woolly ring. The yellowish-white **flesh** is fairly firm and sometimes smells faintly of radish.

Spore print: Rust-brown.
Distribution: Fairly frequent during autumn growing in clusters on the trunks of living, broad-leaved trees, especially beech, often several metres above ground level. It may also occur on fallen, dead trunks.
Possible confusion: The less common *Ph. adiposa* is very similar, but usually grows at the base of beech trees, and the cap bears darker, more numerous and more prominent scales.
Edibility: It is edible, but the quality is mediocre.
Notes: *Aurivella* means 'with a golden skin'.

Pholiota squarrosa **Shaggy Pholiota**

The **cap**, 3–10(15) cm across, is initially bell-shaped, then expanded convex with a raised centre. When young, the cap margin is strongly inrolled and remains so for some time. The straw-yellow or ochre-yellow surface is densely covered with darker, shaggy upturned scales which cannot be wiped off and often overhang and fringe the cap margin. The adnate, crowded **gills** are initially wax-yellow and later rust-coloured. The **stem** can reach a length of 12(20) cm and a diameter of 1–2.5 cm. It is coloured as the cap, and beneath the level of the ring it is covered with abundant darker, recurved scales. Above the ring it is naked. The spreading ring is fibrillose and fringe-like. The **flesh** is yellowish and smells of rotten wood. The taste is not unpleasant, sometimes reminiscent of radish.
Spore print: Rust-brown.
Distribution: A common and widespread species in autumn growing in clusters at the base of living trunks of deciduous trees, very occasionally it may also be found at the base of conifers. One of its preferred hosts is elm. Although it can live as a saprophyte, it can also be a dangerous wound parasite causing a white rot.
Possible confusion: It might be confused with various species of the Honey Fungus complex but these have smooth stems and their colours tend more towards the flesh-coloured or brownish, and in any case their spore powder is white. Within the genus (about thirty species) the Shaggy Pholiota is one of a group all with shaggy cap and stem. Some of them resemble one another closely, and identification can prove difficult.
Edibility: Edible, with some reservations. It should certainly be thoroughly cooked.
Notes: *Squarrosa* means 'with scab-like scales'.

Pholiota destruens

The **cap** reaches a diameter of 4–20 cm. It appears initially hemispherical, then campanulate or broadly convex and finally flattens out markedly. The surface of the massive, fleshy cap is densely covered with large, irregular, cottony white scales on a yellowish-brown background, and these also fringe the margin. The **gills** are crowded and adnate, tending to be whitish at first, then brown and finally tobacco-brown. The short, thick **stem** reaches a diameter of 4 cm, at least in fully-grown fruit bodies which are up to 10 cm long. Towards the base it may be even thicker and tends to be rooted in cracks and crevices. The whitish to pale brown surface bears irregular white cottony scales, and on the upper portion there is a fibrillose cottony ring. The **flesh** of this fungus remains white at all times, except at the base of the stem where it is cinnamon-brown. The taste is mild, though it can be bitter, and there is a malty smell.

Spore print: Dark brown.

Distribution: A rare fungus in Britain found growing in small clusters on the trunks of poplars and sometimes other deciduous trees during autumn. In Europe it is more widespread in the south.

Possible confusion: The very rare *Ph. heteroclita* has a yellowish cap covered with brownish fibrillose scales which are pale ochre towards the edge. It grows singly, principally on birch but less commonly on alder.

Edibility: It is not poisonous but there are specimens with an intensely bitter taste.

Notes: *Destruens* means 'destroying'.

Phaeolepiota aurea

The **cap** can be 5 to 25(30) cm across. Initially it appears almost spherical, but then gradually expands to broadly campanulate and may eventually even be slightly depressed in the centre, while retaining an inconspicuous umbo. The surface, sometimes wrinkled, can be golden-yellow, lion-yellow, reddish-ochre, or even apricot-coloured, and has a fine, almost dusty, granular texture at first, or velvety in mature specimens. The thin **gills** are not particularly deep and are adnexed, often with a decurrent tooth. Initially ochre, they gradually become brownish-yellow. The similarly coloured surface of the **stem** is also granular and finely striate and is sheathed by a large spreading, and at first upstanding, membranous ring which is also covered on the underside with golden-brown granules. The bulbous stem can reach a height of 20(30) cm and is quite massive. As the fungus matures the **flesh** changes colour from white to yellowish, with a hint of red in the stem.

Spore print: Ochre.

Distribution: A widespread but rare species in Britain, it is distributed throughout the northern hemisphere, being found chiefly in the south and south-east. It occurs, often among stinging nettles and usually gregariously, in clearings in all types of woodland during autumn.

Possible confusion: Its striking appearance and especially the funnel-shaped ring covered below with golden-brown granules prevent confusion with other fungi.

Edibility: Edible, but should not be collected in the interests of conservation.

Notes: In the photograph the fungus is not seen in its typical habitat. *Aurea* means 'golden'.

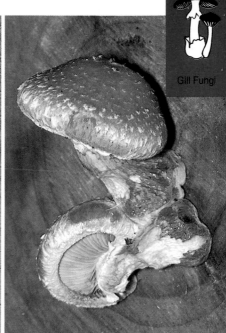

Galerina marginata (Syn. G. unicolor)

The thin-fleshed **cap** up to 4 cm in diameter, is initially convex, later flat. When moist it is honey-coloured, ochre or yellowish-brown with a translucent striate margin. On drying, this hygrophanous fungus becomes pale yellowish-brown. The **gills** are adnate or slightly decurrent, crowded, narrow, initially pale ochre, then rust-brown when mature. The **stem** is cylindrical with a white, fibrillose base, pale honey-coloured near the apex and darker below, the extreme apex being white and mealy pruinose. The ring, borne high on the stem, is generally erect, membranous and soon disappears. Below it the stem has a covering of sparse pale scales. The **flesh** is yellowish in the cap and dark brown in the stem and smells of meal when bruised.

Spore print: Rust-brown.

Distribution: The fungus is both common and widespread, growing in clusters or singly on the trunks of both conifers and broad-leaved trees from August to October.

Possible confusion: *G. marginata* is the smaller but dangerous 'double' of *Kuehneromyces mutabilis*. This latter, however, is scaly beneath its obvious ring, a darker brown, strongly hygrophanous and lacks the mealy smell.

Edibility: *G. marginata* is a dangerous poisonous fungus, containing a substance also found in *Amanita phalloides* (Death Cap).

Notes: The genus *Galerina* comprises about fifty-five species, some very hard to identify, of which at least three are very poisonous. *Marginata* means 'edged'.

Kuehneromyces mutabilis

The **cap** reaches a diameter of 4–5(8) cm. Initially hemispherical, it later becomes broadly campanulate or flattened while retaining a slight umbo. The surface feels moist and during rain the fruit bodies can take up a lot of moisture, causing a striking change of colour. When wet it is a watery, dirty yellowish-brown to cinnamon-brown with a striate margin, but soon becomes pale ochreous from the centre when it begins to dry. The edge has fine striations. The **gills**, which are crowded, adnate or slightly decurrent, are initially yellowish, then rust-brown. The **stem** which can reach a height of 6(10) cm and have a width of 5–10 mm, is solid at first but later hollow and has a tough texture. There is an apical ring which is lost very early, so it is not present on every specimen. Beneath the membranous, spreading ring, often coloured brown by spore powder, the stem is dark rust-brown and somewhat scaly, above it is paler and striate. The **flesh** is pale in the cap, brown in the stem, with a pleasant smell and a mild taste.

Spore print: Ochre-brown.

Distribution: Common and widespread, in deciduous woodland appearing from April until November/December in large clusters on dead stumps. It may occasionally be found on coniferous wood.

Possible confusion: It would be dangerous to confuse it with *Galerina marginata*. The rather similar Sulphur Tuft lacks the ring. The edible *Psathyrella hydrophila* also has a brown, hygrophanous cap, but the stem is white and without a ring.

Edibility: Edible.

Notes: *Mutabilis* means 'changeable'.

123

Hypholoma fasciculare Sulphur Tuft

The sulphur-yellow **cap**, which can reach 7 cm across, is clearly browner in the centre. Initially hemispherical or campanulate, it quickly becomes shallowly convex or flattened. In young specimens there are often yellow remnants of the veil hanging from the margin. The **gills** when young are sulphur-yellow, but as the spores mature they become olive-brown. They are adnate and crowded. The yellowish **stem** can reach a length of 10 cm and a diameter of 5–10 mm. At the apex there is often a vague, fibrillose ring zone but this is frequently made more conspicuous by trapped purple-brown spores. The **flesh** is sulphur-yellow and has a very bitter taste. It is thin above the gills but thicker and more fleshy at the centre.

Spore print: Greyish-violet.

Distribution: The green-gilled Sulphur Tuft is widespread and very common, growing in large clusters on and around rotten tree stumps and on fallen trunks. It is found on coniferous and deciduous wood at almost any time of year, but usually from May until Decmeber.

Possible confusion: Either with *H. capnoides*, which never has greenish-coloured gills and grows on conifers, or with *H. sublateritium* (Brick-red Tuft), another bitter-tasting, inedible species which bears yellowish remnants of the veil on its brick-red cap.

Edibility: For a long time it was thought to be merely inedible, but more recent research has shown that it contains poisons which are also to be found in *Amanita phalloides* (Death Cap).

Notes: The following descriptions of the similar *Hypholoma* species should be studied to avoid unpleasant mistakes. The photograph shows the fungus growing on buried wood in moss. *Fasciculare* means 'clustered'.

Hypholoma capnoides

In mature specimens the **cap** can reach 8 cm across and is completely smooth. Initially hemispherical, it later becomes campanulate or flattened, with the colour a fairly uniformly pale yellowish-brown, without any greenish tones. The adnexed **gills** are pale when young but soon assume a clear smoke-grey colour, which never resembles the greenish-yellow shades of the poisonous Sulphur Tuft. The hollow **stem** up to 10 cm in length and up to 5–10 mm in diameter is yellow-brown towards the base but paler towards the apex. The **flesh** is white with no particular taste or smell.

Spore print: Greyish-violet.

Distribution: Widespread and occasional in coniferous woods, especially on the stumps of spruce and pine. It grows in clusters almost all the year round, but mainly in two flushes from March to May and from September to December.

Possible confusion: Confusion with *H. fasciculare* (Sulphur Tuft), which is poisonous, is possible. Also with *Kuehneromyces mutabilis*, though this would present no danger. The collector should refer to the descriptions of these two species.

Edibility: *H. capnoides* is a popular edible mushroom, though only the caps should be taken, as the stems are often tough.

Notes: It is advisable to refrain from picking this species unless completely certain of its identity. The genus *Hypholoma* comprises about seventeen species growing on wood, mossy turf or peat. Some species are bitter and therefore inedible. *Capnoides* means 'smoke-like'.

Hypholoma sublateritium Brick-red Tuft

The **cap** may reach 8 cm in diameter and is at first hemispherical but later expands and becomes convex. Only the centre of the cap is brick-coloured, and it pales towards the margin to a rather insipid, watery-brown or ochre. In young specimens there are often yellowish-green fibrillose remnants of the veil. Otherwise the surface of the cap is smooth and dry. The **gills** are adnexed, crowded and initially pale yellow in colour, but become olive-grey and eventually dark olive-brown as the spores mature, although the edge is paler. The **stem** can reach a height of 12 cm, and a width of 5–12 mm, is pale yellow at the apex and becomes brown below. On the apical portion just beneath the cap there is a fibrillose cortina which appears dark due to trapped spores. The **flesh** is pale yellowish and slightly bitter.

Spore print: Olive-brown to purple-brown.

Distribution: The occasional but widespread Brick-red Tuft can be found from the end of August until well into autumn. It is found at the base of the rotting stumps of deciduous trees. It is never as common as *H. fasciculare* (Sulphur Tuft) and *H. capnoides*.

Possible confusion: With other species of *Hypholoma*. Confusion with *Kuehneromyces mutabilis* or *H. capnoides* would present no danger as both are good edible fungi.

Edibility: It is suspected of causing health problems, but its bitter taste makes it unsuitable for eating.

Notes: *Sublateritium* means 'almost brick-red'.

Stropharia semiglobata Sticky Dung Round Head

The **cap** of this fungus reaches only 2–3(5) cm in diameter. Initially strongly hemispherical it retains the shape while expanding, a characteristic responsible for its Latin and English names. The cap is viscid and pale yellow with a shiny surface when dry. The broad and fairly distant **gills** are adnate and grey-violet in colour, with a whitish edge. In mature specimens the tall, fragile **stem** reaches a height of about 12 cm, and is very sticky below the ring. It is pale yellow and has an apical membranous ring which tends to disappear with age being barely discernible in many mature specimens. The thin, pale yellow **flesh** has a slightly mealy smell.

Spore print: Violet-brown.

Distribution: A common and widespread fungus which grows in meadows and grassy places on cow and horse dung, appearing from spring to late autumn.

Possible confusion: The size, shape, colour and habitat of this fungus make it easy to recognize, though it can only be distinguished from some very close relatives by use of a microscope. *S. stercoraria* is considered by some authors to be a variety of the fungus under discussion. It has more of an umbo, a scalier stem and hair-like cystidia on the edge of the gills (microscope!).

Edibility: It is not considered edible.

Notes: *Semiglobata* means 'hemispherical'.

Stropharia ferrii (Syn. S. rugosoannulata)

The **cap** about 5–15 cm across, is initially hemispherical, then campanulate and later flattened although the margin is inrolled. When dry the innately fibrillose surface is shiny, when moist it is slightly sticky, and red-brown in colour with a hint of mauve or pink. The mature cap may bear scattered white velar remnants. The crowded thin **gills** are adnexed or adnate, and of a greyish-violet colour. The **stem** can reach a height of 15 cm and with its diameter of up to 2.5 cm adds to an impression of massiveness. It is solid, whitish at the apex, pallid to yellowish lower down, and bears a broad, apical membranous white ring, the upper surface of which is striate and soon coloured dark by spores. The **flesh** is white, odourless and sometimes has a rather earthy taste.

Spore print: Purple-grey-brown.

Distribution: It grows in summer and autumn on plant debris such as straw and on manured ground. In the wild state it is very rare in Britain, where it is now available from seed firms for cultivation on straw bales.

Possible confusion: *S. hornemannii* is very similar and equally rare. It has an obviously viscid cap and is yellowish-brown in colour. The lower part of the stem is strikingly scaly. It too has a pendent, striate ring, but this is transitory. It grows in coniferous and deciduous woods on well-rotted stumps, favouring moss. It is widespread in Northern Europe and rare in Germany.

Edibility: *S. ferrii* is edible.

Notes: It can be bought in the market as the 'brown cap', and it is also easy to cultivate.

Stropharia aeruginosa   **Verdigris Agaric**

The campanulate **cap** measures 5–8 cm in diameter, and is covered with a striking blue-green gluten on which float numerous white fleck-like scales. The margin is also fringed with white veil. In wet weather the scales and gluten may wash off remnants of the veil leaving the surface a pale yellowish colour. The whitish **gills**, which become grey-violet, have a paler edge and are broadly adnate.The coarsely fibrillose **stem** 5–6(10) cm in height, is also at first bluish or greenish with numerous white floccose scales and bears an apical membranous, spreading ring which becomes more conspicuous from the trapped spores. The **flesh** is soft and white.

Spore print: Purple-brown.

Distribution: The Verdigris Agaric is common and widespread and can be found from summer into autumn in deciduous and coniferous woods or in gardens, in grassy verges, or among nettles.

Possible confusion: Confusion is possible with *S. caerulea* or *cyanea* which is very similar and distinction is only possible with the aid of a microscope since it involves the shape of the cystidia on the edge of the gills.

Edibility: It may surprise many collectors, but this poisonous-looking fungus is edible.

Notes: *Aeruginosa* means 'full of verdigris'.

129

Hebeloma radicosum

The **cap**, 6–15 cm in diameter, is fairly thick-fleshed, and glutinous in wet weather, pale ochreous to pale brown, often with darker fibrillose scales. Initially hemispherical, it later expands to become shallowly convex. The margin is at first inrolled, sometimes fringed with the fibrillose remnants of the veil. The **gills** are initially pale clay-coloured, later cocoa-brown, quite crowded, and almost free or sinuate. The solid, tough **stem** is 10–15 cm high and 2–3 cm wide, swollen at the base and prolonged into a long, spindly 'root' (hence the Latin name). Above the thick membranous, spreading ring the stem is white and mealy pruinose, but beneath it there are bands of dark brown fibrillose scales on a pallid background. The whitish **flesh** has an intense smell of bitter almonds or marzipan which is particularly obvious in the region of the gills. It tastes mild but becomes bitter.

Spore print: Clay-brown to tobacco-brown.

Distribution: A rather rare species in Britain, which occurs in autumn in broad-leaved woodland, and if the root is traced down into the soil it can be seen to originate in the underground latrines of small mammals or their decaying bodies.

Possible confusion: *H. radicosum* must be one of the few species of *Hebeloma* which can be identified immediately and with certainty. It is clearly distinguished by its deep-rooting stem, the coarse scales, membranous ring and smell.

Edibility: Inedible because of the bitter taste.

Notes: *Radicosum* means 'rooting'.

Coprinus disseminatus   Trooping Crumble Cap or Fairies' Bonnets

The permanently conical or bell-shaped **caps**, are 0.5–1.5 cm in diameter. The cap is initially creamy-white with a slightly darker centre, but as the fruit bodies mature the colour changes to grey with a brownish-grey centre, fluted or grooved and is very fragile. Unlike many other members of the genus *Coprinus*, the **gills** do not deliquesce into an ink-like liquid at maturity. They are adnate and at first white, but then quickly become grey-violet, and eventually brownish-violet. The very fragile **stem** is thin, whitish, and almost cylindrical.

Spore print: Dark brown.

Distribution: Very common in enormous swarms on and around rotting stumps during spring and autumn.

Possible confusion: Unlike any other fungus of comparable size, its fruiting in swarms of hundreds of fruit bodies and non-deliquescent gills distinguishes it from other members of the genus *Coprinus*.

Edibility: It is not poisonous, but it is without value as an edible fungus.

Notes: *Disseminatus* means 'spread abroad'.

Coprinus micaceus Glistening Ink Cap or Mica Ink Cap

The **cap** reaches a diameter of 2–4 cm, and is at first acorn-shaped, later convex or bell-shaped with conspicuously plicate or striate margin. The yellowish-brown colour is more intense and dense towards the centre, which in young specimens is covered with whitish or cream-coloured glistening mica-like mealy particles. If the cap is observed with a hand lens and tilted in the sun, these particles flash like flakes of mica. The **gills** are sinuate and crowded, and are at first whitish, then grey-brown but eventually dissolve into black ink as the fungus ages. In damp weather this fungus lasts only a few hours before disintegrating into an inky mess. The hollow **stem** can reach a height of 10 cm, though on average it is between 5 and 8 cm, and is white and fragile.

Spore print: Dark brown.
Distribution: This very common fungus fruits in flushes from early spring through until November. It grows in clusters on stumps or at the foot of broad-leaved trees in woods, parks and gardens.

Possible confusion: *C. truncorum* is very similar and not easy to distinguish without a microscope, for the diagnostic feature involves the shape of the spores.

Edibility: Edible, but without any table value.

Notes: *Micaceus* means 'glittering'.

Coprinus picaceus Magpie Ink Cap

The young egg-shaped **cap** is 5–10 cm tall and is uniformly thickly covered with white, fibrillose veil. On expansion the cap becomes broadly campanulate, the velar covering ruptures to form conspicuous white fibrillose scales on an almost black background. These scales are often washed away by rain. When mature, the edge of the cap becomes upturned and dissolves into an inky fluid along with the **gills**. The latter are free, crowded, initially white, then pink, and finally black. The **stem** can reach a height of 25 cm, particularly when the fungus is growing in deep leaf litter, and is 5–15 mm thick. It is white, fragile and hollow, narrowing slightly towards the apex and with the surface ornamented with white fibrillose scales. The **flesh** is whitish, but brown beneath the surface of the cap.

Spore print: Black.

Distribution: Occasional in beech woods on chalk in south-east England, growing in deep humus when present, it may be locally abundant in certain woodland from summer to autumn.

Possible confusion: Hardly likely with any other species.

Edibility: It is hardly worthy of consideration as an edible mushroom.

Notes: The genus *Coprinus* includes about ninety species. They are saprophytes and many grow on dung or manure heaps, others on soil and a few on wood. Many are very difficult to identify accurately without a microscope. Only one species, *C. comatus* (Shaggy Ink Cap), is recommended as a good edible mushroom. *Picaceus* means 'like a magpie'.

Coprinus atramentarius   Common Ink Cap

The **cap**, initially oval has a truncated apex. It expands quickly becoming bell-shaped, the edge often splitting and soon dissolving into a black mass, as with many other Ink Caps. The colour varies between a whitish-grey, ash-grey and a dirty brownish-grey. Towards the centre of the cap, the grey colour gives way to a clear brown shade, and in this region there are small inconspicuous brown scales. In addition, both cap and stem have a striking silky sheen. The **gills** are very crowded and of a light grey colour which soon becomes dark grey until finally dissolving in a soot-black mass. The brittle **stem** reaches a length of 8–9cm, sometimes 10 cm, and is cylindrical, often narrowing towards the apex, and there is a white cottony bulbous base. In young specimens the **flesh** is white, in older fruit bodies greyish-blue.

Spore print: Black.

Distribution: The Common Ink Cap appears in spring and again in autumn in woodlands, by roadsides, in gardens and in parks forming clusters at the base of stumps on buried wood.

Possible confusion: *C. alopecia* differs in spore character, but is rare both in Britain and mainland Europe.

Edibility: Young fungi, whose gills have not yet discoloured, could be eaten, but it does not agree with everyone. It should not be eaten immediately before or after consuming alcohol, since this can have unpleasant consequences such as skin disorders, nausea, etc. which can last for some time.

Notes: *Atramentarius* means 'pertaining to ink'.

Coprinus comatus   Shaggy Ink Cap or Lawyer's Wig

The characteristic shape of the young white fungus can be recognized from afar: it is almost cylindrical. The **cap** is 5–14 cm high and opens slightly to become narrowly, then more broadly, bell-shaped with a turned-up edge. As the cap matures it dissolves away in an inky fluid from the margin eventually leaving only a small central disc of cap tissue at the apex of the stem. The surface of the cap is white covered with brownish, upturned scales at the centre which soon disappear leaving the remainder of the surface covered with white shaggy fibrillose scales. The **gills** are very crowded, and free, initially white, later becoming pink, then grey and finally black before dissolving, with the cap into an inky fluid. The **stem** is cylindrical and hollow, with a club-shaped base. It bears a mobile, transitory ring which often drops off. The white **flesh** is soft and fibrous in the stem.

Spore print: Black.

Distribution: Very common in habitats disturbed by man such as motorway reservations, rubbish dumps, fields, etc. in summer and autumn, either singly or in groups.

Possible confusion: The white, shaggy cap with its strange cylindrical shape makes it difficult to confuse this fungus with any other.

Edibility: The Shaggy Ink Cap is a good edible mushroom, though it should be eaten young before the gills begin to turn pink.

Notes: It should not be mixed with other fungi. The cap can be separated from the stem with a gentle twist. It is hardly ever attacked by the mushroom fly or its larvae. *Comatus* means 'shaggy'.

Inocybe fastigiata

The **cap** reaches 4 to 7 cm in diameter, and is initially somewhat conical becoming bell-shaped as it expands with a fissured edge. Even fully expanded specimens retain their shape. The colour varies between straw-yellow and ochre-brown, with the centre often darker. The surface is dry and disrupts into marked radial fibrils with the white flesh showing through. The crowded **gills** are initially of a greyish-olive colour, but gradually become clay-brown, with a whitish edge. The **stem** reaches 7(8) cm in height and 5–10 mm in diameter, and is slightly enlarged towards the base. It is solid, fairly firm and whitish, gradually becoming pallid brownish below. The **flesh** is white and smells earthy.

Spore print: Brown.

Distribution: *I. fastigiata* is a common and widespread species, which may be found almost everywhere, even by the edge of paths, during summer and autumn.

Possible confusion: The inexperienced collector should avoid all fungi with this conical appearance and clay-brown gills.

Edibility: All *Inocybes* are at best inedible and many are highly poisonous. *I. fastigiata* is very poisonous, containing a high proportion of muscarin, a poison which causes nervous and circulatory disorders. Poisoning shows itself in watering of the eyes and profuse sweating, followed by severe digestive disorders.

Notes: Medical assistance should be sought at the first sign of poisoning. *Fastigiata* means 'pointed'.

Inocybe patouillardii

The **cap** of this fungus is 3–7 cm across, initially conical or bell-shaped and even when expanded, it retains a central umbo. The surface is finely, radially, silky fibrillose and whitish or creamy-ochre becoming blotched with brick-red with age. Only when the fungus takes on this characteristic reddish colour can it be more easily recognized. The **gills** are slightly sinuate and at first a pinkish-white, later olive-brown or rust-brown. The **stem** can reach a length of 4–6(8) cm, and is cylindrical in form, or sometimes with a slight bulb-like thickening at the base. At the apex it is white, but lower down it is whitish, yellowish and, when old or bruised, reddish. The **flesh** is white, becoming red in the stem, and has a fruity smell.

Spore print: Rust-ochre.

Distribution: This rather rare fungus fruits in spring from end of May to early July and is found in association with beech trees on chalky soil.

Possible confusion: *I. patouillardii* grows at the same time as the edible *Calocybe gambosa* (Saint George's Mushroom). It has been known to be confused with the latter and has caused severe poisoning. However, the strong mealy smell of *C. gambosa*, its white gills and spore print and the fact that its flesh does not turn red, should serve as good diagnostic features.

Edibility: Poisonous and dangerous, producing the same symptoms as *I. fastigiata*.

Notes: There are about 150 *Inocybe* species, all of them inedible or poisonous. *Patouillardii* was named in honour of the French mycologist N. Patouillardi.

Inocybe terrigena

The fleshy **cap** can reach 7 cm in diameter and at maturity is shallowly campanulate or shallowly convex with an umbo. The surface is dirty yellow-brown, soon becoming olive-brown and gradually brownish-ochre, with a felty fibrillose, scaly texture. When young the edge of the cap shows evidence of the thick brown veil. The **gills** are adnate with a tooth, at first a yellowish-white then a greenish-yellow and finally a rich olive-brown, with a paler edge. The **stem** is 4–5 cm high, cylindrical in form, sometimes with a bulb-like thickening at the base. It is the same colour as the cap, and has a ring-like cortina. When cut the **flesh** is yellowish.

Spore print: Rust-brown.

Distribution: Uncommon in Britain, *I. terrigena* is widely but unevenly distributed in Europe, where it grows principally on old humus in damp mixed woodland with beech, or in spruce forests on chalky soils during summer until late autumn.

Possible confusion: Not likely with other species. Inexperienced collectors might mistake it for *Tricholoma vaccinum*, which is a more reddish-brown and has a white spore print, or with the *Pholiota squarrosa* (Shaggy Pholiota), which grows tufted at the base of trunks. Both species are described in this volume.

Edibility: It should not be eaten.

Rozites caperatus

The **cap** can reach a diameter of 6–10(12) cm. It is initially dome-shaped, then bell-shaped and finally, almost flat with a central umbo. It is pale yellowish or pale ochre-brown somewhat radially wrinkled and with cobwebby silvery-white fibrils as if covered with a frosty bloom especially towards the centre. The cap margin is very often radially fissured especially in dry weather. The **gills** are crowded and adnate, at first pale yellowish-clay becoming ochre. The massive, solid **stem**, up to 2.5 cm thick, can reach a height of 15 cm. It has fibrillose striations and is of a dirty white colour. There is an apical membranous, slightly striated ring, and remnants of the veil are also found at the base. The soft **flesh** varies from a creamy-white to yellowish-brown in older specimens.

Spore print: Ochre-brown.

Distribution: In Britain chiefly found in the Scottish Highlands, where it is not uncommon in autumn. In Europe it is widespread up to heights of 2,000 m. It grows on acid soils in Scotland. In northern Europe it is found among *Calluna* with scattered pine trees. In central Europe in coniferous woodland (fir, spruce) among mosses and bilberries, but less commonly in oak and beech woods.

Possible confusion: Perhaps with the larger *Inocybe* species. The inedible *Cortinarius traganus* has no ring, a saffron-yellow flesh and an unpleasant smell.

Edibility: An excellent edible mushroom, but unfortunately very often maggoty.

Notes: Of the genus *Rozites* only one species is known in Europe. It is related to the genus *Cortinarius*. The name *Rozites* is in honour of the French mycologist E. Roze. *Caperatus* means 'wrinkled'.

Cortinarius orellanus

The **cap** of this fungus can be up to 8 cm across. Initially it is hemispherical but later expands and retains a more or less marked umbo. Its colour ranges from fox-orange to reddish-brown, and the surface is finely fibrillose with the finest of fibrillose scales although older specimens are sometimes smooth. The edge of the cap is sometimes split. The **gills** are adnate or sinuate and broad, they are fairly thick and distant, their edges uneven and jagged. When young they are pale and when mature a beautiful orange-rust-brown, a vivid cinnamon-brown or orange. The **stem** grows to 9 cm in length and is up to 2 cm thick, cylindrical and generally tapers towards the base. It is pale yellow, brass-yellow or golden-yellow and matt with longitudinal fibrils. Remnants of the veil are not usually in evidence. The **flesh** is fairly firm, pale yellow and a brownish colour at the base of the stem. It smells of radish when freshly cut and has a mild taste.

Spore print: Rust-brown.

Distribution: *C. orellanus* is rare in Britain although widely scattered through Europe. However, it is considered rare in many regions and is common in only a few places. It grows in deciduous woodland (oak and hornbeam) where there is a scattering of pines, in mild localities, but also in highland forests of fir and beech. It seems to favour acid and sandy soils.

Possible confusion: *C. limonius* (q.v.) looks very like it, but *C. speciosissimus* is its closest relative, differing in spore shape.

Edibility: *C. orellanus* is extremely poisonous. Fungi which look even vaguely similar should be avoided.

Notes: In Poland in 1952 there was a mass poisoning incident involving over 130 people, nineteen of whom died.

Cortinarius speciosissimus

The **cap** reaches 6(8) cm in diameter. When young it is mostly conical or bell-shaped, later convex, but always with an obvious, more or less pointed umbo. The edge is occasionally split. It is brownish-orange or reddish-brown in colour, and the surface is finely fibrous or felted, becoming bare when older. In younger specimens lemon-yellow remnants of the veil are sometimes found on the edge of the cap. The **gills** are adnate or adnexed. They are fairly thick, distant and notched on the edge. The colour, like the cap, is brownish-orange, rust-brown when old. The cylindrical **stem** is relatively long, up to 8(10) cm and up to 1.5 cm thick with a slightly club-shaped base, although it is sometimes slightly tapered. It is more or less the same colour as the cap, sometimes paler. When young it is ringed, albeit incompletely, by an ochre to lemon-yellow veil. The **flesh** is pale orange or ochre, yellowish in the centre, and almost odourless.

Spore print: Rust-brown.

Distribution: Rare in Britain, chiefly in the Scottish Highlands. It is widespread and common in the Alps, the sub-alpine areas, and in the Swabian and Bavarian Forests. It is a characteristic species of damp, acid, boggy, sphagnum-rich coniferous woods with bilberry. It appears from August to October.

Possible confusion: With similar fungi of this group.

Edibility: *C. speciosissimus* contains the same poisonous substances as its relative *C. orellanus*.

Notes: The poisons of this group are thermo-stable cell poisons. *Speciosissimus* means 'very attractive, splendid'.

141

Cortinarius limonius

The **cap** grows to 4–6(8) cm in diameter. When young it is hemispherical, when expanded more flatly convex, the edge somewhat inrolled. When moist it is foxy-red or orange-brown, when dry apricot-yellow, paler away from the centre, and when young the edge of the cap bears remnants of the yellow velum. The surface is bare, with at most a few pale yellow fibrils. The **gills** are more or less sinuate, broad and distant. Initially pale wood-yellow, later yellow to rusty yellow. The **stem**, growing to a length of 7 cm and a diameter of 1.5 cm, is more or less cylindrical, tapering both towards the apex and the base. It is yellowish, becoming darker rust-brown below. There is no sign of a ring or cortina, but it is coated quite thickly with yellow fibrils. The **flesh** is yellowish, at the base of the stem foxy-red, and without taste or smell.

Spore print: Rust-brown.

Distribution: Uncommon. Chiefly in northern Britain, *C. limonius* grows in coniferous woodland, in mossy soils with a low lime content. Fruit bodies can be found singly or gregariously from August into September.

Possible confusion: With *C. orellanus*, though the latter has a smooth stem without any remnants of the veil. *C. callisteus*, a species of this group which grows in coniferous woods, has a more club-shaped stem and flesh which is orange-yellow or rhubarb-coloured throughout.

Edibility: The fungus is probably poisonous in a similar way to the previous two species described.

Notes: Again it must be stressed that fungi which have not been definitely identified should never be collected for eating. *Limonius* means 'lion-yellow'.

Cortinarius bolaris

The **cap** of this attractive fungus reaches a diameter of 8 cm. Initially hemispherical, then convex, its dry, pale clay-coloured surface is thickly covered with small, vermilion or carmine-red scales, especially toward the centre. The pale cinnamon **gills** are adnate to slightly decurrent, narrow and not particularly crowded. The **stem** grows to 8 cm in length and 1–1.5 cm in thickness. It is cylindrical, often with a clavate base, though it is sometimes tapered. It is white at the apex, and is covered below with red fibrous scales. The **flesh** is white, turning slightly yellow when bruised. It smells vaguely pleasant and has a mild taste.

Spore print: Light brown.

Distribution: Occasional and widespread in the British Isles, *C. bolaris* is found in most parts of Europe. It prefers mixed woodland of oak and beech in lowlands, from the end of August into autumn.

Possible confusion: Its 'typical' appearance makes it easy to recognize.

Edibility: Inedible, and should not be collected in the interests of conservation.

Notes: *C. bolaris* was formerly placed in a sub-group of the genus *Cortinarius* designated *Inoloma* or *Sericeocybe* because of its dry cap. However, it contains a series of substances which fluoresce blue in ultraviolet light and which are otherwise known only in species of the sub-group *Leprocybe*. *Bolaris* means 'pertaining to a clod of earth'.

143

Cortinarius traganus

The initially spherical then convex **cap** reaches diameters of 4–10 cm. Its lilac-violet colour soon fades to a pale ochre. Older specimens lose their striking colour and fade to a silvery-white. When young the stem and the edge of the cap are still connected by cobwebby remains of the cortina. The broad, sinuate **gills** are of average density, initially foxy-ochre they gradually change to a cinnamon-brown on maturity, with the edges being paler and notched. The **stem** grows to about 10 cm high. It is thick and club-shaped, with a rather bulbous base. It, too, is a vivid violet when young and fades to a pale ochre when older and is covered with remnants of the cobwebby veil. The **flesh** is saffron-yellow with an unpleasant sickly, sweet smell.

Spore print: Rust-brown.

Distribution: In Britain chiefly in the Scottish Highlands where it is occasional in summer and late autumn either singly or in groups on acid soils in coniferous woods.

Possible confusion: *C. camphoratus*, which gets its name from its dreadful smell, is similar. It is paler, the stem more slender, and the violet colour of its flesh is a good distinguishing feature. Young fruit bodies of *C. traganus* might also be confused with the edible *Rozites caperatus*, but the latter lacks the cortina and the unpleasant smell.

Edibility: *C. traganus* is slightly poisonous.

Notes: Aside from the unpleasant-smelling typical form, there are varieties (*var. finitimus* and *var. odoratum*) which smell pleasantly fruity, but which are also inedible. *Traganus* means 'smelling of goats'.

Cortinarius praestans

The **cap** is initially almost spherical and seated on a thick white stem to which it is joined by a copious blue-white cortina. When mature the cap is convex and reaches a diameter of 10–20 cm. When moist the surface is viscid and of a brownish or wine-red colour, usually with a hint of violet. At first it is covered with the pale violet veil, the remnants of which form plaque-like patches. The crowded **gills** are initially pale grey then pale lilac and finally chocolate-brown. The **stem** grows to a height of 15 cm and is 2–5 cm thick. It is massive, club-shaped and has a fibrillose surface which is white, becoming pale violet at the apex. It is often girdled with remnants of the cortina. The white or pale blue **flesh** is characterized by its firmness. There is no strong smell.

Spore print: Pale yellowish-brown.

Distribution: Uncommon. This fungus is mainly found in central and southern Europe. It favours deciduous woods on chalk, in areas with a mild climate. In Germany it is confined to the south, occurring in the alpine foothills. It is rare, but more common in northern Italy (South Tirol).

Possible confusion: The rare *C. cumatilis*, with its varieties, is similar, but it has a violet cortina. *C. durissimus* has a rim to the bulb at the base of the stem and an ochre-coloured cortina.

Edibility: *C. praestans* is edible, but should not be collected in the interests of conservation.

Notes: *Praestans* means 'pre-eminent'.

Cortinarius variecolor

The **cap** grows to 5–15 cm in diameter. Initially hemispherical, it later expands and becomes convex with an inrolled margin. The surface is viscid in wet weather, and when young it is often lilac or violet, but soon becomes foxy-brown, and innately fibrillose, although the violet colour is long retained at the edge of the cap. The adnexed **gills** are thin and crowded, sometimes with a waxy edge. Violet when young, they become rust-brown when mature. The **stem** is 5–12 cm high and 1.5–2.5 cm thick. It is more or less club-shaped, violet with small pointed scales when young, soon becoming smooth and fox-coloured. The cortina is pale lilac and silky. The **flesh** is lilac at first, later white with a hint of lilac. The smell is unpleasantly earthy.

Spore print: Rust-brown.

Distribution: *C. variecolor* is uncommon, generally growing gregariously in conifer-ous woodland. Fruit bodies are formed from July to October.

Possible confusion: Two variants are mentioned in literature. *Var. marginatus* has a rim to the bulbous base of the stem and grows in deciduous woods. *Var. largiusculus* has reddish-violet flesh and an earthy or dust-like smell. It, too, grows in deciduous woodland. Another species which might be taken for *C. variecolor* is *C. nemorensis* which grows in deciduous woods associated with beech and oak.

Edibility: All varieties are inedible.

Notes: The genus *Cortinarius* contains about 450 species. They are mostly mycorrhizal fungi with a cortina, or cobwebby veil, often visible at the edge of the cap or on the upper third of the stem. The spore print is usually some shade of brown. Some species are deadly poisonous. *Variecolor* means 'of various colours'.

Cortinarius violaceus

The very fleshy **cap** is 6–15 cm across, initially hemispherical, later expanding to become campanulate or convex with a small umbo. The surface is dry, uniformly felty and of a beautiful dark violet colour even at maturity. The **gills** are sinuate, fairly distant, often interveined and of the same violet colour as the cap, but become cinnamon-brown at maturity. The dark violet **stem** can reach 12–15 cm in height and 1.5–2 cm in width, but up to 4 cm at the base, which is often inflated and swollen. The surface is fibrillose and there is a violet cortina in young specimens which may later disappear. When the fungus is cut the soft, violet marbled **flesh** is revealed which often smells of calf leather or cedarwood.

Spore print: Rust-brown.

Distribution: In Britain this beautiful fungus is found chiefly in the Scottish Highlands under birch on acid moors with *Calluna*, but even here it is rare. It occurs from Spain to the USSR, but throughout its entire range it is fairly scattered, often rare. In central Germany it is not found, becoming commoner further south at heights over 300m. In Europe it seems not to depend on special soil conditions, and favours damp, shady positions in broad-leaved woodland and spruce/beech forests. In the foothills of the Alps it is often found in pure spruce woods individually and even in groups. It grows from August into the autumn.

Possible confusion: Some authorities distinguish this fungus from *C. hercynicus* which grows in pure coniferous woods, but the two species cannot be separated without the use of a microscope to check their spore size. *C. hercynicus* is not known in Britain.

Edibility: The fungus is edible, but should be spared, because of its rarity.

147

Cortinarius varius

The fleshy **cap**, 8–12 cm across, is at first hemispherical then convex and is sticky to viscid in wet weather. The colour is a striking yellowish, pale orange, or foxy-colour but paler yellow towards the margin. The **gills** are quite crowded, sinuate, broad and a pale lilac shade when young, becoming bluish-violet and later cinnamon-brown on maturity. The solid **stem** is club-shaped, up to 7 cm long, usually smooth, silky, and white, although there is a pale lilac tint at the apex. At maturity the white cortina is coloured brown by falling spore powder. The more or less white **flesh** lacks both a distinctive smell or taste.

Spore print: Light rust-brown.

Distribution: This fungus is rare in Britain, occurring with conifers on chalky soil during autumn. In Europe it occurs in similar habitats particularly in the mountains and the alpine foothills, generally in groups.

Possible confusion: There is a slight possibility of confusion with similarly coloured *Cortinarius* species, but it is easily recognized by its yellow or fox-orange cap, its lilac gills and white flesh.

Edibility: Edible.

Notes: Unfortunately the dirt-covered surface of the cap is difficult to remove. Within the genus *Cortinarius* it belongs to the sub-group *Phlegmacium*. Chemical reagents are a great help in identification. When a drop of alkali (Sodium or Potassium Hydroxide, 20%) or Ammonia (24–25%) is applied to the flesh it turns yellow, or at least brown with a yellow edge. *Varius* means 'changeable'.

Cortinarius crassus

The **cap** is 5–8 cm in diameter but may exceptionally reach 12 cm. It is convex and rounded, later flattened and undulating. In young specimens the edge is inrolled and slightly felty and smooth. The colour ranges from tobacco-brown to ochre. The **gills** are adnate or sinuate, narrow and crowded. They are initially cream, but become a clay colour, then cinnamon-brown. The **stem** is 3–8 cm long and 1.5–2.5 cm thick. It is short and robust, more or less cylindrical, white and fibrillose, frosted at the top becoming brown towards the base. The remnants of the veil on cap and stem are whitish, very fleeting and in mature specimens scarcely visible. The **flesh** is white, becoming slightly brown, with a weak smell and mild taste.

Spore print: Brownish.

Distribution: Very rare and found chiefly in the Scottish Highland pine woods during the late summer and autumn.

Possible confusion: The descriptions of this fungus in literature are very varied. The species described here represent the many problems associated with precise identification and classification: not every fungus that is found can be identified with certainty, however good the available specialist literature may be.

Edibility: One of the edible *Cortinarius* species with white flesh.

Notes: *Crassus* means 'thick'.

Cortinarius auroturbinatus

The **cap** is between 4 and 10 cm in diameter, sometimes up to 12 cm. It is hemispherical at first, but gradually becomes convex and eventually expanded, sometimes with a small depression in the centre and for a long time the margin remains inrolled. The surface is bright chrome-yellow but often becomes foxy-red in the centre, and in wet weather is very slimy but when the cap dries it has a shiny appearance. When young the **gills** are lemon-yellow, but gradually become yellowish-brown with a definite olive tinge and finally rust-brown while the uneven and notched edge remains yellow. The gills are broad, deeply sinuate and fairly crowded. The **stem** can reach a height of 12 cm, and 1–2.5 cm in width enlarging to 2–4 cm or more at the bulbous base. The colour is similar to that of the cap, although not so intense, and when mature it becomes brownish except at the apex. The bulb has a definite rim, usually coloured reddish-brown by remnants of the veil which also clothe the stem; when young these remnants can even surmount the bulb like a volva. The cortina is greenish-yellow. When cut, the **flesh** of the cap and the rind of the stem are greenish-yellow, otherwise the flesh is white, and slightly blue or violet in the upper part of the stem. The smell is spicy, the taste mild.

Spore print: Rust-brown.

Distribution: Rare to uncommon in the south during late summer and autumn, exclusively in beechwoods on chalk.

Possible confusion: The distinction between allied species is not always easy to draw, demanding experience. *C. cedretorum*, for example, is a very close relative.

Edibility: Inedible.

Notes: *Auroturbinatus* means 'golden and top-shaped'.

Cortinarius odorifer

The fleshy, hard **cap** can reach 10 or 12 cm in diameter. At first it is strongly convex, but becomes shallowly convex, finally funnel-shaped and somewhat lobed, with persistently inrolled margin. When moist the surface is very viscid or slimy, but dries shiny, and is easily peeled. The centre is copper-coloured, but towards the margin it becomes more and more greenish, greenish-grey, yellowish-olive or even vaguely violet, but the mature cap is more uniformly reddish-brown. The **gills** are crowded and very regular. They are quite markedly sinuate and yellowish or greenish, becoming olive-brown. The **stem** can be 5–8 cm tall and is 1–2 cm thick, up to 3.5 cm at the bulb. It is always solid and fleshy. The surface varies from yellowish to greenish and is covered with many hair-like fibrils from the cobwebby veil coloured brownish by falling spores. The bulb has a definite rim. The firm yellow-green **flesh** smells strongly of aniseed and has a mild taste.

Spore print: Reddish-brown.

Distribution: Not yet reported in Britain. It is often found growing gregariously on chalky or sandy soils with conifers, in the Alps and the alpine foothills, but scarcely ever below 300 m, from summer until late autumn.

Possible confusion: It vaguely resembles *C. orichalceus*, or even *C. aureofulvus*. The surest identification is provided by the intense smell of aniseed.

Edibility: Edible, but the strong aniseed smell means it is not to everyone's liking.

Notes: *Odorifer* means 'pleasant smelling'.

Cortinarius collinitus

The **cap**, yellowish, ochre or orange-brown and 2–12 cm across, bears a thick layer of mucilage in damp conditions but when dry the surface is shiny. Initially the fungus appears convex or bell-shaped but expands with time, although it never becomes totally flat. The **gills** are sinuate and violet-brown in colour. The **stem**, 6–12 cm high and about 1 cm thick, is distinctly blue, particularly in the apical portion, but becomes more reddish or yellowish toward the base and like the cap it is coated below with mucilage which sometimes gives it a banded appearance. The **flesh** is also a shade of blue, although at first sight it can look yellowish or ochre-coloured.

Spore print: Pale yellowish-brown.

Distribution: Chiefly in the northern pine forests and especially in the Scottish Highlands where it is occasional. It also grows with pines and, exceptionally, in broad-leaved woodland. It is found in autumn.

Possible confusion: This is a particularly variable species. *C. mucifluus* is similar, but the edge of its cap is striate or wrinkled. *C. mucosus* has a white stem, sometimes yellowish-brown when old, and grows in pine woods or among birches and pines.

Edibility: Edible.

Notes: *C. collinitus* and related species belong to the sub-group *Myxacium* within the genus *Cortinarius*. The cap of these fungi, with a few exceptions, is coated with mucilage. Some of these species taste bitter. *Collinitus* means 'slimy, viscid'.

Cortinarius trivialis

The **cap** reaches a diameter of 3–7(10) cm, initially almost round, later bell-shaped and convex with a blunt umbo. Even when the fungus is fully expanded this umbo is still discernible and the margin often inrolled. The brownish surface, often more of a creamy-olive colour, is covered with a layer of mucilage. The **gills**, not particularly crowded, are adnate with a decurrent tooth. When young they are bluish or violet (or at least have a tinge of these colours), later becoming rust-brown or cinnamon-coloured. The solid almost cylindrical **stem** can reach 10 cm in height and a thickness of 1.5 cm, but it tapers towards the base. The upper third is silky-whitish but below the cortina the surface is glutinous and ranges from yellowish, brown or ochre with conspicuous thick whitish bands of scales, sometimes forming almost a snake-like pattern. When moist these bands form slimy rings which sometimes merge. The **flesh** is pale ochre, darker at the base of the stem, odourless, mild and very firm.

Spore print: Rust-brown.

Distribution: This common fungus grows in autumn in deciduous woodland, favouring damp clay soils, especially with alder and willow but also occurs with beech.

Possible confusion: *C. trivialis* is very variable. *Var. squamosipes* has a yellow or olive-green stem with white ring zones towards the apex and brownish ones below. Other than this, the characteristic patterned stem prevents confusion with other species.

Edibility: Inedible.

Notes: *Trivialis* means 'of little value, trivial, ordinary'.

153

Cortinarius armillatus

The **cap** 5–12 cm in diameter is initially bell-shaped then expanded with a prominent obtuse umbo. It is of more or less uniform colour – rust-brown, fox-coloured or brick-red, with fine felt-like scales. The broad **gills** are sinuate, rather distant and when young are a delicate ochre colour, becoming cinnamon-brown at maturity, with the edges generally paler. The **stem** is 6–14 cm long and 1–3 cm thick, more or less cylindrical, often club-shaped. The upper part is pale beige or a reddish-flesh colour, becoming ochre, red-brown or grey-brown below, where the surface is ornamented by one or more bands of vermilion velar remnants. The **flesh** is reddish-white or reddish-yellow to pale brown, has no smell and a mild taste.

Spore print: Cinnamon-brown.

Distribution: *C. armillatus* is a common species found on acid soils with birches, favouring boggy places. The fruit bodies are usually found from July to October.

Possible confusion: Exists with its own *var. luteoornatus*, which is slightly more matt in colour and has yellow or yellow-brown bands of velar remnants on its stem. Otherwise it can scarcely be confused with other fungi, particularly if attention is paid to its association with birch trees.

Edibility: Edible, but not recommended.

Notes: *C. armillatus* belongs to the subgroup *Telamonia* within the genus *Cortinarius*. The fungi of this group range from small to very large, generally in shades of brown, yellow-brown, ochre or violet, and many of them are hygrophanous. Beneath the cortina the stem is often banded. *Armillatus* means 'with a bracelet'.

Cortinarius semisanguineus (Syn. Dermocybe semisanguineus)

The **cap** of this fungus reaches a diameter of 2–8 cm. When young it is bell-shaped, later expanded with an obvious umbo. It is olive-brown or umber, sometimes yellow-brown. The surface is dry and often disrupts into fine scales, especially towards the cap margin. The **gills** are markedly sinuate, and initially a beautiful blood-red, although later becoming cinnamon-brown. The slender **stem**, 3–8(10) cm long and up to 7 mm thick, is cylindrical, and vivid chrome, quince-yellow or brass-coloured, the base sometimes reddish. The **flesh** is yellow and smells slightly of radishes.

Spore print: Rust-brown.

Distribution: *C. semisanguineus* is common, growing gregariously on coniferous woodland on acid soil. It can be found from August until November.

Possible confusion: *C. cinnamomeus* has a similarly coloured cap, but its gills are cinnamon-orange and retain that colour for some time. It, too, is found in coniferous woodland. The lower part of its stem is sometimes covered with brown velum. *C. sanguineus* has a more or less uniformly dark blood-red-coloured fruit body with broad and distant gills. It also grows in damp coniferous woodland.

Edibility: There is a suspicion that it contains similar poisonous compounds to those found in *C. orellanus* and its allies.

Notes: It represents the sub-genus *Dermocybe*, (some recognize it at generic level) containing about twenty-seven species. *Semisanguineus* means 'half blood-red' (because of the gills).

Russula emetica The Sickener

The **cap** can reach a diameter of 5–11 cm, and is initially strongly convex, but gradually expands to the point where it is depressed at the centre. The colour varies from vermilion to blood-red, when old somewhat paler, and the shiny surface can be easily peeled. The distant **gills** are almost free or adnexed to the stem and white. The 1–2 cm thick cylindrical **stem** reaches a length of 7 cm, and is also white, rarely with a hint of red about it. Its **flesh** is solid, but as the fungus matures it gradually develops cavities in the stem and becomes brittle. The white flesh smells rather fruity and has a very peppery taste.

Spore print: White.

Distribution: The Sickener is very common in coniferous woodland on acid soils appearing from July to November.

Possible confusion: There are some other varieties of the Sickener which have pale gills, a more or less white stem, fragile flesh and a sharp taste. In identifying them, their habitat is often of assistance, e.g. *R. emetica var. betularum* (Birch Sickener).

Edibility: Poisonous, together with its varieties.

Notes: The genus *Russula* contains well over 150 species. The caps can be of various colours, they have brittle stems and very brittle gills usually all of one length. The stems are smooth, lacking ring and cortina. *Emetica* means 'causing vomiting'.

Russula quéletii

The **cap** reaches a diameter of 5–8 cm and mature specimens have a depression in the centre, which is a feature common to many *Russulas*. Caps can be coloured a dull wine-red or purple, or even a lemon-green colour. Older specimens are considerably paler, although the centre of the cap remains darker. The surface is rather sticky and shiny and can be peeled almost to the centre. The edge is distinctly grooved. The **gills** are fairly crowded and attached to the stem. They are white when young, turning wax-yellow when mature often with green patches when bruised. The brittle **stem** is up to 7 cm long and 1.5–2 cm thick. It is smooth, cylindrical, broadens gradually towards the base and is carmine or purple-red. Only rarely are specimens found with very pale or almost white stems. The **flesh** is greyish, but beneath the surface it is the same colour as the cap itself. It has a sweet smell, reminiscent of gooseberry jam, but the taste is very peppery.

Spore print: Creamy-yellow.

Distribution: *R. quéletii* is rather uncommon, growing from July to October in coniferous woodland.

Possible confusion: The unbearably peppery flavour distinguishes it from other red, mild and edible *Russulas*. Inexperienced collectors might confuse it with the equally sharp-tasting *R. badia*, but the latter generally has a white stem with red flushes on the surface and it too is found on acid soils among conifers. When rubbed, the gills smell of cedarwood oil.

Edibility: Much too peppery to be edible.

Notes: The gooseberry smell is not always pronounced and is not sufficiently reliable for identification. The name *quéletii* is in honour of the French mycologist L. Quélet.

Russula ochroleuca   Common Yellow Russula

This **cap** is up to 9(12) cm in diameter, at first convex but expands, leaving a slight depression in the centre. The surface, which can be peeled from about half of the cap surface, is yellowish, ochre or light brown in colour, sometimes with a hint of olive which becomes almost greenish in a few exceptional cases. The margin is slightly grooved. The crowded **gills** are white or ivory, later vaguely yellowish with rusty-brown patches in mature specimens. They are adnexed to the stem. The **stem** appears compact and is relatively short (about 5–8 cm) but thick (up to 2.5 cm). Towards the base it is slightly clavate, but otherwise cylindrical. The white or ochre surface has yellow flecks below and becomes greyish when old. In young specimens the **flesh** is white, in older ones it is grey-brown. The smell is fruity, the taste almost mild to moderately peppery or bitter.

Spore print: Cream.

Distribution: The Common Yellow Russula is a widespread and very common fungus growing in both coniferous and deciduous woods during autumn.

Possible confusion: *R. fellea* (Geranium-scented Russula) is similar, but the cap is straw-coloured, the surface peels with difficulty, there is a smell of geranium, and it has a strong peppery taste. *R. claroflava* grows in swamps with birches and has a bright yellow cap and pale ochre spore print.

Edibility: Edible, with reservations. It can be used in mixtures.

Notes: *Ochroleuca* means 'ochre, pale yellow'.

Russula fellea   Geranium-scented Russula

The **cap** reaches a diameter of 5–9 cm, and when it expands a shallow depression forms at the centre. The colour ranges from ochre to straw-yellow, sometimes also a brownish-honey colour, paler towards the edge. The surface is smooth and shiny and can only be peeled at the grooved margin. The **gills** are very pale when young, and dirty cream when old. The **stem** reaches a height of 4–6 cm and a diameter of 1–2 cm, it is paler yellowish-cream. The whitish **flesh** turns yellowish with time, and is brittle, with a sweet smell of geraniums or stewed apple, and has a hot peppery taste.

Spore print: Pale cream.

Distribution: A common species of beechwoods from late summer into autumn.

Possible confusion: Might be confused with the Common Yellow Russula, but the latter is not nearly so hot-tasting, and the flesh in the stem turns grey with age.

Edibility: Inedible because of its hot peppery taste.

Notes: The genus *Russula* contains well over 150 species. See under *R. emetica* (The Sickener) for features common to the genus. For collectors there is one rule: all mild-tasting *Russulas* are edible, all hot and bitter ones are inedible. Species identification requires experience, patience, good specialist books and a microscope; one needs to know the associated trees, exact shade of the spore print, and taste of the flesh. *Fellea* means 'bitter as gall'.

159

Russula foetens   Stinking Russula

With its **cap** reaching 5–18 cm in diameter it is one of the larger members of the genus. When young it is almost spherical, with margin pressed close to the stem, but when mature the cap expands and sometimes becomes slightly depressed at the centre. The margin is coarsely grooved and tuberculate. The surface is light brown to ochre in colour, the centre visibly darker. The surface can be peeled to half way from the margin. When moist it is sticky, when dry smooth and shiny. The **gills** are initially pale, eventually becoming a dirty cream colour, and when bruised they gradually become brownish. Often they bear amber-coloured droplets which later dry to form darker patches. The cylindrical or swollen **stem** grows 9(13) cm in length and is 2–3.5 cm thick. The surface is white, mostly with ochre or brown patches near the base. It is hard, but even early on it develops cavities and later may become completely hollow. The white **flesh** turns brown when exposed to the air and has a sweetish-oily unpleasant smell. The taste is initially bitter to a varying extent but soon very hot and peppery causing one to vomit.

Spore print: White.

Distribution: Fairly common and occurs in both deciduous and coniferous woods in autumn.

Possible confusion: *R. subfoetens* smells less strongly and grows in deciduous woodland. Other than that, it resembles *R. laurocerasi*, not further described in this book, which smells strongly of bitter almonds. *R. illota* differs from both in having yellow to dark violet-brown flecked gill edges.

Edibility: Inedible.

Notes: *Foetens* means 'stinking'.

Russula integra

The **cap** is up to 12(15) cm across, initially convex to bell-shaped, later expanded and flattened with the centre somewhat depressed. It is brown, chocolate-brown, flesh-brown, yellowish or olive-brown, less commonly blood-red, pink or dark purple, often with ochre flecks. The surface is sticky, then shiny when dry, and peels. The margin is slightly downturned, often grooved. The fairly crowded **gills** are adnexed and whitish, almost blue at times, later becoming deep ochre or saffron-coloured. The solid, cylindrical **stem** reaches about 10 cm in height and a thickness of 1–3 cm. The surface, generally pure white, is covered with fine furrows and there are frequently small yellow patches at the base. The **flesh** is also white, readily browning in the stem when bruised with a knife. It is hard and firm, smelling slightly fruity and with a mild taste.

Spore print: Deep ochre.

Distribution: Not uncommon in the Scottish Highlands, from summer to autumn in coniferous woodland.

Possible confusion: *R. integra* is a species with wide-ranging colouration and can be confused with others in this group. The equally mild *R. alutacea* has a more violet or wine-red cap, fading to ivory-white, and a white or reddish stem. *R. olivacea* has a completely pink stem. Before the gills turn brown, *R. integra* can also be confused with *R. erythropoda*, though the crab-like smell is diagnostic for the latter species.

Edibility: A very good edible mushroom.

Notes: *Integra* means 'entire'.

The **cap** can reach a diameter of about 15 cm. It is initially hemispherical but expands until eventually the centre becomes slightly depressed. The surface can be greyish-violet, bluish-lilac, greenish-yellow or greenish-lilac, with violet and green generally occurring together, with patches in various shades of lilac. The upper surface when moist is greasy, with fine radial veining. The surface is easily peeled, revealing the superficially violet-coloured flesh of the cap. The narrow **gills** are crowded, forked near the stem, adnexed, later slightly decurrent of a dull white colour. They are soft and malleable and not brittle when a finger is run across them as in most other *Russulas*. The **stem** grows to a height of 10 cm and a thickness of up to 2.5 cm, and is cylindrical, tapering towards the top. The basic colour is white, though some specimens show a violet flush. The **flesh** is white, commonly turning brown in old specimens. In the cap it is firm and elastic, in the stem solid with the occasional cavity, later quite spongy. It is without smell and tastes very mild.

Spore print: White.

Distribution: This very common *Russula* can be found in summer and autumn almost everywhere in coniferous and deciduous woodland, especially near beeches.

Possible confusion: There are several varieties of *R. cyanoxantha*. *R. grisea* is very similar in cap colour but the gills are distinctly cream and are brittle.

Edibility: Edible.

Notes: *Cyanoxantha* means 'bluish-yellow'.

Russula cyanoxantha, fm. peletereaui

Differs from the above only in that its **cap** is more or less green from the start. All other features are similar or identical. The habitat is also the same.

Edibility: Edible.

Possible confusion: It is often taken for *R.* aeruginea, but the latter is usually found beneath birches. Its **cap** grows to 5–10 cm, is grass-green, pale green or grey-green, often very pale. The **gills** are initially white, later creamy-yellow. The **stem** is also white, often with rusty flecks at the base. The **flesh** is mild, though the gills can taste rather hot and peppery. When raw it induces severe vomiting and can produce symptoms of poisoning even after being heated to a high temperature. Another representative of the group is *R. virescens*, with its surface cracked and tessellated. Its habitat is usually under oak, beech and birch. It, too, is edible. These *Russulas* are confused again and again by incautious collectors with *Amanita phalloides* (Death Cap). The features are very different and easily seen, however; *Russulas* have no ring, no bulbous swelling of the stem base, no volva, and their flesh is smooth and fragile. To avoid one of the non-poisonous but occasionally very hot species, it is sufficient to take a tiny fragment of flesh or gill and chew it briefly. The hot *Russulas* are quickly recognizable. Various reagents can be a good aid to identification, but working with these chemicals demands experience and goes beyond the normal process of identification by the collector. For the mycologist, however, these tests are essential.

Russula aurata   Golden Russula

The **cap** is up to 9(10) cm in diameter, and is hemispherical when young, but later flatly convex or slightly depressed. It is fiery-orange or red, though these colours are not always present, or may be patchily developed. The surface is sticky, and peels partially when moist, shiny when dry. The edge is smooth at first, later slightly grooved. The brittle **gills** are crowded and adnexed, pale when young, eventually becoming a deep butter-yellow. The edges are typically, though not always, lemon or chrome-yellow. The firm, fleshy **stem** grows to 9(10) cm in height and to a thickness of up to 2.5 cm. It is white to pale yellow and typically club-shaped, though it sometimes has an evident tinge of chrome-yellow. It is often wrinkled, with firm, whitish **flesh** which softens and develops cavities when older. It is almost odourless and has a mild taste.
Spore print: Ochre-yellow.

Distribution: This rare *Russula* can be found from summer until late autumn in deciduous woods. It is widespread in the temperate zone, although in Europe there are large areas where it is not at all common.
Possible confusion: It is easier to distinguish from its relatives than are many other *Russulas*, because of the chrome-yellow colour of the gill edge and from the yellow tinge to the stem.
Edibility: It is edible, but should be conserved in areas where it is rare.
Notes: *Aurata* means 'golden-yellow'.

Russula lepida

The **cap**, 10(12) cm across is initially hemispherical, for a long time convex, then later depressed. It is mostly vermillion, dark blood-red, pink or flesh-coloured, often becoming paler toward the margin. The surface, which can scarcely be peeled, is smooth, matt, dry and has a whitish frosting. The brittle, crowded **gills** are white or pale cream, adnexed or more broadly attached. The **stem**, cylindrical and often very short, is up to 7(8) cm long and 3 cm thick, becoming more or less obviously wrinkled with age. The surface is white, mostly tinged with red or pink, especially near the base. The white **flesh** is very firm but brittle and granular. The flavour is not hot, but it can be quite bitter, particularly in the gills.
Spore print: Pale cream.
Distribution: It is widespread and locally common, growing in deciduous woodland,

especially with beeches, even in dry weather during early summer and autumn.
Possible confusion: *R. lepida* often grows in close proximity to *R. amarissima*, which has very bitter-tasting flesh. The cap colours are very similar, the centre often having ochre patches. *R. pseudointegra* also has the same cap colours, but its gills stay pale for a long time and then become yellow to saffron. Its stem lacks all hint of pink colouration and it has a strong fruity smell and a markedly bitter taste. It grows in broad-leaved woodland.
Edibility: Because it is so difficult to distinguish from the bitter-tasting species, it should not be eaten.
Notes: *Lepida* means 'pretty'.

Russula paludosa

This fungus is one of the largest of the genus, its **cap** reaching a diameter of almost 15 cm. When young it is bell-shaped, sometimes with an umbo, and later flat with depressed centre. The glowing, blood-red colour of the surface, reminiscent of a rosy apple, is most striking. The colour is usually even more intense towards the centre, often varying from cherry-red to pale red and generally with a number of ochre or yellowish patches. The surface can be peeled. It is smooth and shiny, sometimes with radial veining and in really mature specimens grooves become evident at the edge of the cap. The narrowly attached **gills** are fairly crowded, rather thin and elastic, their pale colour later becomes deep butter-yellow and their edges can sometimes be red. The stocky **stem** is 4–10(15) cm tall and often 1.5–4 cm thick, and varies from cylindrical to club-shaped. The white surface often has a reddish tinge of varying intensity, and is finely veined or striate. The **flesh** is white and solid, firm in the stem. The taste is mild and slightly sweet, though the gills of young fruit bodies are sometimes rather peppery. It does not have a very marked smell.

Spore print: Pale ochre.

Distribution: Not uncommon in pine woods in the Scottish Highlands, but rare elsewhere tending to grow in boggy sites from June into autumn.

Possible confusion: Could be mixed up with the unpleasant Sickener and other hot peppery species, so caution is required.

Edibility: A very good edible species.

Notes: *Paludosa* means 'pertaining to or growing in swamps'.

Russula erythropoda or Russula xerampelina

This species represents a group of fungi with varying colours which all share a crab-like smell. The **cap**, between 10 and 12 cm in diameter, is almost spherical when very young, but later expands and becomes shallowly convex. When mature, the edge is finely grooved. The colour varies from carmine, purple, vine-leaf or dark red, the centre often being darker (even black). The surface is very sticky when moist but when dry it is without a sheen and peels to half way. The adnexed **gills** are initially a pale creamy-white, later a dull ochre colour, and bruise brown. The **stem** grows to 6–9 cm high and can be about 3 cm thick. It is often stocky, cylindrical or club-shaped and carmine-pink in colour on a white background or, more rarely, completely red. When bruised it becomes a dirty brown colour. The white **flesh** is brownish in the centre of the stem and quickly turns brown when exposed to the air. The smell is of fruit, but some minutes after picking and in older specimens it develops a crab-like smell.

Spore print: Light ochre.

Distribution: Widespread and common in coniferous woods (pine) from summer into autumn.

Possible confusion: Four species are distinguishable, according to their habitat. *R. elaeodes*, with its green and olive colours, grows in deciduous woods, such as beech, oak and birch. *R. faginea* occurs in beech woods. Its cap tends to be more brown, wine-brown, yellowish in the centre. *R. graveolens* is of similar colouration with a white stem, turning brownish-yellow later. It prefers to grow under oak. *R. pascua* is a small species growing among alpine dwarf heaths.

Edibility: Because of intense smell of crab not highly prized, but edible.

Notes: *Erythropoda* means 'red-footed'.

167

With a maximum **cap** diameter of 10(12) cm, this is a medium-sized *Russula*, but it seldom reaches this size. Initially hemispherical it expands markedly and becomes depressed in the centre, the cuticle retracting from the margin to expose the gills which then resemble teeth. The surface can be peeled to about half way. The colour varies considerably, usually it is flesh-coloured, but it can also be lilac, or a strong red, or brownish to reddish-brown, often dull with dark olive-grey markings. Sometimes the edge is white and, as the fungus becomes older, becomes grooved. The soft **gills**, often forked near the stem are adnexed or slightly decurrent, white, and quite often with brownish edges. The **stem** is 1.5–2.5 cm thick. It is cylindrical, generally tapered towards the base. The surface is whitish, with brown patches near the base and often with a hint of yellow colouration about it. The **flesh** is white and also inclined to have rusty patches. For a long time it is very firm, almost hard, and in dry weather it splits and shows cavities. It has a mild taste and almost no smell.

Spore print: White.

Distribution: The Bare-toothed Russula is one of the common and widespread *Russulas* and can be found as early as May in deciduous woods.

Possible confusion: All *Russulas* with a reddish or red cap should be subjected to the previously mentioned taste-test, since otherwise there is a risk of eating *R. emetica* (The Sickener) or other unpleasant or poisonous species.

Edibility: A good edible species which can be used alone or in mixtures.

Notes: *Vesca* means 'edible'.

Russula puellaris

The **cap** of this small fungus is 3–5(7) cm in diameter. Convex when young, it is later depressed in the centre. The colour is typically fleshy-violet to salmon-purple, with a varying amount of brown. The centre of the cap, however, is always more intensely coloured, sometimes almost black, while the edge is always paler, often flesh-pink. The ochre or wax-yellow colour of the flesh is also typical. Most of the surface can be peeled, it is moist, shiny and viscid. The edge is broadly and unevenly ribbed and translucent. The **gills** are moderately crowded and adnexed or free. They are watery-cream, becoming pale yellow and finally deep ochre. The fragile **stem** is clavate, 3–5(10) cm long and 7–15 mm thick. The surface, which in mature specimens is veined and wrinkled, is initially white but soon turns yellowish from below, finally acquiring ochre patches. The **flesh** is fairly fragile in the cap, while in the stem it has a firm rind and a spongy or hollow centre. It is whitish or yellowish and turns yellow very suddenly. It has a slight fruity smell and a very mild flavour.

Spore print: Pale cream to cream.

Distribution: Not uncommon in both deciduous and coniferous woodland. It grows gregariously, but also singly, from summer into the autumn.

Possible confusion: A hot-tasting but similar-looking species found under birches is *R. versicolor*. The cap is often the same colour, but rarely has the same penetrating wax-yellow, and the edge of the cap is not so broadly grooved. Attention should be paid to the habitat.

Edibility: *R. puellaris* is edible.

Notes: *Puellaris* means 'girlish, dainty'.

Lactarius vellereus   Fleecy Milk Cap

The **cap** reaches a diameter of 10–12 cm. The flesh is particularly thick, hard and firm. From the initially convex shape it gradually develops a depressed or funnel-shaped cap which always has a slightly downturned edge. A good diagnostic feature is the woolly, felted or downy surface with its creamy-white colour showing scattered yellowish marks. The **gills** are crowded when young, later less so. They are slightly decurrent, white, but become pale ochre-yellow with increasing maturity. A few are forked and they are occasionally linked by cross-veins. When bruised or cut copious white milk exudes. The **stem** rarely exceeds 5–6 cm in height and 2–5 cm in width. It is usually cylindrical, less commonly tapered towards the base, and has the same hard, firm flesh as the cap. It also has the same felted, woolly and cream-coloured surface which bruises pale ochre.

If the compact, hard, whitish **flesh** is cut, white milk exudes. Without the flesh this tastes mild, while the flesh burns on the tongue and in the throat.

Spore print: Whitish.

Distribution: Common and widespread from summer into autumn, often in very large numbers in deciduous woodland (beech, oak).

Possible confusion: With other white or whitish hot-tasting Milk Caps, particularly *L. piperatus*, which lacks, however, the characteristic woolly surface. Also possible with *L. pargamenus*, which has adnate gills.

Edibility: In spite of the hot taste, it is eaten by many collectors.

Notes: *Vellereus* means 'fleecy' (because of the cap surface).

Lactarius piperatus

One of the medium-sized Milk Caps, its **cap** reaches a diameter of 13–16 cm. Initially convex, it expands, becomes flattened, and finally depressed and slightly funnel-shaped. The whitish, smooth, almost naked surface is often flecked with ochre in mature specimens. The inrolled margin becomes undulating in older specimens. The narrow **gills** are very crowded, slightly decurrent and white, cream or ivory. Bruising produces yellowish-brown patches. The **stem** is 3–8 cm high and 1–3 cm wide, is cylindrical, sometimes tapered towards the base, and coloured like the cap. It feels smooth and is sometimes longitudinally striate near the base. The **flesh** is white, hard and odourless. The white milk burns the tongue and throat immediately, as does that of many related species.

Spore print: Whitish.

Distribution: *L. piperatus* is common and widespread in mixed broad-leaved woodland (hornbeam, beech, oak and birch). It often occurs in large colonies which can be found from June to August or September.

Possible confusion: *L. vellereus* (Fleecy Milk Cap), *L. pargamenus* and *L. glaucescens* are similar, with their greenish or bluish-coloured flesh. These species are very hot-tasting.

Edibility: Because of its very hot peppery taste this fungus is useless. In some countries, however, it is prized as an edible species as it is said to lose its peppery taste when grilled, fried or roasted.

Notes: Reagents are useful for identification purposes, since they turn the surface and stem of various species different colours. *Piperatus* means 'peppery'.

Lactarius deliciosus   Saffron Milk Cap

The **cap** of this fungus reaches a diameter of 5–12 cm. When young it is shallowly convex and soon becomes expanded with a central depression and finally funnel-shaped when fully mature. The margin, however, remains rather persistently inrolled. The surface is a rosy-orange with darker concentric zones and is greenish only in places. When moist it is greasy and slippery. The **gills** are almost the same colour as the cap but become greenish on bruising. They are crowded, of varying length, narrow and slightly decurrent. The **stem** is 3–7 cm long and 1–2.5 cm thick, cylindrical, and sometimes tapered visibly towards the base. It, too, is coloured like the cap, but the surface has small, darker, shallow pits. The **flesh** is white and orange in the rind of the stem, which soon becomes hollow. The milk is carrot-coloured but gradually turns paler and is eventually greenish. It tastes mild.

Spore print: Light ochre.

Distribution: The Saffron Milk Cap is found almost exclusively under pines and spruce. It is uncommon in England but more frequent in Scotland from August to October.

Possible confusion: There are other Milk Caps growing under pines and firs with orange to wine-red milk and a similar appearance. Identification demands careful study of the distinguishing features. Generally speaking the change or non-change in colour of the milk plays a part. All these Milk Caps are edible. Confusion with the Woolly Milk Cap (*L. torminosus*) should not occur because of the habitat.

Edibility: The Saffron Milk Cap has a delicate flavour and is a much sought-after edible mushroom. Since they are often heavily infested with maggots, it is a good idea to cut them through on the spot.

Notes: *Deliciosus* means 'delicious'.

Lactarius deterrimus

The **cap** is 3–10 cm across, convex when young, later expanded, and eventually depressed in the centre or shallowly funnel-shaped, the edge of the cap often remaining inrolled. It is an orange-flesh colour, often darker reddish-orange with greenish areas. When bruised, it becomes initially orange-red, then green. The cap surface is sticky when moist. The **gills** are slightly decurrent, crowded, pale ochre, later orange-ochre, and flecked with green. The 3–6 cm long **stem** is 1–2.5 cm thick and more or less cylindrical. Its orange surface which is seldom pitted often has flecks of a darker orange. The **flesh** is pale yellow, white at the centre of the stem, a dark green under the surface of the cap, spongy in the stem and fragile. The orange-red milk slowly turns wine-red in the course of a few minutes. The taste is slightly bitter.

Spore print: Light ochre.

Distribution: This Milk Cap is found chiefly with spruces, but also associated with pines *en masse*. It is widespread in Europe and can be found from August to the end of October.

Possible confusion: Possible with *L. deliciosus* (Saffron Milk Cup) and *L. semi-sanguifluus*, both of which grow under pines.

Edibility: *L. deterrimus* is edible, but not especially tasty and often bitter.

Notes: The genus *Lactarius* contains over eighty species. Many of them have a hot or very hot taste and are inedible. They are mycorrhizal fungi and similar in features to the *Russulas*: brittle flesh, more or less brittle gills, and releasing milk when cut. *Deterrimus* means 'of little value'.

Lactarius torminosus   Woolly Milk Cup

The **cap** up to 12(15) cm in diameter is initially convex, then flattened and finally shallowly funnel-shaped. The margin remains inrolled for some time and is densely covered with long, shaggy hairs. The colour is carmine-red, flesh-red, or flesh-pink, later fading to a pale ochre shade, with darker, watery concentric zones. The initially white **gills** are decurrent and gradually pale flesh-coloured. The **stem**, 4–8 cm long and 1–2 cm thick, is cylindrical or slightly thicker towards the base. A delicate white frosting can be seen over its entire surface, which is paler than that of the cap but when bruised it becomes rusty flesh-pink. The **flesh** is white with a pink tinge in the cap and a strong flesh-tint in the stem, which becomes hollow. It smells vaguely fruity and has a hot peppery taste. The copious white milk is hot and burning on the tongue.

Spore print: Pale yellow.

Distribution: It is found with birches and is very common and widespread during late summer and autumn.

Possible confusion: *L. pubescens (L. blumii)*, which tastes equally hot, has a very shaggy edge to its cap and whitish to very pale flesh-pink colouration, without zones. It grows in grassy places under birches.

Edibility: Inedible, because of the hot bitter taste.

Notes: *Torminosus* means 'causing colic'.

Lactarius scrobiculatus

The **cap** grows to 10–20 cm in diameter, is initially hemispherical or convex with a navel-like depression, later becoming more or less funnel-shaped. The margin remains inrolled and short hairs make it look slightly felted. The fibrillose surface varies in colour from a dull yellow with light shades of ochre to a golden-yellow. Fibrillose scales on the surface are arranged in concentric rings. The centre of the cap usually remains smooth and has watery patches. The **gills** are crowded and slightly decurrent, varying from white to cream-yellow, but become a dirty reddish-brown where bruised. The **stem** seldom exceeds 4–6 cm and its considerable thickness of 3.5 cm gives the fungus a stocky and massive appearance. Its yellowish-white surface has numerous shallow, darker pits. The whitish **flesh** is hard, smells fruity or perfumed, and has a hot peppery taste. The milk, initially white, has an unbearably hot, burning taste, and rapidly takes on an intense yellow colouration.

Spore print: Light ochre.

Distribution: A rare species found in the Scottish Highlands in the native pine forests. In Europe it occurs in Scandinavia, south Germany and in the Alps, often in groups, in spruce forests on mainly chalky soils from July to October.

Possible confusion: The less common *L. citriolens* looks very similar, but has fewer pits on the stem and grows with birch. *L. repraesentaneus* grows in damp spruce forests, but also under birches but has milk which becomes violet on exposure to air.

Edibility: The fungus is suspect and is probably slightly poisonous. Because of its extremely hot taste it cannot be recommended for cooking.

Notes: *Scrobiculatus* means 'pitted'.

175

The **cap**, up to 15(20) cm in diameter, is initially convex and later expanded with a central depression. When young the margin is cleary inrolled, and even in mature specimens is generally curved down. The uniform orange or foxy colour of the cap is usually darker towards the centre, and the surface has a finely velvety smooth and dry texture. The **gills** are crowded and adnexed or slightly decurrent, and retain their whitish or pale ochre colouration even when mature, although when bruised they turn an intense brown colour. The **stem** can be up to 12 cm tall and 1.5–3.5 cm thick, is fleshy and usually cylindrical, often swollen about the middle. Its surface is the same colour as the cap, but generally paler and with a pale frosting. The whitish **flesh**, sometimes shaded with the colour of the stem, turns yellowish from the base upwards as it matures and has rust-brown patches where bruised. It has a fishy smell or that of a Jerusalem artichoke. The white milk becomes brownish-grey and sticky when it dries. It tastes mild but has a bitter aftertaste.

Spore print: White or very pale.

Distribution: A rare species of deciduous woodland, often associated with oak during autumn. It is not at all common in Denmark, Sweden or the North German Plain, but in central and southern Europe it is widespread even at heights above 1,000 m. It prefers the moister deciduous and coniferous woods and appears from July to October. Unfortunately it has become less numerous in recent years.

Possible confusion: A smaller variety of *L. volemus, var oedematopus* has a dark reddish-brown or copper-red cap.

Edibility: A popular edible species, but it should be left in the interests of conservation.

The **cap** is up to 8(10) cm across. When young it is conical, then shallowly convex, with a depression surrounding a characteristically pointed umbo. It is persistently and uniformly dark red or red-brown with an innately grained appearance. The crowded **gills** are decurrent. Initially white with a flesh-pink tinge, later rust-red to pale ochre with dirty patches, and when old they may have a dusting of white spores. The more or less cylindrical **stem** is 4–8 cm long and 5–20 mm thick, its pale colour gradually becoming pale red, and in the middle is the same colour as the cap. The initially white **flesh** soon becomes reddish from the cortex of the cap and stem inwards. It is firm and soon becomes hollow in the stem. Its smell is not distinctive. The abundant unchanging white milk tastes immediately resinous but soon is very hot and burning to the tongue and in the throat.

Spore print: Whitish.

Distribution: A very common and widespread species during early summer and autumn, generally in large numbers, on acid soils in pine woods and less commonly under birches.

Possible confusion: The edible *L. camphoratus* smells of curry especially after drying. The slightly bitter *L. badiosanguineus* has a deep chestnut-red cap with a darker centre and a stem of the same colour. Its gills are orange, and it is unknown in Britain. The mild-tasting *L. sphagneti* has similar cap colouration and grows in sphagnum bogs with spruce and pine.

Edibility: Inedible.

Notes: *Rufus* means 'red'.

177

Lactarius lignyotus

The **cap** grows to 2–7(10) cm in diameter. Initially it is conical or convex with an umbo, later expanded, but always with a pointed umbo seated in a central depression. The margin, which is usually paler or even whitish, is inrolled when young and finely crenulate. The black or dark brown velvety veined wrinkled surface is, however, characteristic. The **gills** are decurrent when old, and initially pure white, but later become a pale ochre, and where bruised show pink or pinkish-red discolouration. The **stem** is cylindrical, very slender, up to 12 cm tall and 5–10(20) mm thick, and at the apex is deeply grooved. The colour is uniformly dark and velvety like the cap even to the extreme apex. The base is paler or even whitish. The **flesh** tastes mild and is only slightly bitter. Initially white it changes to a pale pink, then salmon-pink and finally, after some time, to ochre-yellow. The abundant, mild or slightly bitter, white milk is rather watery and only colours in contact with the flesh.

Spore print: Pale ochre.

Distribution: A very rare species of the Scottish Highlands in the native pine forests during autumn. In central Europe it is a characteristic species of old acidic mountainous coniferous forests (spruce and fir) and is absent from the plains.

Possible confusion: *L. picinus* is similar, even as to habitat. It has neither a wrinkled cap nor stem and lacks the colour contrast between gills and stem. Its milk is initially mild-tasting, then burning.

Edibility: Edible.

Notes: *Lignyotus* means 'black'.

Lactarius necator *(Syn. L. turpis)* Ugly One or Ugly Milk Cap

The **cap** reaches 6–20 cm in diameter, and is convex with a central depression, later becoming shallowly funnel-shaped, with the edge persistently inrolled. The surface is dark olive-green or almost olive-black, sometimes olive-yellow or olive-brown, with the centre generally blackish. It often has a zoned appearance. In young fruit bodies the edge of the cap is yellowish-green, with a downy or felt-like covering. When moist the surface is slimy or sticky. The **gills** are fairly crowded, and decurrent, initially milky-white, and later straw-yellow to pale ochre. In damp weather the edges of the gills often bear water droplets, when dry they have dirty olive-coloured or brown patches. The **stem**, 3–8 cm long and 1–2.5 cm thick, is sturdy, cylindrical and often tapered towards the base, though sometimes the base is thickened. Its surface is paler than the cap and near the apex is a paler olive-green or yellow colour, but it turns brown or black from the base up. The **flesh** is firm, but fragile, initially white, later becoming slowly brown when cut. It has a mild flavour at first which then becomes very hot and burning, like the watery-white milk.

Spore print: Creamy-yellow.

Distribution: Very common and widespread in association with birch, on poor acid soils during late summer and autumn. It is widespread in Europe where it grows with spruce and birch, less commonly under pine, but also in peaty areas in deciduous woodland.

Possible confusion: Can hardly be confused with any other species.

Edibility: It is inedible, and if eaten raw causes stomach and intestinal problems with vomiting.

Notes: *Necator* means 'murderer'.

Gill Fungi

179

Paxillus involutus Roll Rim

The **cap** grows to 7–15(20) cm in diameter. When young it is shallowly convex, but later when expanded has a slight depression in the centre. At first the edge of the cap is tightly inrolled, then down turned and often slightly ribbed. The surface is sticky or glutinous when moist; silky; downy or felted when dry. The colour varies between olive-brown, rust-brown and red-brown. The **gills**, linked by veins, fork where they join and run down the stem and are easily separated from the flesh of the cap. They are at first a yellowish-wood colour, later a more intense rust-brown with dark brown patches when bruised. The 5–8 cm long and 1–2 cm thick **stem** is more or less cylindrical, or sometimes tapered. The surface is a similar colour to the cap, often with a fine frosting. The yellowish-white **flesh** browns like other parts of the fungus. It is soft with a sour smell and taste.

Spore print: Rust or ochre-brown.
Distribution: The Roll Rim is widespread and very common in heathy places with birch during summer and autumn. In Europe it is also common and widespread from June to October in almost all woodlands, parks, gardens, etc.
Possible confusion: *P. filamentosus* is similar, but lighter in colour and the surface of the cap is covered with darker fibrillose scales. The gills do not discolour, or do so only slightly.
Edibility: For a long time this fungus was considered edible, but if eaten raw or insufficiently cooked it causes very severe poisoning. If eaten regularly, allergic reactions can occur which may even lead to death.
Notes: *Involutus* means 'rolled in'.

Paxillus atrotomentosus Velvety Black-stemmed Roll Rim

The **cap** of this fleshy fungus grows to 8–15(20) cm in diameter. When it first emerges it is convex, but becomes excentric or even lateral with age and even in mature specimens the edge remains obviously inrolled. The uniformly dark brown surface is dry and downy. The soft **gills** are decurrent, crowded, often forked and interconnected with colour ranging from pale yellow to pale ochre. The **stem** is 4–9 cm long and often very thick (2.5–4 cm), which gives the fungus a massive and sturdy appearance. The stem, which is seldom centrally placed and may even be lateral is very obviously velvety, and the colour is dark brown or almost black. The pale yellow **flesh** is thick, soft, often watery and slightly brownish near the base. It has a pleasant smell and a sour taste.
Spore print: Rusty-brown.
Distribution: Occasionally growing from rotting conifer stumps in autumn, often in tiers. In Germany, from the end of spring and during autumn, one can find the fruit bodies at the base of living trunks, on roots and stumps of coniferous wood, and rarely on deciduous wood.
Possible confusion: None.
Edibility: It can hardly be considered for eating; only very long cooking enables it to be eaten.
Notes: The genus *Paxillus* comprises about five species. Most authorities place them with the *Boletales*, since they are considered more closely related to the boletes than to the gill fungi. *Atrotomentosus* means 'black-felted'.

Pleurotus eryngii

The **cap** is 3–10 cm across, initially hemispherical, with an umbo, later expanded and depressed, sometimes with irregular undulations. The margin is thin and inrolled for some time. The surface can be dirty white, greyish, brownish or speckled grey or brown on a whitish background, and is delicately felty when young. The **gills** are deeply decurrent and, in places, interconnected by veins, initially whitish, later with a greyish-ochre tinge. The **stem** is 4–6(10) cm long and 1–2(3) cm thick. It is excentric or almost central, rooting, and more or less whitish in colour. The **flesh** is almost white, smells faintly pleasant and tastes mild.

Spore print: White.

Distribution: Not found in the British Isles. It is very rare north of the Alps, occurring mainly in southern and south-western Europe, generally in open country, on the roots of larger umbelliferous plants such as *Eryngium campester*. It is often found in spring, but usually from the end of summer until well into autumn.

Possible confusion: Because of its occurrence on umbelliferous plants it is scarcely possible to confuse it with any other fungus.

Edibility: It is a very good edible species.

Notes: The genus *Pleurotus* comprises about eight species in Europe. They generally have lateral or excentric stems, often with large fleshy white, brownish or bluish fruit bodies. They are saprophytes or parasites on wood, or root sometimes on herbacious plants. Two species possess a veil. Aside from these 'veiled species' they are good edible mushrooms. *Eryngii* means 'pertaining to Eryngium'.

Pleurotus ostreatus   Oyster Fungus

The **cap** can reach a diameter of 5–15 cm and is semicircular or shell-shaped. The upper surface is completely smooth and slightly shiny with a dark violet or slate grey-blue colour, although often discoloured with grey-brown or grey shades. The somewhat decurrent **gills** are more or less crowded, of very varied length and interconnected by transverse veins near the stem, and they are creamy-white, then ivory. The whitish **stem** is very short and laterally attached to the cap, and has a white woolly base. With many Oyster Fungi, however, the stem is rudimentary. The **flesh** is white, thick, tender when young, later tough and fibrous, with a pleasant taste and smell.

Spore print: Pale lilac.

Distribution: The Oyster Fungus is widespread and common, growing as a saprophyte or parasite on deciduous, more rarely coniferous trees, often in dense clusters with fruit bodies in tiers one above the other. Fruit bodies may be found throughout the year but more abundantly in autumn.

Possible confusion: There are some colour variations in this species. *P. pulmonarius*, for example, has a paler coloured cap and yellowing flesh with a weak aniseed smell.

Edibility: Edible.

Notes: Cultivated in large numbers on wood of beech and poplar, on straw and other plant material. The amateur, too, can cultivate them with great success. They are a real alternative to fresh wild mushrooms. *Ostreatus* means 'oyster or shell-like'.

Lentinellus cochleatus

The **cap** grows to 2.5–7(9) cm across, is funnel-shaped, often one-sided and irregularly lobed while the margin is thin, and sometimes slightly inrolled. The colour is dull or reddish-brown to pale leather-yellow. The crowded **gills** are deeply decurrent, with a saw-toothed edge, initially white, later pale flesh-coloured. The **stem**, which is ribbed, is 3–9 cm long and 5–15 mm thick, tapered towards the base, where it is usually fused with stems of other fruit bodies. The surface is the same colour as the cap, though lower down it is a darker red-brown. The **flesh** is thin, whitish or pale red, leathery and tough with an aniseed smell and a mild taste.

Spore print: White.

Distribution: The fungus is widespread but uncommon. It grows on deciduous stumps during July and on into autumn.

Possible confusion: Many authorities make mention of another varieity, *var. inolens*, which simply lacks the aniseed smell. Apart from Britain it is known in other parts of Europe, such as France, Czechoslovakia and Germany. *L. omphalodes* mainly grows on twigs or buried wood, particularly alder. It is generally smaller, lacks the aniseed smell and tastes hot. *L. vulpinus* also grows in dense clusters on trunks. It is usually larger, but with shorter stems. It, too, lacks the aniseed smell.

Edibility: Edible, but very tough.

Notes: The genus *Lentinellus* is represented by nine species in Europe. They have excentric or lateral stems and saw-toothed gills. They grow on wood or woody debris. No poisonous species are known. *Cochleatus* means 'snail-like with spiral shell'.

Omphalotus olearius **Copper Trumpet**

The **cap** is 6–12(14) cm across. When young it is convex, as it matures it flattens out and becomes distinctly funnel-shaped, with the margin rather persistently inrolled. The surface with innate fibrils can be a beautiful orange-yellow to orange. The **gills** are closely crowded, markedly decurrent and an attractive saffron-golden-yellow. Even in darkness the fungus can be seen, as the gills have luminous properties. The massive, more or less excentric **stem** is up to 15 cm long and 2 cm thick, tapering towards the base, with colour ranging from that of the gills to that of the cap. The yellow-orange-coloured **flesh** is tough with a slightly unpleasant smell and an astringent taste.

Spore print: Yellowish-white.

Distribution: This fungus is essentially a species of southern Europe, where it is found on trunks of deciduous trees, especially olive. In Germany it is extremely rare and occurs only in areas which have a very warm, favourable climate; in the Upper Rhine Plain, in the Main-Neckar district and occasionally in central Germany. It grows during summer and autumn. In Britain there are very few records, chiefly in south-east England where fruit bodies were collected on oak.

Possible confusion: Its clustered growth form on wood makes this very unlikely. In the Mediterranean a brownish-red capped form is found. The more orange-coloured variety is regarded by some authorities as a sub-species or as a species in its own right. It grows on oak.

Edibility: Poisonous.

Notes: *Olearius* means 'pertaining to the olive tree'.

Chroogomphus helveticus

The **cap** seldom exceeds 4–7 cm in diameter. It remains rounded and convex, and this form is retained even in mature specimens. The orange or orange-brown surface is only viscid in damp weather, otherwise it feels extremely dry and rather fibrillose, felted or scaly. The **gills** are decurrent, at first light pink contrasting with the colour of the cap, but as the fungus matures the colours become very similar, and when old become blackish. The **stem** grows to about 8 cm in height, is more or less cylindrical, often tapered towards the base. It is the same colour as the cap. In young specimens there is a cobwebby dry cortina, and on the upper half of the stem of older specimens this is still visible as a zone of darker fibrils. When bruised or damaged the surface of the stem and the orange-coloured **flesh** turn reddish.

Spore print: Olive-brown.

Distribution: Not known in Britain. In Europe it occurs in Switzerland, as the scientific name might suggest, but it grows scattered and not very commonly under spruces and stone pines, on which it seems to be dependent, in fairly high mountainous areas, but also in the foothills of the Alps. It appears from July or August to October.

Possible confusion: There are two subspecies. *Ssp. helveticus* usually has a more pronounced umbo, and grows on acid humus-rich soils under stone pines. *Ssp. tatrensis* has a less pronounced umbo and grows under spruce; it is the more common and widespread of the two.

Edibility: Edible. Because of its rarity it should not be picked.

Chroogomphus rutilus

The **cap** reaches 4–10 cm in diameter. At first it is conical or hemispherical, then flattened with a slight umbo. The colour of the cap is reddish or copper-brown, often greyish or brownish-orange. When moist it is clearly viscid, when dry it is somewhat shiny. The margin remains persistently inrolled. Young specimens have a thin, fibrillose cortina. The **gills**, which are markedly decurrent, are at first concealed beneath the cortina, and are easily separated from the flesh of the cap. They change with age from pink to a reddish-saffron colour, but soon they have a black dusting of spores. The dry **stem** is up to 8 cm high and 5–20 mm thick, solid, very firm and tapers towards the base. Its fibrillose surface is the same colour as the cap with a vague zigzag pattern. When cut the **flesh** is yellowish, darker in the stem, and at the base a golden-yellow. It lacks a distinc-

tive smell and has a pleasantly mild taste.

Spore print: Dark brown to blackish.

Distribution: Fairly frequent in coniferous woods in Britain. It is widespread in the entire temperate zone. A *var. testaceus* is reported to occur in broad-leaved woodland. It, too, grows from July and August to October.

Possible confusion: With *Ch. helveticus*. Otherwise the two fungi, with their dry caps, stems and habitats are hardly liable to confusion with other fungi.

Edibility: Edible.

Notes: The genus *Chroogomphus*, which in Europe consists of the two species described and their subspecies, was separated from the genus *Gomphidius* because of the dry, fibrillose cortina. *Rutilus* means 'reddish-yellow'.

Decurrent Gills

187

Gomphidius glutinosus

The massive, fleshy **cap** can reach a diameter of up to 12 cm. Initially it is convex but gradually it expands until almost flat. The grey-brown to violet, dark-flecked surface is characteristic. When young it is covered with a thick layer of transparent mucilage which also covers the gills. This viscid skin is easy to remove. The very thick and distant **gills** are markedly decurrent, originally white but become more and more of a dirty, sooty grey as the spores mature. The sturdy **stem** is usually thicker at the base, while near the apex there is an obvious ring zone left by the glutinous veil, which often traps the black spores. It is almost as slimy as the cap, even if the mucilage is not so thick. The upper part is white, towards the base it becomes more and more glowing yellow. The firm **flesh** is of a similar yellow in the stem base, otherwise white and soft with a pleasant taste and smell.

Spore print: Black.
Distribution: In Britain widespread but less common than *Chroogomphus rutilus*. It is spread through the temperate zone of the northern hemisphere and throughout Europe, in southern and central Europe principally in mountainous areas. Fruit bodies are formed during summer and autumn in conifer woods either singly or in groups.
Possible confusion: Its thick layer of mucilage and contrasting brownish-violet and glowing yellow colouration, make it hard to confuse. *G. maculatus* is found with larches; the base of its stem turns wine-red.
Edibility: Good for eating according to some authorities, while others do not recommend it.
Notes: The mucilage is very tough and like glue. *Glutinosus* means 'sticky'.

Gomphidius maculatus

The **cap** is 3–5(8) cm across, and is roundish, but soon flattens and becomes shallowly convex and sometimes depressed. The surface, which cannot be peeled, is viscid, greyish-pink or vaguely brownish, sometimes flesh-coloured, while the centre is often darker with yellowish patches and black flecks. The margin is thin, uneven, and undulating. The **gills** are decurrent and forked, initially white, but soon grey and eventually blackish. When bruised they take on a wine-red colour. The slimy veil, visible when young, soon disappears and is absent in mature specimens. The **stem** is 6–7 cm long and about 1 cm thick. In contrast with the surface of the cap there is neither a slimy cortina nor a layer of mucilage, but it shows the unmistakeable feature of pink or reddish droplets on the whitish apical portions, and, further down dark red spots. The **flesh** is white, soft, fibrous in the stem and yellowish at the base. It turns reddish when cut, has no smell and has a mild flavour.

Spore print: Dark olive.
Distribution: *G. maculatus* is widespread but rare in Britain and is always found in association with larch. In Europe it occurs in mountainous and sub-alpine situations, only with larches. Outside its natural habitat it occurs in larch plantations, but less commonly. It fruits from July to October.
Possible confusion: It has one very close relative. *G. gracilis*, and they are very hard to tell apart. Bruises on the latter turn black immediately.
Edibility: Edible.
Notes: *Maculatus* means 'marked'.

Phylloporus rhodoxanthus

The fleshy **cap**, 3–9 cm in diameter, is initially hemispherical, later irregularly expanded and flat with a thin, undulating margin which is inrolled. The dry, soft-felted surface with its purple or reddish olive-brown colour is reminiscent of *Xerocomus subtomentosus*. The underside bears thick **gills** with initially blunt, undulating edges and an intense lemon or golden-yellow colouration. In mature specimens they turn rust-brown when bruised. They are interveined, broadly attached, often running down the stem and can easily be removed from the flesh of the cap. The firm, slender **stem** is 4–9 cm long, 1–2 cm thick, reddish-yellow or brownish-purple, downy-fibrillose, tapering at the base, and almost rooting. The soft **flesh** is yellow, wine-red beneath the cap and in the stem; when broken it turns a dark purple-red. It has an unobtrusive but pleasant smell and a mild flavour.

Spore print: Olive-yellow or rust-yellow.
Distribution: Rare in Britain, chiefly in the south in deciduous woods. It is found all over Europe, but is very scattered and nowhere common. It fruits during late summer and autumn either singly or in small groups especially in deciduous woodland, and less commonly among conifers.
Possible confusion: The similar *Boletinus cavipes* has a stem with a ring, grows under larches, and is poroid below.
Edibility: It is edible, but should be spared in the interests of conservation.
Notes: Its features place it somewhere between the gill fungi and the boletes, and its classification has posed something of a headache; at one time it was grouped with the *Clitocybes*.

Cantharellus friesii

In form and colour it is very similar to the Chanterelle, though it never reaches the same size. The thin-fleshed **cap** reaches at most 4, rarely 5 cm in diameter, and initially hemispherical it becomes flattened or even markedly depressed or funnel-shaped. It is orange-yellow or reddish-orange, and the margin can be very undulating and wavy. The thick blunt **gills** are deeply decurrent, forked and interlinked. Their colour, which is at first like that of the cap, becomes greyish-yellow at maturity. The 2–3.5 cm long **stem** reaches a diameter of at most 5–10 mm, and tapers towards the base, where there is also a fine white felty covering; elsewhere it is pale orange or yellowish. The **flesh** is faintly orange in the cap and white to yellowish in the stem. It smells like the genuine Chanterelle and has a sour taste.
Spore print: Straw-yellow.

Distribution: It is rare in Britain and in the rest of Europe occurring scattered in deciduous woodland on acid soils, singly and in clusters, during summer and autumn.
Possible confusion: It closely resembles the true Chanterelle, but that is more yellowish, lacking the reddish shades. The habitat is also similar.
Edibility: It is edible, but should be left in the interests of conservation.
Notes: The name *friesii* is in honour of the Swedish mycologist Elias Fries.

Hygrophoropsis aurantiaca False Chanterelle

The shallowly convex **cap**, 2–4(8) cm across, gradually expands and becomes slightly depressed at the centre with the margin remaining inrolled. The surface is usually orange-yellow, but is sometimes more or less brown, and has a fine, downy texture. The **gills** are decurrent, crowded and both regularly and repeatedly dichotomously forked. They are the same colour as the cap. The **stem**, up to 8 cm tall when mature, is cylindrical, and is the same colour as the cap. The **flesh** is soft, elastic with a slightly earthy smell and the taste is not unpleasant.

Spore print: White.

Distribution: The False Chanterelle is very common and widespread during late summer and autumn, generally in coniferous woods or on heathland but also in mixed woodland, growing on fallen needles or on wood.

Possible confusion: For beginners, confusion is possible with the True Chanterelle, which never grows on wood, has far less regularly forked gills, and smells of apricots.

Edibility: Edible with some reservations.

Notes: The False Chanterelle has a relationship with the genus *Cantharellus*, and the common name emphasizes this superficial similarity. The genus *Hygrophoropsis* contains four species. They are fungi with more or less funnel-shaped caps, a felted surface and inrolled margin when young. The gills are thin and regularly forked. Spore print is whitish. *Aurantiaca* means 'orange-coloured'.

Cantharellus cibarius Chanterelle

The **cap** grows to 2–10(12) cm in diameter. Initially hemispherical, it becomes flattened and often depressed at the centre. The matt surface is egg-yellow to orange-yellow, sometimes paler or very pale. The edge remains inrolled for some time but gradually becomes undulating and wavy. The thick irregular, gill-like wrinkles or **pseudo-gills** are deeply decurrent, irregularly forked, and coloured as the cap. The massive **stem** is 3–6 cm long and up to 2 cm thick and yellowish, is paler and less intensely coloured than the cap. The pseudo-gills are so deeply decurrent that one has the impression that the stem widens upward. The **flesh** is compact, fairly fibrous in the stem and pale yellow. It has a strong smell of apricots and a slightly sour taste.

Spore print: Light ochre-yellow.

Distribution: This widespread fungus grows in coniferous and deciduous woodland, on acid soils. Fruit bodies can be found as early as June but fruiting is mainly in autumn. In Europe numbers have unfortunately become much reduced in recent years, especially near centres of population, possibly due to over-exploitation.

Possible confusion: In beech woods there is a rare, paler, more compact variety, *C. cibarius var. amethysteus*, whose cap surface is covered with thick lilac or violet scales. There are also similarities with *C. friesii* and *Hygrophoropsis aurantiaca* (False Chanterelle).

Edibility: A very much sought-after edible fungus.

Notes: *Cibarius* means 'edible, pertaining to food'.

Cantharellus tubaeformis

The thin-fleshed **cap** forms a deep, open, pierced funnel which is continuous with the hollow stem. It is 2–6 cm across, with its edge down-turned, delicately wavy, undulating and lobed. The surface is finely scaly and coloured somewhere between brownish and greyish-yellow. The irregular, forked and broad wrinkles or **pseudo-gills** are decurrent, and various shades of yellowish-grey. The hollow **stem** is up to 8 cm long and 8 mm thick, cylindrical with longitudinal grooves, and yellowish-brown. The **flesh** is thin, white, with hardly any smell and a mild taste.

Spore print: White.

Distribution: Occasional during autumn in both deciduous and coniferous woods. It often appears in surprisingly large numbers, in rows or rings.

Possible confusion: There is a pure yellow variety, *C. tubaeformis var. lutescens*. Both could be confused with *C. lutescens* (= *C. xanthopus*) but that has only vague wrinkles on the underside of the cap.

Edibility: It is edible and much sought after in some regions.

Notes: The genus *Cantharellus* comprises species which are not typical gilled fungi. The pseudo-gills or veins are not so easily separated from the cap as the gills of true gilled fungi. The genus comprises five species. *Tubaeformis* means 'trumpet-shaped'.

Cantharellus lutescens (Syn. C. xanthopus)

The thin-fleshed, lobed **cap** can reach 3–5 cm in diameter and is trumpet-shaped. When young it is distorted with an umbilicus which later develops into a funnel with a small perforation into the stem. It is brownish-yellow or dark brown, sometimes with fine, fibrous scales. One can scarcely refer even to **pseudo-gills**: rather they are indistinct and irregular wrinkles which are barely visible. The colour range is pinkish-violet, salmon-coloured or yellowish-orange. The thin **stem** can be 8 cm long and 5–10 mm thick, hollow and often longitudinally grooved. The golden-yellow surface is smooth. The **flesh** is thin, tough, yellowish and smells strongly of fruit, but is later unpleasant. It has a mild taste.

Spore print: White.

Distribution: This fungus is not uncommon in the native pine forests of the Scottish Highlands where it can be found among *Calluna*, usually growing gregariously. It appears during late summer and autumn.

Possible confusion: With other *Cantharellus* species. *C. tubaeformis* has obvious pseudo-gills and lacks the striking smell.

Edibility: Edible, but in Britain should not be collected due to its rarity. The use of the dried, powdered mushroom as a flavouring for soups and sauces is recommended in areas where it is abundant.

Notes: *Lutescens* means becoming yellow.

195

Gomphus clavatus

The habit of *G. clavatus* vaguely resembles that of a large Chanterelle. The solid, fleshy **fruit body** is up to 10 cm tall and 6 cm across, and is top-shaped though sometimes it looks like a truncated club or is elongated on one side and ear-shaped. In young specimens the upper surface is coloured violet or purple, in older ones it is flesh-coloured, and finally ochre or clay-coloured, sometimes with a tinge of yellow. The **pseudo-gills** fork and branch to the point where they resemble a network which runs down to the base of the fruit body, so that there is only the mere suggestion of a **stem**. The **flesh** is whitish and of a soft, tender consistency. It smells and tastes spicy.

Spore print: Ochre to rust-coloured.
Distribution: Its status in Britain is uncertain and if it occurs it is very rare. In Europe it is found in mixed and coniferous woodland and shows a preference for chalky soils. It tends to occur between 400 and 1,400 (1,800) m rather than in valleys and is more common in south Germany and very rare to the north. Mature fruit bodies can be found from August to October.
Possible confusion: Unlikely.
Edibility: It is a good, productive edible mushroom. Unfortunately its numbers have become much reduced in recent years.
Notes: It grows in clusters or gregariously, often in fairy rings. The genus *Gomphus* is represented in central Europe only by this one species. *Clavatus* means 'club-shaped'.

Craterellus cornucopioides   Horn of Plenty

This fungus cannot be divided in the customary way into **cap** and stem, but forms a continuous funnel, usually running down to a point. In the upper part, where the lobed edges of the trumpet bend outwards to form a vague limb, the diameter can be up to 10 cm. In damp woods in autumn this dull-coloured fungus is often difficult to spot as its colour varies from a sooty-grey or black to a blackish brown with a hint of lilac. The cap surface bears small fibrillose scales. The **stem** is not clearly distinguishable. The fertile spore-producing layer lacks either gills or **pseudo-gills**. Rather it consists of an ash-grey, uneven, vaguely wrinkled surface, which just blends into the stem. The **flesh** is very thin, dark grey, with no particular smell and a slightly astringent taste.

Spore print: Yellowish.
Distribution: Occasional in damp places in deciduous woods on chalky soil. One should look particularly under beeches, where it is often found in large numbers during autumn.
Possible confusion: The uncommon *Pseudocraterellus cinerus* is slightly similar. Its colours are just as dark and inconspicuous, but it has definite 'gills' on the spore-producing layer. The equally rare *Pseudocraterellus sinuosus*, on the other hand, is fleshier, and more irregularly fluted.
Edibility: The Horn of Plenty has a very good flavour. Cleaning them can be rather troublesome. They are best used dried.
Notes: The genus *Craterellus* is represented in central Europe by just the one species. *Cornucopioides* signifies that the shape is reminiscent of a 'Horn of Plenty'.

Hydnum repandum **Hedgehog Fungus**

The **cap** can reach a diameter of 10–12 cm, sometimes even 15 cm. After expanding, the compact, stocky fungus takes on a rather irregular and undulating form. The surface, with its typical pale yellow, bread-roll or flesh colour, turns yellow when bruised and as the fungus ages. It feels slightly felted or suede-like. The margin remains inrolled for some time. The irregular brittle **spines** are crowded and slightly decurrent. They can be detached from the flesh of the cap, and if touched they easily break off. They can be white, or yellow like the cap. The **stem** can be 8 cm long and 3 cm thick, and generally tapers towards the felted base. The **flesh** is white, thick and firm, but fragile and turns pinkish-yellow. The smell is slightly fruity, and the taste a little hot or bitter after a short interval.
Spore print: White.
Distribution: Occasional and widespread, growing in deciduous and coniferous woodland, preferring chalky soils, generally occurring gregariously sometimes with several specimens being fused together. Found between late summer and late autumn; in southern Europe it continues to grow until early winter.

Possible confusion: In some areas *H. repandum var. rufescens* is more common. It is rather smaller and both cap and spines are more orange-coloured. The characteristic spines on the underside should exclude any further confusion with other fungi.

Edibility: Edible, but flavour is bitter and hot when old. Best used as a flavouring.

Notes: The genus *Hydnum* consists of three taxa, which can be regarded simply as varieties of a single species differing chiefly in colour. *Repandum* means 'bent backwards or upwards' (because of the edge of the cap).

Sarcodon imbricatum

The **cap** can reach the considerable size of 30 cm in diameter. At first it is hemispherical to flat with a slight umbilicus, but finally becomes slightly depressed at the centre. In young specimens the edge of the cap is still inrolled. The most obvious feature is the coarsely tessellated, scaly cap surface. These upturned scales tending to be in concentric rings stand out against the pale russet background since they are dark brown or almost black. The scales become darker towards the tip. The **spines** on the underside of the cap are 5–10 mm long, crowded and slightly decurrent, initially white then a greyish-brown or brown. They are easily detached from the flesh of the cap and are very fragile. The short, massive **stem** can reach 8 cm in length and 2–2.5 cm in thickness. It, too, has a grey-brown surface. The **flesh** is initially white, but becomes gradually grey-brown as the fungus matures. Older specimens smell rather unpleasant. The flesh is crumbly and sometimes tastes slightly bitter.

Spore print: Red-brown.

Distribution: In Britain most likely in the native pine woods of the Scottish Highlands, but it does occur sporadically elsewhere during summer and autumn.

Possible confusion: There are a few bitter-tasting species which can be confused with it. *S. scabrosum* has a rather paler cap and less upturned scales. The base of its stem is blackish. *S. amarescens* is another, more bitter species.

Edibility: It can be poisonous when raw and should therefore be well cooked. Only young specimens are suitable for eating. When dried, it can be made into a good powder for flavouring.

Notes: *Imbricatum* means 'like roof tiles'.

Strobilomyces floccopus

The **cap** has a diameter of 5–15 cm. In young specimens it is almost spherical, in older ones expanded and shallowly convex. At first the margin of the cap is inrolled and linked to the stem by a whitish-grey woolly cortina, which later ruptures, usually leaving part on the stem as a ring zone and the rest hanging in tatters from the edge of the cap. The latter is covered by a grey or dark brown layer which breaks as the fungus matures to form conspicuous thick upturned scales. The fibrils of the individual scales come together at the point. The **tubes** are 1–3 cm long and slightly decurrent, but rather shorter near the stem. At first they are whitish-grey, then grey or dark brown and when bruised they become reddish then black. The **stem** is 8–15 cm long and 1–3 cm thick. It is firm and often slightly twisted. Beneath the cap it is whitish-grey, further down dirty grey-brown. The grey-white **flesh** turns reddish when first broken, then grey or black.

Spore print: Black.

Distribution: A rare fungus of beech-woods on chalk in Britain, fruiting in autumn. In northern Europe it also prefers deciduous woodland, but in central and southern Europe it is also found in mixed and even coniferous woods. The fungus is not common, does not occur everywhere, and is sometimes absent for years.

Possible confusion: It is distantly reminiscent, with its scaly cap surface, of *Sarcodon imbricatum*, but the latter has spines beneath the cap.

Edibility: It could be eaten, but the flesh has a peculiar smell and a poor flavour.

Notes: It is the only representative of its genus in Europe. *Floccopus* means 'with a floccose foot'.

Porphyrellus porphyrosporus

The **cap** of this tough bolete with its dreary snuff-brown to sepia colour, reaches a diameter of 6–12 cm, in some specimens 16 cm. Young fungi have a hemispherical cap, but it expands and becomes convex. The margin is initially turned down and is a pale grey-brown, later dark brown with reddish patches. The surface is at first finely velvety, later smooth and always dry. The **tubes** are sinuate, initially quite short but reaching 1.5 cm in length as the fruit body matures. Their colour varies from grey-brown to dirty brown, and like the cap they turn dark brown when bruised. The cylindric or clavate **stem** is a similar colour to the cap but whitish and felty at the base. It is velvety in young specimens, smooth in older ones. The **flesh** is white to greyish-white, sometimes reddish or blue-green, and firm.

Spore print: Red-brown.

Distribution: This rare species occurs on poor sandy soil in coniferous woodland as well as on rich humus in beech woods. However, in Europe it favours spruce forests in mountainous regions and is less common at lower altitudes. Fruit bodies can be found from June to October, singly or in groups.

Possible confusion: Easy to identify because of its dreary appearance.

Edibility: The flesh is fibrous and tastes bitter even after cooking, but it is not poisonous.

Notes: Since the form varies, mycologists used to distinguish two species, the form occurring in coniferous woods (*P. pseudoscaber*) and that occurring in deciduous woods (*P. porphyrosporus*). Recent research indicates that this division is not justified.

Tylopilus felleus   Bitter Boletus

The **cap** is 5–15 cm in diameter, hemispherical when young, later expanded and convex. The surface is dry, finely velvety, and difficult to peel from the flesh. It is pale snuff-brown, dull brown or grey-brown with a slight tinge of olive colour. The **tubes** are long and do not reach the stem, they are whitish when young but soon become clear pink. The **pores** are roundish, the same colour as the tubes and on bruising, and when old they acquire brown patches. The **stem** is 4–12 cm long and 1–4 cm thick, is more or less club-shaped, a little paler than the cap and bears a characteristic coarse-meshed network of olive-coloured, raised veins which cover the whole of the stem. The **flesh** is whitish, sometimes a pale pink, soft or watery, olive-brown or olive-green beneath the surface of the cap. It lacks a strong smell, but has a very bitter taste.

Spore print: Dirty pink or pinkish-brownish-ochre.

Distribution: In Britain it fluctuates in abundance from year to year, sometimes common, sometimes occasional. In central Europe it is common and gregarious in all types of coniferous woodland on poor, acid soils, but is also found in deciduous woodland on and around rotten stumps. It grows from June to October.

Possible confusion: Particularly when young it can be confused with Ceps. If the features of the species are compared carefully there will be no need to taste them. There is also another, mild variety, *var. alutarius.*

Edibility: It is inedible largely because of its extraordinarily bitter taste: a single fungus can ruin an entire meal. It may also cause stomach and digestive upsets.

Notes: *Felleus* means 'bitter as gall'.

Boletus edulis   Cep or Penny Bun Boletus

The **cap**, 5–25 cm across, is initially hemispherical then later shallowly convex or expanded. It is naked or finely felted, and somewhat viscid when moist. The colour varies from whitish, to dark brown but is generally of a uniform colour, often with a paler zone at the edge of the cap. The **tubes** are quite long, depressed around the stem, white or whitish when young, then pale yellow and finally yellowish-olive-green. The **pores** generally are the same colour as the tubes. They are very small when young, then roundish. The **stem** is 4–20 cm long and 2–6(10) cm thick. At first it is swollen, then elongated with the base remaining swollen, or more or less cylindrical. The surface is mostly whitish or light brown, always paler than the cap, and white towards the base. It is covered with a fine, pale network of varying extent. The **flesh** is white, beneath the cap slightly pale pink or reddish. It has a pleasant smell and a mild taste.

Spore print: Olive-brown.

Distribution: Not uncommon in Britain, in all types of woodland. It is widespread in central Europe. It forms mycorrhizal relationships and is found from the plains up into the mountains, where it is more common. It prefers poor acid sand and silica-rich soils, but also occurs on chalk where there is an acid surface layer. It is quite commonly found with *Amanita muscaria* (Fly Agaric). Mostly from September to October.

Possible confusion: With *Tylopilus felleus* (Bitter Boletus). There are a further seven species closely related to the Cep, which are distinguished by, among other things, their association with various species of tree.

Edibility: A good edible mushroom.

Notes: *Edulis* means 'edible'.

Boletus pinicola

The **cap**, 10–20 cm in diameter, has a uniformly, deep brownish-red or chestnut-brown colour. The surface is smooth or downy but slightly viscid when wet. With time the **tubes**, initially white, change via yellow to a yellowish-olive colour. The **pores** are generally the same colour as the tubes, very small when young, later roundish or angular. A reddish or yellowish-brown network covers the thick, very hard **stem**, becoming paler towards the apex. The **flesh** is white, slightly reddish beneath the surface of both the cap and stem. Like all Ceps, it tastes mild.

Spore print: Greenish-yellow.

Distribution: A rare species of pine woods, as the Latin name indicates. It is widespread in Europe, and particularly in the Alpine countries, where it occurs at heights over 2,000 m. It is rare in north German pine plantations. Some authorities also record the fungus under spruce and beech. The fruit bodies mainly occur in two flushes, one in May and July, then again in the autumn.

Possible confusion: Because of its reddish-brown cap surface and its habitat, it is relatively easy to distinguish from the other Ceps-like species.

Edibility: All Ceps-like species taste good, either alone or mixed with other mushrooms.

Notes: Some authorities distinguish yet another variety, *var. fuscoruber* ('dark red'). Its stem is rather more swollen and brownish-red. It is found even in early summer. *Pinicola* means 'living with pines'.

Boletus regius

This compact fungus has an initially spherical **cap** which gradually expands to 6–15 cm. It is reddish or blood-red on a pink or pale yellow background, with hair-like fibrils. In shaded positions it is very pale yellow or pink. With age it loses this reddish shade and is then a dirty, light leather colour with a smooth, bare, often cracked or tessellated surface. The **tubes** are pale yellow, becoming deep lemon-yellow or golden-yellow, and finally olive-greenish. They are attached to the stem and depressed around it in older specimens. The **pores** are the same colour as the tubes. They do not discolour when bruised or only rarely turn a faint blue. The club-shaped **stem** is lemon-yellow, sometimes with a faint carmine-red colour at the base. A very fine network covers the greater part of its surface. Towards the base the mesh often becomes elongated or vein-like. The **flesh** is pale to deep lemon-yellow, a deeper yellow particularly at the apex of the stem and over the tubes. Under the cap surface it often becomes slightly pink. It does not discolour. At the base of the stem there is often a striking purple-carmine-pink colouration. It has a slight smell and a mild taste.

Spore print: Olive-brown.

Distribution: A rare fungus of deciduous woods in south-east England. In Europe is typical of mild, low-lying areas and sheltered, south-facing positions in hornbeam and beech woods, growing on grassy, chalky soils from May to September. It is very scattered in central Europe and has recently become much reduced in numbers.

Possible confusion: With other equally rare, yellow-pored boletes, such as *B. fechtneri* or *B. speciosus*.

Edibility: Edible, but should always be spared because of its rarity.

Boletus calopus

The **cap**, up to 20 cm in diameter, is hemispherical when young but expands and becomes convex, when the margin is at first down-turned. The colour of the surface is olive-grey, light grey or brownish-grey, sometimes clay-coloured or milky-coffee colour. It is finely downy, matt and not viscid. The long, lemon-yellow **tubes** become olive-coloured and depressed around the stem. The **pores** are the colour of the tubes, and turn blue when bruised. The **stem** is 6–8 cm long and 2–5 cm thick with a swollen base sometimes almost cylindrical. It usually shows several colours. From the apex downwards sometimes to beyond half way it is yellow, and below that an attractive carmine-red, the base being generally brownish or brown. The surface is covered by a raised whitish or pallid network. The **flesh** is yellowish-white, intensely blue when bruised and appearing marbled as a result. The taste is astringent at first, then usually bitter.

Spore print: Light ochre to olive-brown.

Distribution: In Britain widespread but possibly less common than formerly, in south-east England, chiefly in deciduous woodland with beech and oak. In Scotland sometimes in coniferous woodland.

Possible confusion: *B. albidus* is similar, but lacks the reddish colour on the stem.

Edibility: Because of the intense bitter taste it is inedible.

Notes: *Calopus* means 'beautiful foot'.

Boletus albidus (Syn. B. radicans)

The **cap** is 6–20(30) cm across. When young it is hemispherical and cushion-shaped, later convex with an overhanging, membranous edge which is initially inrolled. The surface is whitish with dirty grey and brownish-grey shades, similar to those of the Devil's Boletus. When roughly handled it darkens slightly. It is very finely downy and sometimes tessellately cracked. The **tubes** are at first pale lemon-yellow, then olive-yellow with shades of olive-green. When broken they turn blue, and are depressed around the stem. The **pores** are the colour of the tubes, roundish to angular, and also bruise blue. The **stem** is 8–12 cm long and 3–5 cm thick, with a swollen base but then becoming more or less cylindrical with a pointed root-like base. It is dull yellow to lemon-yellow and often olive-grey or olive-brown towards the base, sometimes with a few brownish patches. It has a very fine network the same colour toward the apex, but it also often lacks reticulation. The **flesh** is lemon-yellow and whitish above the tubes. When cut it turns blue, particularly in the stem. The smell is weak, the taste slightly bitter and unpleasant.

Spore print: Olive.

Distribution: Occasional, chiefly in the south of England in deciduous woodland on chalk particularly with beech and oak during late summer and autumn. In Europe it is concentrated in the south in warmer regions and does not occur at higher elevations. In Germany it is relatively rare and its numbers are falling. It appears from July to October.

Possible confusion: Possible with *B. calopus*, among others, but should not happen because of the differently coloured stem.

Edibility: Not poisonous, but inedible because of its bitter flavour.

Notes: *Albidus* means whitish.

207

Boletus impolitus

The **cap** reaches 5–12(20) cm in diameter, and is initially hemispherical, then convex but often flattened in the centre. It is pale ochre to clay or light tan, sometimes brown at the edge. It is silky-hoary, later smooth, and not viscid. The **tubes** are pale yellow to golden-yellow, becoming yellowish-green with an olive tinge later; they do not change colour when bruised. The small **pores** are the same colour as the tubes and roundish. The **stem** is 5–15 cm long and 2–5 cm thick, and is at first swollen below, later more or less cylindrical with a thickened base. Initially the same colour as the cap, it later becomes increasingly yellow, but is seldom uniformly coloured, often having only a yellow apex. The surface is innately fibrillose and is often rough with fine dots but lacks a reticulate network. Often it has red patches, stripes or dots. The **flesh** is white to pale yellow and golden-yellow especially above the tubes and in the stem. It does not turn blue when cut, and is soft, has a sour smell, and a mild taste.

Spore print: Olive-ochre.

Distribution: Occasional in deciduous woodland in southern England especially with oak during summer and autumn. In central Europe it is found in similar situations with oaks and hornbeams on chalky soils. In Germany it is uncommon especially in the north. It is mycorrhizal with oak, but it has also been found under other deciduous trees and even under pines. It appears from June to October.

Possible confusion: Scarcely likely.

Edibility: Edible but should be left because of its rarity.

Notes: *Impolitus* means 'unsmoothed, unpolished'.

Boletus satanas   Devil's Boletus

The **cap** can reach a diameter of 25 cm. Initially it is hemispherical, then convex or cushion-shaped, when old it is more expanded and irregularly lobed. Young specimens are whitish-grey, but when older tend to be more ochre, buff or sepia, often with dirty grey patches, rarely with a vague hint of pink. It has a matt surface which is slightly downy, or innately fibrillose, later becoming bare and then vaguely sticky or viscid. The **tubes** are pale yellow at first, becoming greenish-yellow and a weak blue-green when cut. Only in very young specimens are the **pores** yellowish, but they soon redden and rapidly becoming completely red. The **stem** grows to a length of 5–12 cm and is markedly swollen and bulbous (4–10 cm), and in young fruit bodies almost spherical. It is basically yellow but covered with a definite red network, which finally becomes dark blood-red. The mesh is fine and hexagonal and sometimes extends down to the yellow base of the stem. The **flesh** is whitish, yellow to pale ochre, turning fairly blue when broken and very rarely reddish. When young it has little smell, but when old it smells of rotten meat.

Spore print: Olive.

Distribution: Rare, chiefly in the south of England in beech woods on chalk during summer and early autumn. In Europe it is definitely more common in the south. It prefers dry, south-facing slopes in beech and oak woodland, appearing from June to October. This bolete should be conserved.

Possible confusion: With other red-pored boletes, such as *B. rhodoxanthus*, *B. luridus* and *B. erythropus* (Red-stalked Boletus).

Edibility: Poisonous, causing stomach and intestinal disorders, especially if raw.

Boletus luridus

The **cap** is 5–25 cm across, initially hemispherical to convex, then expanded, but seldom flat. The surface is finely downy, with an olive-brown colour, sometimes more olive-yellow to almost leather-yellow, but becoming blue-black when bruised. When moist it is slightly viscid, otherwise dry. The **tubes** are a pale olive-yellow, later yellowish-green or a dirty olive-colour, and when cut become greenish-blue. A good diagnostic feature, though not always present, is the persistent red colour in a line above the tubes, as seen when the cap is cut. The **pores** are initially yellowish when young, but soon have a tinge of red and are eventually a vivid red colour. The initially swollen **stem** is later more cylindric, 4–20 cm long and 1.5–5 cm thick, and a light to orange-yellow, with an obvious red network. The mild-tasting **flesh** is pale yellow, sometimes with red at the base of the stem.

It becomes rapidly and intensely blue on cutting.

Spore print: Olive-brown.

Distribution: Occasional in deciduous woodland on chalk soils during summer and early autumn. This fungus is widespread in Europe, from the plains to the high mountains. In Germany it tends to prefer mild positions, favouring oak, hornbeam and beech woods on chalky soils. It fruits from May and June to September.

Possible confusion: With *B. erythropus* (Red-stalked Boletus) and other red-pored boletes.

Edibility: The fungus is edible, but it contains poisonous compounds which are destroyed by heat during cooking. It is nevertheless not advisable to consume alcohol with them.

Notes: *Luridus* means 'pale'.

Boletus erythropus   Red-stalked Boletus

The **cap** is 8–20 cm in diameter, hemispherical when young, later a convex or cushion-shape, and when older more or less flat. The colour is mainly a uniform dark brown, but can be olive-brown to almost black. It is finely felted, matt, dry, and when moist only slightly viscid. The **tubes** are pale or olive-yellow, finally yellowish-green, and turn very blue when bruised or cut. The **pores** are only yellow when very young and quickly change to a uniform red colour. When bruised they also become intensely blue. The **stem** grows to a length of 4–15 cm and is 2–6 cm thick. Swollen when young, it soon becomes more or less cylindrical, but is usually relatively thick. The background colour is yellow, thickly dotted with small red flecks. The **flesh** is yellow or deep yellow and slightly marbled when moist, turning an immediate deep blue when bruised or cut. It has a slight smell

and a generally mild flavour.

Spore print: Olive-brown.

Distribution: Fairly common and widespread in deciduous and coniferous woodland during summer and autumn. In Europe from the plains to the high mountains. It prefers acid, chalk-free soils. It is found from mid-May until October in spruce woods or in mixed beech, fir and spruce woodland, also in boggy places and in deciduous woods.

Possible confusion: The very rare *B. quéletii* has an olive-yellow to olive-brown cap with reddish shades and a more or less smooth stem, yellowish at the top, reddish below. It prefers chalky soils, but is not so tied to them as is *B. luridus*.

Edibility: A good edible mushroom.

Notes: *Erythropus* means 'with a red foot'.

211

Boletus rhodoxanthus

The **cap** grows to 7–20 cm in diameter, is hemispherical when young, then convex or cushion-shaped, and is later more flattened. It is whitish or brownish-grey, when old a dirty brownish-yellow, but generally with a tinge of pink or reddish toward the margin. It is bare, or at most slightly downy, generally rather sticky. The **tubes** are deep, light yellow to yellow, yellowish-green when mature and easily bruise blue. The **pores** are initially the same colour as the tubes, but they quickly become red or carmine. The **stem** is 6–16(20) cm long and 2–6 cm thick, and is initially swollen, later more or less cylindrical, sometimes tapering slightly towards the base. Its yellowish surface, purple or carmine-red near the base, is covered by a fine red, purple or blood-red network. The **flesh**, firm in the cap, soft in the stem, is a vivid lemon yellow, deeper in the stem and above the tubes. It turns slightly blue, and it is wine-red near the base. It has little smell and a mild taste.

Spore print: Olive-coloured.

Distribution: This attractive, red-pored Boletus occurs in similar habitats to *B. satanas* but is generally less common. It is unknown in Britain.

Possible confusion: Beginners might confuse it with the Devil's Boletus. The other, very rare, 'purple' boletes such as *B. rhodopurpureus*, *B. lupinus*, *B. splendidus*, etc. are very hard to distinguish.

Edibility: Poisonous at least when raw. Because of its rarity it should not be collected.

Notes: *Rhodoxanthus* means 'pink and yellow'.

Boletus splendidus

The **cap** grows to 5–10 cm in diameter. It is cushion-like when young, then convex, often uneven with an overhanging margin. Initially milky-coffee-brown, then brown with tinges of pink here and there. Slightly downy when dry and young, smooth when older. In young specimens the **tubes** are very greyish-yellow, the **pores** yellow, but soon becoming red or carmine. The **stem** is 4.5–8 cm long and 2–4(6.5) cm thick. It is more or less cylindrical and tapered towards the base, while the yellowish surface is covered by a very fine red network. Towards the base the colour becomes a fiery red or purple, the reticulation and the background being of uniform colouration. The basal mycelium is yellow. The **flesh** is light yellow, reddish inside at the base of the stem becoming slightly blue in the cap. Larval tunnels are reddish. It has a slightly sweet, perfumed smell.

Spore print: Olive-coloured.

Distribution: In fairly warm deciduous woodland especially in sunny situations, near oaks and beeches. The fungus in the photograph was found in a sunny, dry position with beeches on chalky soil. Its distribution is insufficiently recorded but it is known to occur in Czechoslovakia, France and Italy. Very rare. It grows during summer and autumn.

Possible confusion: Described in literature, but not always in the same sense; thus the complex of species has various names: *B. satanoides*, *B. lupinus*, *B. purpureus*, *B. le-galiae*. *B. satanoides* and *B. purpureus* have been recorded in south-east England in deciduous woodland, both are very rare.

Edibility: Unknown.

Notes: This photograph was included to indicate some of the problems involved in precise identification of critical species.

Xerocomus chrysenteron Red-cracked Boletus

The **cap** is 3–12 cm across, and at first markedly convex cushion-shaped to almost hemispherical, but later it becomes more flattened and sometimes even depressed at the centre. It is brown, yellowish-brown, sometimes with an olive-brown shade, greyish-ochre and sometimes slightly reddish. The surface of the cap is dry, matt, finely felted or velvety and when dry it cracks in a tessellated pattern, when the thin reddish upper layer of otherwise yellowish flesh is visible. The **tubes** are initially pale yellow, then greenish-yellow to olive-green, becoming blue when bruised. The **pores** are the same colour as the tubes, large and angular. Sometimes they are also flecked with brown and become more or less blue when bruised. The **stem** is 3–10 cm long and 5–20 mm thick. It is generally cylindrical and tapered towards the base. It is mostly red or brownish on a yellowish background, often with longitudinal striations. The soft, tender **flesh** is whitish or vivid yellow but distinctly reddish under the surface of the cap. When broken it becomes pale blue. It smells and tastes pleasant.

Spore print: Brownish-olive.

Distribution: Widespread and common throughout Europe, occurring in both coniferous and deciduous woodland and on all types of soil in June to November. In Britain found in deciduous woodland.

Possible confusion: The 'false' Red-cracked Boletus (*X. truncatus = X. porosporus*) is extremely similar but paler, found in parks and deciduous woods. It is principally distinguished by its truncated spores.

Edibility: The fungus is edible.

Notes: The genus *Xerocomus* comprises about ten species.

Xerocomus badius Bay Boletus

The **cap** is initially hemispherical, then cushion-shaped and convex, and finally somewhat flattened. It grows to a diameter of 5–10(15) cm, varying from chestnut-brown to lighter reddish-brown or even olive-brown with many specimens almost black-brown. It is usually matt, dry and downy, but in damp weather it is distinctly viscid. The **tubes** are depressed around the stem and are a strikingly pale, later olive-yellow to dirty olive-green, and bruise a greenish-blue colour. The **stem** grows to a length of 5–12 cm and is 1–4(5) cm thick. It is very variable in form, often more or less cylindrical wth a slightly pointed base, but it can also be slightly swollen. It is yellowish-brown, and innately streaky, the top of the stem often yellowish and the base often white and cottony. The whitish-yellow **flesh** is brownish beneath the surface of the cap and turns more or less blue when bruised. It is very firm when young. It has little smell and a mild taste.

Spore print: Olive-brown.

Distribution: The Bay Boletus is common and widespread in both coniferous and deciduous woodland. Often found as early as June or July, but more plentiful in autumn.

Possible confusion: It is sometimes mistaken for a Cep by beginners, but it lacks the reticulated stem, and the flesh and the tubes of the Cep do not turn blue.

Edibility: Edible.

Notes: *Badius* means 'bay-brown'.

Xerocomus spadiceus

The **cap**, 3–10 cm across, is cushion-shaped, later shallowly convex, with the centre flat or even depressed. The edge is often quite thin and inrolled. It is dark brown or reddish-brown, without olive shades, but when young it generally has a yellowish, finely felted covering. When dry it cracks exposing the pale yellow flesh. The **tubes** are initially pale yellow, then golden-yellow, and become blue when touched. In mature specimens there is generally a depressed area around the stem. The **pores** are the same colour as the tubes, strikingly labyrinthine when young and angular when mature. They become bluish when bruised and then finally brownish. The **stem** is 4–9 cm long and 1–2 cm thick, is more or less cylindrical, sometimes with a pointed base. Over its whitish or yellowish surface there are light brown, coarse ridge-like markings which often come together in an incomplete network. The **flesh** is whitish, but yellowish near the tubes and in the stem. In fresh specimens it becomes blue, particularly above the tubes, when cut. It tastes mild.

Spore print: Olive-brown.

Distribution: Probably not uncommon in woodland. In Europe it grows in deciduous and coniferous woodland on deep humus among mosses. Generally in groups, but also singly, from July to October.

Possible confusion: This species is often confused with *X. subtomentosus* and was formerly regarded as a variety or subspecies of it. Many authorities distinguish between a coniferous woodland form and a deciduous woodland form, this differentiation resting largely on a positive or negative reaction to ammonia of the cap surface.

Edibility: Edible.

Notes: *Spadiceus* means 'date-brown'.

Xerocomus subtomentosus

The **cap** is 3–12 cm across, almost hemispherical when young, soon cushion-shaped with a flattened centre, sometimes with a slight depression. The colour is olive or olive-brown, and particularly when young is covered with a mustard-yellow down which generally disappears with age. The **tubes** are vivid yellow, finally turning greenish-yellow or a brownish colour and are relatively long. The **pores** are the same colour as the tubes or more intensely yellow, relatively large and become only very slightly blue when bruised. The **stem** grows to a length of 6–10 cm and 1.5–2.5 cm thick, and is more or less cylindrical, and covered with or has a scattering of small brownish flecks on a uniform pale yellow background. There is no obvious reticulation. The **flesh** is whitish-yellow, firm when young, but soon becomes soft and spongy. It has little smell and a mild taste. Bluing is not always present, and in very young specimens scarcely perceptible.

Spore print: Olive-brown.

Distribution: Common in Britain in deciduous and mixed woodland. It is found throughout Europe in deciduous and coniferous woodland, and occasionally even occurs outside woodland and for some years after it has been cut down. The fruit bodies are found in large numbers from August to October.

Possible confusion: With *X. spadiceus*, q.v. *X. chrysenteron* differs in that it has reddish colouration on the stem and beneath the cap surface.

Edibility: Edible.

Notes: In moist weather it is very quickly covered by a white then vivid yellow mould, which particularly attacks *X. subtomentosus*, but also other boletes. *Subtomentosus* means 'rather felted'.

Boletinus cavipes

The **cap** is 5–15(20) cm in diameter, initially convex, then cushion-shaped, often with a low, blunt umbo, less commonly with the centre slightly depressed. It is yellow-brown, golden-brown, dark brown or reddish-brown, and covered with dense upturned fibrillose scales. In young specimens the edge of the cap has hanging from it whitish remnants of the partial veil. The **tubes** are yellow at first, then greenish-yellow, relatively short and can only be removed from the cap with difficulty. The **pores** are the colour of the tubes, initially large, compound, irregular, then elongated, vaguely gill-like with cross-connections. The **stem** is 5–8 cm long and 1–2.5 cm thick, almost cylindrical or slightly club-shaped, and hollow. Above the peronate ring it is the same colour as the tubes, and below it is covered with small or rather coarse scales. The **flesh** is pale yellow, and does not change colour when bruised. It has only a slight smell and an unremarkable taste.

Spore print: Olive-ochre.

Distribution: *B. cavipes* is a mycorrhizal fungus of larch and hence restricted in its distribution to that of its mycorrhizal partner, mainly in mountainous or sub-alpine regions. It is also found in plantations in lowland areas, though it is less common there. It grows from July to October on soils with a degree of acidity. This bolete is rare in Britain, mainly in the south in larch plantations.

Possible confusion: Easily recognized and confusion is unlikely.

Edibility: Edible, but should be conserved.

Notes: *Cavipes* means 'with a hollow foot'.

Chalciporus piperatus Peppery Boletus

The **cap** reaches a diameter of 2–6(10) cm. It is hemispherical, then cushion-shaped, and later rather flat. The colour ranges from coppery-reddish-brown through yellowish-brown to foxy-ochre-brown. The surface is finely grained and when moist it is slightly sticky. The **tubes** are attached to the stem, sometimes slightly decurrent, and orange-brown, yellowish-brown or cinnamon-red in colour. The **pores** are the same colour as the tubes. The **stem** is 4–7(10) cm long and 5–10 mm thick. It is cylindrical, of uniform thickness or tapered slightly towards the base. The surface is the same colour as the cap and hymenophore, or paler. It is smooth and dry. The unchanging **flesh** is yellowish, often with a reddish tinge, and chrome-yellow in the stem. The taste is hot and peppery.

Spore print: Cinnamon-brown.

Distribution: Common and widespread in Britain in deciduous woodland and most commonly with birch. Widespread in central Europe, but not equally common everywhere. It occurs on soils with an acid content from the plains to the mountains, preferring coniferous woods on sandstone. Under similar circumstances, though less commonly, it also grows in deciduous woodland, from summer into the autumn.

Possible confusion: *Ch. amarellus* (False Peppery Boletus) has similar colouration, but paler, more pink to copper-red with a mild or slightly bitter-tasting flesh. It is considerably less common, more frequent in the south (Alps), and grows under fir and spruce. Some authorities regard it merely as a variety of the Peppery Boletus.

Edibility: It is sometimes used as a flavouring, otherwise it is scarcely of value.

Notes: The genus *Chalciporus* contains four species. *Piperatus* means 'peppery'.

Suillus luteus   Slippery Jack ←●

The **cap** grows to 5–10(15) cm in diameter. When young it is hemispherical, then cushion-shaped with a slight umbo, later expanded. At first, the surface is very slimy and viscid when moist, but shiny when dry. It is dark brown or yellowish-brown, sometimes paler with a grey or violet tinge, and the skin is easily peeled. The **tubes** are pale yellow, later yellow to dirty olive-yellow. They are attached to the stem or slightly decurrent. The **pores** are the colour of the tubes and often exude whitish droplets. The **stem** is 3–6 cm long and 1–2.5 cm thick, more or less cylindrical, rarely thickened at the base or tapered upward. A membranous velum initially links the stem with the edge of the cap. It is whitish on the outside, soon becoming dirty brown, and yellowish inside. When ruptured it forms a membranous, pendent ring. Beneath it the surface often has a brownish coating. The **flesh** is white to yellowish, tending to become brown from the base up, firm and fibrous in the stem and soft and tender in the cap. It has a fruity smell and a rather sour taste.

Spore print: Rusty ochre-brown.

Distribution: Slippery Jack is common and widespread both in Britain and the rest of Europe, in coniferous forests, especially with pine. It can be found in groups during autumn.

Possible confusion: Easy to recognize from its habitat and membranous ring.

Edibility: The fungus is edible. It is said to provoke in some people an allergic reaction similar to *Paxillus involutus* (Roll Rim).

Notes: The genus contains about twenty species. They are mycorrhizal fungi associated with conifers, which generally have viscid caps, with or without a veil and often exude droplets from the pores and apex of the stem. *Luteus* means 'yellow'.

Suillus grevillei ←●

The **cap** is 3–10 cm in diameter, initially hemispherical, then cushion-shaped (sometimes with an umbo), later expanded and almost flat. The surface is a vivid light yellow with variations to golden-brown with a darker centre. It is slimy or viscid when moist and shiny and smooth when dry. The **tubes** are yellow, later dull olive to brownish-yellow, attached or slightly decurrent. The **pores** are the same colour as the tubes. The **stem** is 6–10(12) cm long and 1–2.5 cm thick, is either cylindrical or slightly thickened towards the base and club-like. A yellowish veil at first joins it to the edge of the cap, and when ruptured this forms a thick cottony ring zone on the stem. Apart from this, the stem is yellowish with brownish fibrils. The **flesh** is also a vivid yellow, although sometimes paler, and turns a vague pinkish-violet colour when cut. It smells pleasantly fruity and tastes mild and sometimes slightly sour.

Spore print: Yellowish-brown, variable.

Distribution: Not uncommon in larch plantations in Britain. The fruit bodies often grow gregariously from July to October.

Possible confusion: *S. aeruginascens* has a similar habitat, but the cap, pores and stem are more or less grey. Its flesh is whitish. *S. tridentinus* has a similar form, but is orange or cinnamon-brown in colour. Both species grow with larches, prefer chalky soils, and are less common.

Edibility: All three species are edible.

Notes: Grevillei is named honouring the Scottish mycologist R. K. Greville.

Suillus granulatus

The **cap** is 4–10 cm across, initially hemispherical but flattening with age. It is brown or yellowish-brown in colour, becoming paler. When moist the surface is viscid, when dry smooth and shiny, peeling easily. The **tubes** are whitish or yellowish, attached or slightly decurrent. The **pores** are the same colour as the tubes, and exude milky droplets. The **stem** is 4–10 cm long and 1–2 cm thick, and more or less cylindrical, less commonly thickened below or tapered again towards the base. The yellowish-white surface is covered, completely or just the upper half, with similarly coloured or yellowish granules from which exude milky droplets, which turn sooty and dark as they dry. The **flesh** is also yellowish-white, firm at first, later soft and watery. It has a pleasantly sour smell and a mild taste.

Spore print: Ochre-yellow.

Distribution: It is common and widespread in both Britain and the rest of Europe, always occurring under two-needled pines on dryish, chalky soils, sometimes gregariously, in clearings, on woodland margins, from June to November.

Possible confusion: With *S. collinitus* which has pink-coloured mycelium at the base of the stem, and is also edible.

Edibility: The fungus is edible.

Notes: The skin of the cap should be peeled before cooking, as with all viscid boletes. *Granulatus* means 'granular'.

Suillus plorans

The **cap** is 3–15 cm across, at first hemispherical, then cushion-shaped, rarely with an umbo. It has brownish fibrils on an ochre or orange-brown, sometimes more yellowish, background. It is viscid when moist, but quickly dries and has innate fibrillose spots. The **tubes** are brownish-orange, then olive-ochre, becoming a lighter, dirty yellow in older specimens. The **pores** are the same colour as the tubes or darker, relatively small and roundish. When young they exude milky-white droplets which dry brown. The **stem** is 4–10(12) cm long and 1–2.5 cm thick, the base is generally quite thick and it tapers towards the apex. It is solid, more rarely with cavities or hollow. Its dirty ochre to orange surface is covered with granular dots which secrete milky droplets, which later dry blackish. The **flesh** is also orange, more yellowish above the tubes and at the stem apex, firm in the stem and soft in the cap. It has a vaguely fruity almond-like smell and a slightly sour taste.

Spore print: Olive-brown.

Distribution: This fungus does not occur in Britain. It is associated with the five-needled Stone Pine, a conifer of alpine regions, and therefore is only found in the Alps (central Alps), parts of Siberia and the Carpathians. Fruit bodies are formed during summer and autumn.

Possible confusion: A close relative is *S. placidus*, growing under both Weymouth Pine and Stone Pine. It is whitish in colour and is described and illustrated on pages 226–7.

Edibility: It is edible, but should be spared in the interests of conservation.

Notes: *Plorans* means 'weeping' (because of the tear-like droplets).

Suillus bovinus   Jersey Cow Boletus

The **cap** reaches a diameter of 3–10 cm, and is initially cushion-shaped with a pallid slightly inrolled margin, but later expands to become irregularly flattened and depressed. It is a clay-pink-cinnamon or ochre-brown and when moist the surface is very viscid but quickly dries. The **tubes** are pale greyish-yellow to olive-yellow or olive-brown, broadly adnate or decurrent and difficult to separate from the flesh of the cap. The **pores** are the same colour as the tubes or have a dirtier appearance, and are large, compound and irregular. The **stem** is 3–6 cm long and 5–15 mm thick, fleshy, usually cylindrical or slightly swollen below. The surface has a similar colour to the cap, though often paler, and is almost always saffron-yellow at the apex, with brownish streaks below. Th **flesh** is pale yellow, to brownish, turning a pinkish-flesh colour as it dries but is often vinaceous in the base of the stem. It has a pleasant, fruity smell and a sour taste.

Spore print: Pale olive-brown.

Distribution: The Jersey Cow Boletus is common and widespread in Britain and the rest of Europe. It prefers poor, acid soils in coniferous woodland, where it grows beneath pines from August to October.

Possible confusion: Inexperienced collectors could mistake it for *S. variegatus* (Variegated Boletus), the cap of which is covered with rough, felty scales and which has small pores.

Edibility: The Jersey Cow Boletus is edible.

Notes: *Gomphidus roseus* is generally found in the same places, both species requiring the same soils and tree species. It is possible that the two fungi are interdependent. *Bovinus* means 'pertaining to the cow'.

Suillus variegatus   Variegated Boletus

The **cap** is 6–15 cm in diameter. Initially hemispherical with the margin markedly inrolled, later cushion-shaped, but soon expanding. The yellowish-brown to orangey-ochre surface is covered with darker fleck-like scales especially toward the margin and looks as though it had been strewn with sand. In moist weather the cap is only slightly viscid, otherwise it is dry. The **tubes** are dirty pale yellow with tinges of orange and finally turn yellowish-green. The small **pores** are darker and dirtier becoming cinnamon and turning slightly blue when bruised. The **stem** is 7–10 cm long and 1.5–2.5 cm thick. Initially slightly swollen, it later becomes cylindrical, often with a thickened base. It is paler in colour than the cap and more orange-brown towards the base, and a more vivid yellowish-orange at the apex. The **flesh** is yellowish or pale orange-tinged throughout with blue, or becoming slightly blue above the tubes or not at all. It has a slight smell and a mild taste.

Spore print: Olive-brown.

Distribution: Common and widespread throughout Europe growing in coniferous woods under pines on acid soils. The fruit bodies are formed from June to November.

Possible confusion: With *S. bovinus* (Jersey Cow Boletus), though the latter has a smooth cap which is very viscid when moist.

Edibility: It is edible, but is not regarded as particularly good.

Notes: *Variegatus* means 'variegated'.

Suillus placidus

The **cap** reaches 3–13 cm in diameter, initially hemispherical or cushion-shaped and later expanded with a blunt umbo or with a slight depression in the centre. The white or ivory-coloured cap, yellowing from the edge inwards, is viscid and sticky when moist, but shiny and smooth when dry. When bruised it slowly turns violet. The skin peels and the **tubes** are the colour of the cap, only becoming lemon-yellow when mature. The **pores** are the same colour as the tubes, and exude milky-white, later brownish or reddish droplets, which are finally seen as brownish-red specks. The **stem** is 5–15 cm long and 0.5–3 cm thick, more or less cylindrical, and with its white surface dotted with pale, reddish-brown granules. Small droplets can very often be seen at the stem apex. The **flesh** is white, yellowish in outline and sometimes violet-grey when exposed to the air. It has an inconspicuous smell and a mild flavour.

Spore print: Dull ochre.

Distribution: Not native in Britain but has been found in Arboreta on several occasions. In southern and central Europe the fungus can be found from the coast to altitudes of 2,100 m, though there are gaps in its distribution. It is rarer in the north German Plain than in the central Highlands. It seems to have no particular soil preference but is dependent both on the native Stone Pine and on the Weymouth Pine, introduced around 1700 from North America.

Possible confusion: *S. plorans*, described on page 222, is closely related.

Edibility: *S. placidus* is a good edible mushroom, but it should be spared in the interests of conservation.

Notes: *Placidus* means 'mild, pleasant, calm'.

Leccinum aurantiacum

The **cap** grows to 5–20(25) cm in diameter. When young it is hemispherical, then cushion-shaped, flattening out when mature, with a slightly overhanging edge. The surface is orange-red, brownish-red or brownish-orange and slightly viscid in damp weather, otherwise finely felted and quick-drying. The **tubes** are whitish for some time, finally becoming grey, or dirty olive-grey, or yellowish-grey, and are depressed around the stem. The **pores** are the colour of the tubes, and turn brown at the slightest pressure. The tall cylindrical or clavate **stem** reaches 5–20 cm in length and is 1–5 cm thick. It is whitish or pale, ornamented thickly with prominent scales which are initially whitish, but soon turn orange and then brown. The undamaged surface of the stem develops light ochre patches when bruised. The **flesh** is white but quickly turns grey-violet or purple-grey and finally black. When cut it turns wine-red or violet, sometimes greenish-blue at the base. In the stem it is firm and fibrous, in the cap it becomes soft. It smells and tastes pleasant.

Spore print: Brownish, with a tinge of olive.

Distribution: Rare in Britain but widespread in Europe, probably occurring everywhere. It grows from June until October under aspens. On the continent in recent years the species has become much reduced in numbers.

Possible confusion: This is a genus rich in variety. Identification is sometimes very difficult, and the habitat is often very important. *L. atrostipitatum* grows under birches. *L. piceinum* under spruces, *L. quercinum* under oaks, *L. vulpinum* under pines.

Edibility: All these species are edible.

Notes: *Aurantiacum* means 'orange-coloured'.

Leccinum scabrum　Brown Birch Boletus

The **cap** is 5–15 cm across. When young it is hemispherical, then cushion-shaped and sometimes flat at the centre. The edge of the cap does not overhang the pores. The surface is light grey-brown to reddish grey-brown, later often brown, smooth, and dry, but rather viscid when moist. The **tubes** are whitish, later dirtier and rather pale grey, unchanging when broken, relatively long, deeply sinuate around the stem and easily detached from the flesh of the cap. The **pores** are the same colour as the tubes, and do not change colour when bruised. The elongated cylindrical clavate **stem** reaches 5–15(20) cm in length and is 1–2.5(3.5) cm thick. Its whitish surface is densely covered with scales, initially pale grey, but later grey to blackish. The mycelium is white. The **flesh** is whitish, later more greyish-white, and pale brown when dried. When bruised or broken it is unchanged or becomes flushed with pink. It is relatively firm when young but soon becomes spongy. The flavour is mild.

Spore print: Yellowish-brown, cinnamon-coloured.

Distribution: Widespread and common in Britain and Europe within the range of the birch, with which it forms a mycorrhizal partnership, growing from June to October.

Possible confusion: *L. variicolor* has a stem which turns blue when cut; *L. oxydabile* has firmer flesh which colours pink and a different cap structure; *L. melaneum* is darker, with tinges of yellow below the surface of cap and stem; all parts of *L. holopus* are pale or whitish.

Edibility: The fungus is edible.

Notes: *Scabrum* means 'rough'.

Leccinum carpini (Syn. L. griseum)

The **cap** is 3–15 cm across, initially hemispherical, then cushion-shaped, or occasionally somewhat flattened. It is grey, grey-brown, yellow-brown, olive-brown or blackish-brown, very variable and with all shades of these colours. It is often an ochre-yellow at the edge and in the centre. It is slightly velvety or frosted, when young typically with depressions and wrinkles, and when older dry, cracked and tessellated. When moist it becomes slightly sticky. The **tubes** are whitish at first, then yellowish-grey. When touched or bruised they become violet-grey. At the stem they are deeply sinuate. The **pores** are the same colour as the tubes, and if bruised they become greyish-violet or blackish. The **stem** reaches 5–16 cm in length and is 0.8–3(4) cm thick. It is initially very swollen, then cylindrical but narrowing towards the apex, and pointed at the base. It has longitudinal ribs on a whitish to yellowish-grey background, coarsely dotted initially with grey, later deep brown to black granular scales, and darkening everywhere when bruised. The **flesh** is whitish to pale yellow and when cut turns rapidly reddish to violet, then black. It is firm, later soft in the cap.

Spore print: Dirty brown.

Distribution: In Britain widespread, but rather rare in association with hazel and hornbeam, less often with oak. Widespread in central Europe, if scattered, and not extending beyond the northern and eastern boundary of beech and hornbeam. It grows from June to October, generally gregariously, in deciduous woodland, especially with hornbeams and oaks.

Possible confusion: *L. scabrum* (Brown Birch Boletus) is not so massive, its flesh does not blacken, and its habitat is different.

Edibility: The fungus is edible.

The **cap** has a diameter of 5–12 cm. When the fungi grow singly, their caps are regular and almost circular in shape. Often, however, they grow tightly packed together, when their caps are irregular, twisted and lobed, and often fused. In young specimens the cap is smooth, in older ones it is split or tessellated. It is fleshy and entirely creamy-white in colour. The **pores** are initially white, later yellowish with a hint of green, 1–3 mm deep and decurrent. They are roundish and very small. The **stem** of this polypore is 3–5 cm long, its diameter 1–3 cm. It is smooth and solid, but rather fragile, and often excentric, but specimens are also found with a central stem. The **flesh** is white, often turning yellowish when bruised. It has a solid but fragile consistency and a pleasant taste and smell.

Spore print: White.

Distribution: Its occurrence in Britain is doubtful. In Europe *A. ovinus* is found from July to October in coniferous forests in mountain locations. It occurs on both sandy and chalky soils and can be very numerous. It is found in association with spruce.

Possible confusion: *A. similis (= subrubescens)* is very similar, a species little known in central Europe. *A. confluens* can also look similar. From above it could be mistaken for *Hydnum repandum* (Hedgehog Fungus), but the latter has spines on the underside of the cap.

Edibility: It is an edible and tasty fungus, whose flesh unfortunately is often riddled with maggots.

Notes: *Ovinus* means 'pertaining to sheep'.

Laetiporus sulphureus **Sulphur Bracket, Chicken of the Woods**

The **caps** often measure 10–50 cm across and are flat, fan-shaped brackets, often in tiers one above the other. The colour of the cap ranges from tile-red or yellowish-red in the case of young specimens via sulphur-yellow in mature specimens to dirty white when old. The **tubes** are sulphur-yellow and only 2–4 mm long. The small **pores**, the same colour and 3–5 mm in length, exude yellowish droplets in young fruit bodies. The **flesh** is a vivid yellow, soft and very juicy when young, when old it is whitish, dry, cheesy and easily crumbled. It has an aromatic smell, but the taste is sour, even bitter when old.

Spore print: Pale cream.

Distribution: Common and widespread in Britain on such hosts as oak, chestnut, willow and yew. This fungus, with a worldwide distribution, is common in southern and central Europe. It can be found from May until autumn in deciduous woodland with oaks. Host trees are principally living and dead deciduous trees, especially oaks, willows and various fruit trees, but also sycamores, alders, ashes, poplars, limes, robinias, walnuts, horse-chestnuts and sweet-chestnuts. Less commonly it grows on conifers, especially on larches in the Alps and north Germany.

Edibility: Juicy, young fruit bodies are soaked in water to remove the sour taste, then sliced and dipped in breadcrumbs before frying. They taste very good.

Notes: This beautiful and striking fungus is a great destroyer of wood. Its persistent mycelium causes intense brown rot. The heart wood is transformed into a reddish-brown, crumbling mass, the trunk becomes hollow and sooner or later falls. *Sulphureus* means 'sulphur-yellow'.

Fomitopsis pinicola

The **fruit bodies** of this large polypore which lasts for several years grow on the tree as broad, flat, woody brackets, up to 25 cm radius, 15 cm thick where they join the trunk, and 10–40 cm in diameter. The upper surface is concentrically zoned, furrowed and unevenly wrinkled. It displays a range of colours depending on age. Young specimens are initially covered with an orange-yellow to red-brown, resinous crust, almost reminiscent of *Ganoderma lucidum*. Later the crust turns black or dark grey, but toward the margin zones remains red and the extreme margin is yellowish-white. Fresh, growing fruit bodies frequently exude watery droplets from their thick, swollen margin and from their pores. The underside, which turns grey or brownish-red when bruised, has small round **pores**, pale yellow in colour, 3–4 per mm. If the fungus is cut, the pale wood-coloured layers of **tubes** can be seen, each layer 5–10 mm thick. Above the tubes is the 2–6 cm thick corky or woody cortex or **flesh** of the cap, which is pale ochre with indistinct zones and a sour smell.

Spore print: Pale cream.

Distribution: Although very common in Scandinavia, Denmark, central and southern Germany and the Alpine countries, in north Germany, Holland, northern and western France it is very scattered. In Britain known from a single record. It attacks living trees through wounds, but is more common on dead wood, causing a brown rot which reduces it to small fragments. It prefers coniferous wood, mainly spruce and fir, but can also be found on deciduous trees.

Possible confusion: Old specimens look like *Fomes fomentarius* (Hoof Fungus).

Edibility: The fungus is not edible.

Fomes fomentarius Hoof Fungus or Tinder Fungus

The **fruit bodies**, often hoof-shaped and persisting for many years, reach a diameter of 10–30(50) cm and a height of 7–15(25) cm. The surface is covered by a 1–3 mm thick hard horny crust the colour of which varies with age. The young fruit body has a red-brown, then hazelnut-brown surface ornamented with darker, undulating bands and grooves. During the winter the crust becomes a uniform and persistent milky-grey or dark grey with only the growth zone showing nut-brown colouration. Old specimens are grey to dark grey with irregular concentric grooves or ridges. The underside is flat, with a grey or grey-brown frosting, much darker when bruised, with fine, roundish **pores**, 2–4 per mm. Most of the fungus consists of the many-layered (3–10 mm per layer), rust-brown tubes. The layers of **tubes** correspond to periods of growth, which can occur several times per year. Above the tubes is a brownish-white marbled, crumbly and fragile heart, which contrasts sharply with a yellow-brown, tough and fibrous layer of 2–5 mm, from which in former times the much sought-after tinder was obtained.

Spore print: Whitish.

Distribution: In Scotland and northern England it is very common and grows almost exclusively on birch. It is absent over most of the remaining country but occurs again in the south-east on beech and less often sycamore and other deciduous trees.

Possible confusion: It is sometimes confused with the *Ganodema* species.

Edibility: The fungus is not edible.

Notes: *Fomentarius* means 'pertaining to tinder'.

This polypore grows at the base of oak trees, and is often of considerable size; 10–40(60) cm in diameter, 5–20 cm in radius and 3–10(15) cm in thickness. The **fruit bodies** appear in summer as thick brackets just above ground level at the base of the trunk. The uneven upper surface is initially covered by yellowish-white down, and exudes numerous yellowish droplets. With age the down disappears and in the mature fungus a thin, bare, brownish-red crust is formed. Only the blunt yellowish-white growing edge then exudes the brownish droplets. Similarly, it is only when the fungus has grown large that the chestnut-brown, 5–20 mm long **tubes** develop in a single layer on the underside. The **pores** are quite small, 3–5 per mm, roundish and brown with a silvery sheen when fresh. The thick, rust-coloured **flesh** is at first soft and juicy with vague zones, later becoming hard and fibrous or cork-like.

Spore print: Whitish, then yellowish.

Distribution: Not uncommon in Britain, on various species of oak including some which are evergreen. It is rare in north Germany, and its northern limit is southern Scandinavia. Elsewhere it is scattered or rare, favouring mild districts, where it appears from summer until autumn at the base of the trunk of large oaks. It occurs very rarely on sweet chestnuts, beeches and even firs. The white rot caused by the fungus only attacks the roots.

Edibility: It is inedible.

Notes: *Dryadeus* means 'living with trees'.

Piptoporus betulinus **Birch Bracket or Razor-strop Fungus**

The annual **fruit bodies** are semicircular and slightly hoof-shaped and attached to the host by a thick, short lateral stem-like structure. The upper surface is convex and cushion-shaped, with its blunt edge turned down over the pores, smooth and unzoned. Initially it is whitish, then grey-brown to pale brown, covered with a thin, leathery, membrane which can be removed. Occasionally fruit bodies develop which are bell-shaped or cucumber-like, longer than they are broad or variously distorted. They are 5–20(30) cm in diameter, 7–15 cm in radius and reach a thickness of 2–5 cm. The white **tubes** are strikingly short in comparison with the thick flesh (1–8 mm), from which in mature fruit bodies they are easily separated. There is only a single layer of tubes, the fruit body decaying in winter. The **pores** on the whitish undersurface develop tardily and are later yellowish-grey to light brown and small (3–4 per mm). The white **flesh** occupies most of the fruit body and is tough and rubbery.

Spore print: Whitish.

Distribution: Widespread in the northern hemisphere and common wherever birches grow. Strictly dependent on the birch, it is never found on other trees. It mostly attacks elderly or weakened trees, gaining access to the trunk through wounds or damaged branches. Severe brown rot then develops in the wood and the trunk snaps.

Possible confusion: None.

Edibility: It is said to be edible when young, but bitter and inedible when old.

Notes: *Betulinus* means 'pertaining to the birch'.

Pycnoporus cinnabarinus

The **fruit bodies** are annual, more rarely biennial, their flattened **caps** either semicircular, kidney-shaped or spatulate, 2–10 cm in diameter, 2–8 cm in radius, and 5–20 mm in thickness. The upper surface of young fungi is downy, that of older ones naked, rather uneven or wrinkled, without zones or with a zone only visible at the margin. Young specimens are a vivid orange or vermilion, older or dried-out ones are paler. The fairly long **tubes** (3–7 mm) are indivisibly fused with the flesh and are the same red as the upper surface, while the roundish or angular **pores** (2–3 per mm) are an even more intense red. The **flesh** is vermilion to pale yellowish-orange, with vague zonation, soft at first, then tough and leathery, with little smell or taste.

Spore powder: White.

Distribution: In Britain there are very few records of this striking polypore. Although widespread in Europe, it avoids almost entirely that part of north-west Europe influenced by the oceanic climate (British Isles, Belgium, Netherlands, Denmark), whereas in central Europe it is commonly found in the plains, highlands and mountains (up to the tree line). Its preferred hosts are deciduous trees such as birch, copper beech, wild cherry, rowan, alder, willow, hornbeam and oak. Occasionally it favours conifers, above all silver fir. It prefers sunny positions.

Edibility: It is inedible.

Notes: The magnificent red colour of this fungus is caused by the red pigment cinnabar. Even the mycelium within the wood is coloured red. *P. cinnabarinus* is a saprophytic fungus, i.e. it affects only dead wood.

Fistulina hepatica Beefsteak Fungus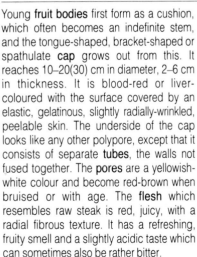

Young **fruit bodies** first form as a cushion, which often becomes an indefinite stem, and the tongue-shaped, bracket-shaped or spathulate **cap** grows out from this. It reaches 10–20(30) cm in diameter, 2–6 cm in thickness. It is blood-red or liver-coloured with the surface covered by an elastic, gelatinous, slightly radially-wrinkled, peelable skin. The underside of the cap looks like any other polypore, except that it consists of separate **tubes**, the walls not fused together. The **pores** are a yellowish-white colour and become red-brown when bruised or with age. The **flesh** which resembles raw steak is red, juicy, with a radial fibrous texture. It has a refreshing, fruity smell and a slightly acidic taste which can sometimes also be rather bitter.

Spore powder: Pale reddish-brown.

Distribution: The Beefsteak Fungus is common in Britain and is widespread in Europe, its northern limit coinciding with that of the oak. In Germany it is found everywhere from the plains to the lower mountain regions. It grows near the base of old oak stumps, or quite high up the trunk. The sweet chestnut is another host, while other deciduous trees are less frequently attacked. Fruit bodies are formed during summer and autumn.

Possible confusion: *Buglossoporus pulvinus* has a similar form and spore colour, and is initially just as fleshy and juicy and turns red. The fungi are not, however, related and are easy to distinguish with careful examination of the pores.

Edibility: Edible when young, but opinions as to its worth differ.

Notes: *Hepatica* means 'liver-like'.

This complicated very branched polypore can reach a diameter of 30–50 cm. From one thick, fleshy and whitish stem there arise innumerable branches, each of which ends in a small, circular **cap**. These reach 1–4 cm across, can be pale yellow or brownish, and almost always have a definite depression in the centre. The scaly surface is covered by fine fibrils. The underside bears short **tubes**, 1–2 mm long. The **stems** and the branches which bear them are in part covered by decurrent **pores**. The **fruit bodies** are soft-fleshed, short-lived and particularly in rainy weather soon begin to rot and decay. They are also generally attacked by larvae. The smell is slightly mealy and the taste mild.

Spore powder: Whitish.

Distribution: Inhabits deciduous woodland areas in the temperate zone in Europe. In Britain very rare, found mostly in the south-east, associated with oak. In Germany, occasional, from the coast as far south as the foothills of the Alps, especially around old trunks or stumps of oak and beech, but it can be found growing on the ground without any apparent connection with wood. It may occur as early as June and continues into autumn.

Possible confusion: It has a certain similarity of structure with *G. frondosa*. The latter, however, has many caps which are clearly fan-shaped and overlapping, grey-brown in colour, and spring from a short, fleshy, branched stem.

Edibility: This fungus is edible.

Notes: Beneath the ground is found the underground sclerotium of the fruit body. It is an irregular, knotty and branching structure enclosing thin, living tree roots. Every year, new fruit bodies grow from it. *Umbellata* means 'umbrella-like'.

Trametes versicolor **Many Zoned Bracket**

The invidiual **fruit bodies** are 3–8(10) cm in diameter and of similar radius. They are flat and leathery, in tiers one above the other. The colours vary considerably and occur in narrow zones ranging from yellowish, brownish, or blackish, usually with a paler whitish margin. Towards the centre the surface is coloured greenish by algae, elsewhere it is finely velvety, coarsely hairy, or naked with a silky sheen in alternating bands. The **pores** are small, roundish or angular, sometimes torn and almost tooth-like. They vary from white to yellowish, and later light brown. The whitish **flesh** is thin, tough and leathery.

Spore powder: White.

Distribution: *T. versicolor* is very common and widespread, both in Britain and Europe and is one of the most important fungi involved in the decomposition of wood. In Germany it is densely distributed from the coast to the Alps. It colonizes almost any deciduous wood and is only rarely found on coniferous substrates. It can be found throughout the year.

Possible confusion: This species has transitional forms towards other *Trametes* species which can cause a problem of identification. Very similar, and sometimes growing alongside it, is *T. hirsuta*. This has a covering of white silky-grey hairs, and creamy-coloured pores which develop a greyish tint. It grows especially on beech in sunny exposed situations.

Edibility: Inedible.

Notes: *Versicolor* means 'many coloured'.

Stereum hirsutum   **Yellow Hairy Stereum**

This beautiful, colourful fungus forms thin undulating, wavy-tiered irregular **brackets**, which are broadly attached to the wood and have a characteristic yellowish-orange edge when young. The individual **fruit bodies** are 2–10 cm across, ochreous or yellowish-brown to pale grey-brown with a yellowish edge. The surface is zoned and covered with hairs. The underside or **fertile layer** is smooth, a vivid orange-yellow or ochre, less commonly with a pinkish tinge, but when old and dry assumes a greyish or brownish colour. The **flesh** is thin, membranous, tough and leathery.

Spore print: Whitish.

Distribution: *S. hirsutum* is widespread in Europe and common everywhere including Britain. It grows on fallen trunks of deciduous trees and is one of the first fungi to colonize them; it especially favours fallen branches, stacked trunks and stumps of such hosts as oak and beech, causing a white rot, but it is also found on many other trees but only very rarely on conifers. Fruit bodies occur at any time of year.

Possible confusion: The illustration probably represents the most common form of this fungus, which varies considerably according to the time of year and the age of the fruit body. There are evidently several races, among them some in which the hymenium turns red when wounded.

Edibility: The fungus is inedible.

Notes: The *Stereum* species grow on wood and can be recognized from their smooth fertile layer, which forms neither tubes, pores, spines or gills. *Hirsutum* means 'hairy'.

Schizophyllum commune   **Split Gill**

The **cap** is 1–4 cm across, and fan-shaped but more complicated forms arise when several fruit bodies become fused together. The upper surface of the cap is whitish-grey with shaggy or felt-like hairs. Sometimes there is a hint of lilac. When moist it is more of a dirty grey-brown, with a vaguely zoned appearance. The undulating edge is slightly turned under. The **gills** give the fungus its name ('split gill') since they appear to be split lengthways. They are also fairly distant and of uneven length, reddish-grey or slightly violet in colour. The **fruit body** is virtually sessile with only a rudimentary **stem** and often occurs in clusters or tiers. The gills radiate out from this point.

Spore print: White to slightly reddish.

Distribution: Apparently on the edge of its range in southern England during autumn, on fallen or felled trunks of decidu- ous trees, especially beech and perhaps less frequent than formerly. It is one of the earliest fungi to colonize such substrates. Living trees are also attacked, as are conifers. It has a very wide distribution in temperate and tropical regions of the world.

Possible confusion: Very unlikely if the gills are carefully studied.

Edibility: Inedible.

Notes: In dry conditions the halves of the gills cover the spore-producing hymenium, expanding again as humidity increases so that the spores can be liberated. Such movement to protect the fertile portion from drying out is rare among fungi.

Clavariadelphus ligulus

The small, club-like **fruit body** grows to a height of 5–8 cm, and some may have a truncated apex and are somewhat irregularly grooved below. The 'head' is about 5–15 mm wide, and the fungus tapers visibly towards the base to about 3–5 mm, where the shaggy, felted, white mycelium can also be seen. The hollow fungus is initially yellowish-white, later ochreous or brownish with more or less noticeable brownish-salmon or brownish-violet tones. The surface is smooth when young, later uneven or wrinkled, often with longitudinal furrows. The **flesh** is whitish, and the flavour is either mild or quite bitter.

Spore print: Cream.

Distribution: In Britain a rare fungus of coniferous forests or with birch during autumn, often in vast swarms but also singly.

Possible confusion: The colour and shape are reminiscent of *C. pistillaris* (Giant Fairy Club), which is larger but also yellowish or orange, but its habitat in deciduous woodland helps to prevent confusion. The spores of *C. ligulus* are also distinctive.

Edibility: The fungus is edible, with reservations, since it is not very tasty and often bitter.

Notes: There are seven species in Europe belonging to the genus *Clavariadelphus*, and individual identification can sometimes pose problems. Information regarding habitat can be helpful but should not on its own be treated as decisive. *Ligulus* means 'tongue-like'.

Clavariadelphus pistillaris   Giant Fairy Club

The club-shaped **fruit body** can reach 20 or even 25 cm in height. When young it is more or less cylindrical, but very soon becomes club-shaped with a broad, rounded 'apex' and a narrow base. At the apex it is 2–5(8) cm wide. When young the initially smooth surface is pale yellow, gradually becoming yellow-brown, ochre, vinaceous-brown with salmon or violet tinges. In the course of maturation it becomes more and more deeply and longitudinally wrinkled. Young, yellow fruit bodies turn dark brownish-purple or wine-red when bruised. When cut, young specimens have firm, white **flesh** which becomes increasingly spongy with age. When bruised it discolours like the surface. The smell is very pleasant, but the taste is bitter.

Spore print: Cream.

Distribution: In Britain a rare fungus in the southern beech woods on chalk. In Europe it occurs in deciduous woodland with oak, beech and chestnut, in northern Europe also with hazel. It prefers rich, chalky soils and fruit bodies can be found during autumn.

Possible confusion: *C. truncatus* looks very similar but is a more reddish-brown and its top is abruptly truncated. The species described, *C. ligulus*, is smaller and often grows in spruce woods.

Edibility: Inedible.

Notes: *C. pistillaris* should not be picked owing to its rarity. *Pistillaris* means 'pertaining to clubs'.

Sparassis crispa   Cauliflower Fungus or Brain Fungus

The whole **fruit body** is reminiscent of a coarse bath sponge, a lax cauliflower or a brain-like object. The fungus consists of many high branched ribbon-like, curly, closely intertwined lobes which can eventually be traced back to a single white **trunk** which is sunken in the ground and thus difficult to see. Mature specimens can be 30 or even 40 cm in diameter and weigh several pounds. Initially it is pale buff in colour, but gradually becomes paler and eventually looks dirty brownish-white. The **flesh** is white and waxy with a spicy smell and a pleasant, nutty flavour.

Spore print: Pale ochre.

Distribution: The Cauliflower Fungus is not uncommon in Britain. It is a parasite on the roots of pines and other exotic conifers causing rot in the trunk. In elderly trees, it can cause considerable damage to the heartwood in the lower part of the trunk.

After infected trees have been felled, the fungus can continue to form fruit bodies for some years on and around the stumps. The fruit bodies are formed during late summer and autumn.

Possible confusion: With *S. nemecii* in Europe, a species which grows with spruces and firs. It is not so curly, having only smooth-edged, slightly undulating, straw-yellow lobes to its branches. It is also more profuse and massive.

Edibility: The Cauliflower Fungus is edible and prized by many collectors. Its interior often conceals small creatures which can only be removed with much labour, as well as sand and grass debris enclosed by the growing fungus.

Notes: The fertile layer forms on the underside of the ribbon-like lobes. *Crispa* means 'curly'.

Ramaria largentii

The much-branched **fruit body** can grow to a height of up to 17 cm and is often broader than it is high. From an often massive **trunk** there develop very densely-packed branches which end in short, blunt, toothed or broken-looking tips, the number dependent on the age of the fruit body. The trunk is whitish at the base and an attractive yellow where it meets the lower boughs. In young specimens the **branches** are generally a deep orange, more intense towards the tips, becoming paler with age and finally becoming a pale creamy-orange colour. When the spores are mature the branches have a creamy-yellow-ochre dusty appearance. The **flesh** is dirty white, sometimes slightly coloured just below the fruiting layer. The smell is generally of rubber. The taste is mild, the tips of older specimens slightly bitter.

Spore print: Yellowish-ochre.

Distribution: This beautifully coloured coral fungus, not often reported in Europe, grows particularly in spruce forests in the mountains, forming its fruit bodies from August to September. The specimen pictured was photographed near Moosburg in Upper Bavaria. It is not known in Britain.

Possible confusion: Identifying individual coral species is often very difficult, and because of the similarities they are frequently wrongly identified by the layman. *R. aurea* is not such an intense orange colour and when young generally has yellow tips. It grows in deciduous woodland, especially near beech.

Edibility: Value unknown.

Notes: Without specialist knowledge and study of the microscopic features, identification of most *Ramaria* species is impossible.

Ramaria flava

The **fruit body** reaches a height of 15–20 cm and a diameter of 10–15 cm. From a thick, white **trunk** grow dense, bushy branches, which divide several times. They are more or less cylindrical, but can also be compressed. The branches often have two blunt tips or irregularly foreshortened ends. They are a glowing, light primrose-yellow or light egg-yellow. When young the lower branches and those above the trunk often have a tinge of sulphur-yellow, when old they are creamy-ochre. When bruised they sometimes become a yellowish wine-brown. The **flesh** is moist, dirty white and, especially in the trunk, marbled. It does not change colour. It has an acrid smell and a mild taste, though the tips, particularly when old, are bitter.

Spore print: Yellowish-ochre.

Distribution: In Britain it is rarely found, but in central Europe it is one of the largest and most common species, growing in deciduous, coniferous and mixed woodland, especially near beeches and spruces. July to September.

Possible confusion: As already discussed under *R. largentii*, there are similar fungi which can only be correctly identified with the aid of a microscope. *R. obtusissima* resembles this species externally because of its similar colouration, particularly in the case of young fruit bodies. *R. flavobrunnescens* is smaller.

Edibility: Can be used when young in mixtures with other fungi, but risk remains of mistaken identification.

Notes: The coral fungi produce their spores over the surface of the branches. In many books, are described as good edible fungi, but there are poisonous species and the beginner should avoid all coral fungi for this reason. *Flava* means 'yellow'.

Ramaria formosa

The species name *formosa* has nothing to do with the Chinese island and gives no hint as to the origin of the fungus. The word is Latin and means, more or less, 'beautifully shaped'. The **fruit body** can be up to 15(17) cm high and 4–12 cm across, most specimens being 8–10 cm high. From the **trunk**, which is white at the base, grow dense coralloid branches which divide into two or three at the ultimate tips, which are fairly blunt. The trunk is yellowish-ochre towards the apex, with a tinge of pink. The branches are salmon-pink, yellowish at the tips and later ochre below in part due to the presence of the mature spores. The **flesh** is white, pinkish in outline, moist but not watery, marbled and unchanging.

Spore print: Yellow-ochre.

Distribution: *R. formosa* grows only in deciduous woods on chalky soils, often under beeches, where it can be found from summer into autumn. It is rare in Britain.

Possible confusion: This fungus, at least when young, is easily recognizable from the gradation of colour (base white, branches salmon-coloured, tips yellow). With older specimens identification is really difficult and poses problems even to experts. *R. mairei*, also poisonous, has pale branches with longitudinal wrinkles and the tips are flesh-coloured or violet.

Edibility: It is poisonous, causing severe gastro-intestinal problems.

Notes: The collector of edible fungi could apply the rule of thumb that species with pure white flesh in the trunk are poisonous, while all those with marbled flesh can be eaten.

Calocera viscosa   Yellow Antler Fungus

This beautiful fungus has an antler-like or coral-like appearance. The many-branched **fruit body**, which grows to a height of 3–7 cm, is egg-yellow or orange and from the short, whitish, felted base a long root-like portion often penetrates deep into the wood on which the fungus is growing. The fungus is tough, with a firm gelatinous texture and is greasy or sticky in damp weather. When dry, the tough elastic **flesh** takes on a hardened horn-like consistency, but when damp conditions return it expands once more.

Spore print: Light yellow-ochre.

Distribution: The Yellow Antler Fungus grows in clusters of varying size in coniferous woodland on rotting stumps, roots, and on fallen wood. It is found throughout the year, but particularly between July and January. It is very common and widespread in Britain.

Possible confusion: Similar, but considerably smaller, is *C. cornea*. This species is only 5–10 mm high, generally with an unbranched or only slightly forked fruit body. It occurs on deciduous wood, where it often grows in swarms. Various coral fungi can also be confused with the species, but none has the elastic texture of the Yellow Antler Fungus.

Edibility: One should refrain from eating it, since it is edible but tough and indigestible. Some similar-looking corals are edible, some are clearly inedible or poisonous.

Ramaria botrytis

This attractive-looking fungus is very varied in appearance, reaching 10–20 cm in height. From a robust **trunk** grow branches of varying thickness which branch more and more finely, like coral, and terminate in truncated or pointed tips. The trunk is whitish, particularly towards the base, near the apex and into the branches creamy-white or pale brownish-white, later more ochre-yellow from the brown spores. Older specimens are pale ochre or a brownish-leather colour. The tips are very pale red to deep purplish-wine-red when young, becoming paler lower down when old. The **flesh** is dirty white, perhaps slightly reddish in the tips, but otherwise unchanging. It has a pleasant, fruity smell and a mild taste.

Spore print: Light ochre.

Distribution: Rare in Britain but quite common in Europe, growing in deciduous and coniferous woodland, especially under beeches on chalky and sandy soils.

Possible confusion: To date, two other similar forms or species are mentioned in literature, *R. botrytis fm. musaecolor* and *R. rubipermanens*. They have been reported in Italy and in Bavaria, but they could well be present in the rest of Germany and be confused by inexperienced collectors and amateur mycologists with the typical *botrytis* because of their similarity. Intensive study of the species is necessary for precise differentiation.

Edibility: This coral fungus is said to be the tastiest of all, but it should be spared in the interests of conservation.

Notes: It should be noted that the clubs or branches of coral fungi are roundish or flattened and are entirely covered by the fertile layer, the hymenium. *Botrytis* means 'grape'.

249

Clavulina cristata   **White-crested Coral Fungus**

The whitish **fruit body**, with its numerous, irregular branches, reaches a diameter of about 4–6(10) cm. The very short **stem** can reach a diameter of 1 cm. From this grow more or less slender branches which are flattened towards the apex and there divided into many small delicate crested tips. These smaller branches are whitish, especially towards the tips, and very fragile. The **flesh** is also whitish, sometimes rather bitter and earthy.

Spore print: White.

Distribution: White-crested Coral Fungus is widespread and common, growing in deciduous and coniferous woodland on the forest floor. It is found from August until October.

Possible confusion: There are a whole series of varieties of this white coral. Their fruit bodies can look very different, for instance, with tooth-like or bristle-like tips, with forking branches or truncated ends, often thick-growing. *Cl. cinerea* is also similar in habit with a bushy growth form, but is grey in colour, especially below. *Cl. rugosa*, also white, grows singly and has a broad twisted fruity body, often with only a few branches

Edibility: The fungus is inedible. It is not known to be poisonous, but the crested corals and all other whitish relatives are of no value to the collector.

Notes: White-crested Coral Fungus and *Cl. cinerea* are often attacked by another parasitic fungus, *Roselinia clavariae*, which causes them to become dark grey in colour. *Cristata* means 'comb-like or crest-like'.

Ramariopsis pulchella

The **fruit bodies** are quite small and dainty, 1–2 cm tall, bright violet, becoming pale as they dry. The thin, delicate branches have few rounded axils and short, violet tips. At the base the frail fruit bodies have a clearly distinct, if very short **stem**, the red-brown colour of which is often covered by a felty, white layer which is easily wiped away. The **flesh** is rather waxy, but firm and without any particular smell.

Distribution: This fungus is not common in Europe (England, France, Italy, Switzerland, Germany), and it needs a sharp eye as well as good fortune to spot this tiny violet species. From mid August until late autumn it grows singly, less commonly gregariously but scattered, on bare earth in dampish places.

Possible confusion: This pretty coral is easy to recognize from its small size, the relatively sparse branching, the fairly firm flesh and the violet colouration. *Clavaria zollingeri* and *Clavulina amethystina* are similar in colour, but considerably larger (2–7 cm) and generally more branched, growing more strongly and having fragile or very fragile flesh.

Edibility: Inedible.

Notes: Definite identification of club-shaped and coralloid fungi without a microscope and specialist knowledge is possible only in very few instances. The specimen illustrated was identified by an acknowledged expert in this group of fungi, Herr E. Schild, Brienz, Switzerland.

Lycoperdon perlatum   Common Puff-ball

It is club-shaped with an enlarged head narrowed below into a stalk-like base. The whitish surface is covered by prominent white spines, each of which is surrounded by a ring of small warts. The spines are easily rubbed away or fall away at maturity leaving a meshwork of the smaller warts covering the surface of the **fruit body**. The fungus is up to 8 cm high and 2–4 cm thick. When young it is white. Later, when the spores are almost mature, the surface becomes dry, papery and brownish. On the **stem portion** the warts become smaller, and less dense. The interior of the head is soft and white when young but gradually becomes olive-brown and powdery as the spores mature. The interior of the stem, however, takes on a sponge-like consistency, so that the body can only be cut through with a very sharp knife. As with all puff-balls, the mature spores are dispersed through a small apical pore or opening at the centre of the head.

Spore powder: Olive-brown.

Distribution: It is very widespread and common in deciduous and coniferous woods, generally in large groups, from June to October.

Possible confusion: L. foetidum (The Stinking Puff-ball) has fine brownish or black hair-like spines united at their tips into almost stellate groups, and grows principally on acid soils. It is equally common. Calvatia excipuliformis, described later, is larger but covered with scurfy spines.

Edibility: Edible when young and while the interior is still white.

Notes: Perlatum means 'widespread'.

Lycoperdon pyriforme

The initially white surface of the narrowly club-shaped **fruit body** is covered with small, mealy particles or scurfy spines. It is up to 4 cm high and to 2.5 cm wide across the head and less robust than L. perlatum. The fruit body, however, has a more or less marked umbo, and is ripe when the fungus becomes brownish in colour. The surface is then usually more or less smooth. The interior of the head remains white for some time in young specimens, but eventually turns a yellowish-olive-brown. Finally the spore mass becomes brownish and powdery and the spores are dispersed through an apical pore. The interior of the stem has a spongy texture of very small 'cells'.

Spore powder: Olive-brown.

Distribution: L. pyriforme is very common and widespread and always grows on wood, especially on rotting stumps and usually in large swarms. Highly decomposed beech stumps are a favourite habitat. Sometimes fruit bodies appear to grow on soil, but then they are always attached to roots or buried wood by conspicuous white chords of mycelium. It can be found from August to November in the fresh condition but old fruit bodies can persist throughout the year.

Possible confusion: Can arise with all its white relatives bearing granules or spines on the surface. L. perlatum (Common Puff-ball) does not grow on wood.

Edibility: Inedible.

Notes: Pyriforme means 'pear-shaped'.

Lycoperdon umbrinum

The mature **fruit body** is pear-shaped and about 4–5 cm in diameter. The dark surface is covered by dense spines and granules, initially creamy-yellow, later brownish and finally almost black. At the base of the **stem**, white, branching threads of mycelium can be seen. In the head the fertile tissue is usually white but turns more and more olive-yellow and finally on maturity becomes powdery and almost blackish-brown. The spores are dispersed through a small apical pore in the centre of the cap.

Spore powder: Reddish-brown.

Distribution: Uncommon in Britain but distribution uncertain. It prefers slightly acid soils rich in new humus. It is found in coniferous woods in the mountains, only occasionally in deciduous woodland, where it generally grows gregariously. No reliable distribution data is as yet available.

Possible confusion: It is often confused with other dark-coloured puff-balls. Exact identification is usually possible only with a microscope. *L. foetidum* and *L. molle* are particularly similar.

Edibility: It could be eaten when young, but should be spared.

Notes: As with all puff-balls spores are dispersed by rain drops falling on the thin papery mature fruit bodies. *Umbrinum* means 'umber-brown'.

Lycoperdon echinatum

The **fruit body** is pear-shaped with a diameter of 4–5 cm, rarely more than 6 cm, and a height of about 5 cm. The surface is covered by a dense layer of elongated fibrillose spines up to 6 mm long, joined at their tips into groups. When the spines drop off a reticulate pattern is seen. There is no properly differentiated **stem**, rather the fungus tapers uniformly towards the base. The whole fruit body is a brownish colour. The interior of the head is initially white but becomes purple-brown and powdery at maturity. Spores are dispersed as indicated for previous puff-balls.

Spore powder: Lilac-grey to dark brown.

Distribution: It is widespread, but rather uncommon in deciduous woods in autumn. At maturity the fruit bodies become thin and papery and the fertile head contains cottony threads holding the powdery spores. Raindrops hitting the head cause it to act like bellows puffing out clouds of spores.

Possible confusion: The particularly long spines are very distinctive and make it easy to recognize. Other brownish species, such as *L. molle* and *L. umbrinum*, have only fine granular warts on the surface. Once the spines have fallen, no particular pattern is left.

Edibility: Scarcely edible. It could be eaten while the flesh is still white.

Notes: *Echinatum* means 'spiny like a hedgehog'.

Scleroderma citrinum

The **fruit bodies** reach a diameter of 3–10(15) cm and are more or less spherical, sometimes with a flattened centre. The entire surface, which consists of a thick, leathery, ochre or yellowish-brown skin, is cracked, tessellated, and ornamented with darker scales. If young specimens are cut through, the central fertile area is initially yellowish-white, but this quickly changes to reddish-violet with fine white marbling, then to a slate-grey colour, finally becoming purplish-black and powdery. In fully mature specimens a jagged, roundish opening appears in the centre of the sphere through which the spores are dispersed.

Spore powder: Purplish-black.

Distribution: *S. citrinum* is widespread and common throughout the British Isles where it tends to grow on poor, acid soils especially on heathland, but also in deciduous woodland. Its fruit bodies appear as early as July and on into the autumn.

Possible confusion: *S. verrucosum* is very similar, but its skin is scarcely thicker than 1 mm even when young. It has a well-formed stem with root-like strands of mycelium. *S. areolatum* is even more similar and requires microscopic study to confirm its identity.

Edibility: Slightly poisonous. Nevertheless some collectors use young specimens as a flavouring. One should refrain from this, as consumption can cause unpleasant digestive disorders.

Notes: *Citrinum* means 'lemon-yellow'.

Calvatia excipuliformis

The **fruit body** is generally long-stemmed with a swollen head, less commonly pear-shaped or top-shaped. It reaches a height of 7–12(15) cm, with the head mostly up to 10 cm in diameter. The fungus is very variable in form and size, but always higher than it is wide and always with an obvious **stem**. The exterior is covered with fine spines or scurfy dusty granules on a cream to ochre background. The junction between head and stem is often marked by a groove and lower down the surface becomes smoother. The skin is thin and fragile and when mature falls off in irregular flakes, while the surface of the 'stem' remains intact. The fertile interior of the head is initially white, turning dark cocoa-brown and powdery when the spores are mature. In the stem portion the structure is cellular and brown.

Spore powder: Olive-brown.

Distribution: *C. excipuliformis* can be found fairly frequently from early summer until late autumn in deciduous and coniferous woodland, but also away from woods in meadows.

Possible confusion: Larger specimens can resemble *C. utriformis*. Smaller specimens are often mistaken for *Lycoperdon perlatum* (Common Puff-ball), but the latter has more prominently spiny fruit bodies.

Edibility: This large fungus is considered edible, even if its skin remains leathery after prolonged cooking. It can be eaten as long as the flesh is completely white.

Notes: *Excipulum* means 'goblet, vessel' and *forma* means 'shape' (because of the shape of the fruit body).

Calvatia utriformis

The **fruit body**, more broadly pear-shaped than spherical, can reach a diameter of 12–15(20) cm. The upper portion generally appears a little depressed or flattened. Young fungi are covered with fine **spines** which are often fused at their tips in groups. In older fruit bodies, however, these warts disappear and the surface becomes cracked into more or less hexagonal areas. Toward the base the fungus is plicate and folded with thick anchoring strands of mycelium. At first the fruit body appears whitish, but soon turns a greyish-white and when old often has a more or less golden-yellow colour. The interior of the young fruit body is initially white and fleshy, but becomes a greenish-yellow, then a dark olive-brown and powdery as the spores mature. This spore mass is said to smell vaguely of carbolic, but such claims concerning smell should be treated with caution and not regarded as an important diagnostic feature.

Spore powder: Dark brown.

Distribution: More common in the north, occasional elsewhere, chiefly in fields and heathland from summer until late autumn. The old empty cup-shaped sterile base often persists for many months.

Possible confusion: *C. excipuliformis*, described here, can vaguely resemble it but has a more clavate shape. *Langermannia gigantea* (Giant Puff-ball) is considerably larger, has a smooth upper surface, and more spherical shape.

Edibility: It is edible so long as the inside is still white.

Notes: *Utriformis* means 'looking like a water-skin'.

Langermannia gigantea **Giant Puff-ball**

The white, spherical **fruit body** can be up to 100 cm in diameter and can weigh 20 or even 25 kg, though generally they are considerably smaller than this. The surface is predominantly white but on closer inspection one can see that it can also be slightly yellowish or brownish-yellow. Despite its large size it has a very fragile surface which can be damaged by even slight pressure. When fully mature the outer surface falls away in large pieces and the cottony interior is revealed, i.e. the gleba. This is white and fleshy when young but when mature is brown and cottony holding the powdery spores.

Spore powder: Olive-brown.

Distribution: *L. gigantea* is occasional and widespread. It grows in meadows and pastures, waste places among nettles, woods, etc. from early summer into autumn.

Possible confusion: This large fungus cannot be confused with others. Its development, too, proceeds so rapidly that even shortly after its first appearance it has reached dimensions way beyond that of other puff-balls.

Edibility: As long as the flesh is completely white, it is a sought-after and very tasty edible fungus. It is cut into slices and fried like cutlets, either with or without breadcrumbs.

Notes: *Gigantea* means 'gigantic, enormous'.

259

Geastrum sessile

The *Geastrum* species (The Latin name meaning 'earth star'), of which one species is here depicted and discussed as representative of the entire group, are among the most beautiful and striking of the fungi. The growth habit is typical of all *Geastrum* species: a spherical spore sac surrounded by stellate rays. Initially the **fruit body** has a closed structure but in the course of development the outer layer splits, giving rise to a number of pointed rays which either spread out flat or have their tips turned under, resulting in a star-like appearance. The rays which may be slightly arched and especially if rolled under at the tips, raise the peridium or spore sac above the surrounding humus, etc. At maturity the spore sac ruptures at the tip, leaving a pore through which the spores are dispersed. *G. sessile* is, when opened, 2–5 cm across. The outer layer of the fruit body splits into five to eight pointed rays. These are yellowish-ochre in young specimens and rolled under, while the spherical spore sac, 1–1.5 cm in diameter, is grey-brown in colour, with a central pore seated on a raised, slightly pointed mouth.

Spore powder: Cocoa-brown.

Distribution: *G. sessile* is uncommon or local in deciduous woodland. In central Europe there are about twenty-five different species of *Geastrum*, most of which are quite rare. They fruit in autumn.

Possible confusion: Species of *Geastrum* are impossible to confuse with other fungi.

Edibility: They are inedible, and because of their rarity they should certainly be left in the interest of conservation.

Notes: *Sessile* means 'sitting'.

Cyathus striatus

The **fruit body** of young specimens is closed and top-shaped or funnel-shaped and the outside is covered with tufts of shaggy reddish-brown hairs. Gradually an opening develops at the apex, that is to say, the covering of hairs splits, and beneath it a thin, white membrane becomes visible, the so-called *epiphragma*. As maturation continues this membrane also ruptures and exposes the shiny, greyish-white interior which is coarsely plicate or fluted. On the rim one cannot overlook the fringe of shaggy hairs. In the base of the funnel there are several egg-like, lenticular spore sacs, each about 3 mm in diameter and known as peridioles, which are attached by short **stalks** to the sides of the cup and bedded in a jelly-like material. Within these sacs the spores mature. The fruit bodies have an overall diameter of 1–1.5 cm and are about 1 cm high.

Spores: White.

Distribution: Occasional, mainly in woodland which is rich in humus, among mouldering leaves, on rotting branches, and rotting deciduous stumps.

Possible confusion: There are a number of other *Cyathus* species in central Europe, of which *C. olla* is similar. In this species, however, the inside of the cup is shiny and smooth, without fluting. *C. olla* occurs in gardens and on cultivated land. It, too, grows on the remains of dead plants and on charcoal.

Edibility: The fungus is not edible.

Notes: The peridioles are ejected for up to 50 cm by the force of raindrops falling into the funnel-shaped fruit bodies. A fine thread on the peridiole is then pulled free and becomes wrapped around nearby vegetation. The spores are released as the peridiole decays. *Striatus* means 'striated'.

Phallus impudicus   Stinkhorn

The complete fungus expands in a few hours from the so-called 'witches egg', an oval spongy or gelatinous structure half buried in the ground. The fungus consists of a pendent bell-shaped **cap**, 3–4(6) cm across, with a perforated apex. It is covered by the dark green gleba, which smells very unpleasantly of rotting flesh and contains the spores. Most of this slime is eaten by insects, which are primarily responsible for the dispersal of the spores. When this glutinous mass is removed, a honeycomb network is revealed, reminiscent of a morel. The head stands atop a white **stem**, up to 20 cm tall and 2–4 cm thick, which is a very fragile sponge-like structure, hollow inside. At the base the remains of the jelly-like 'egg' form a volva-like structure.

Spore mass: Greenish and glutinous.
Distribution: The Stinkhorn is very common throughout the British Isles in all kinds of woodland, parks, gardens, etc. Its presence, often from early summer, is easy to detect, for the smell carries to distances of 15–20 m.

Possible confusion: *Ph. hadriani* is similar in structure and growth, but it has a pink or violet-coloured egg and grows with dune grasses.

Edibility: The fungus is inedible. Again and again one comes across collectors who dig up the eggs, cut them through and eat the inner core raw, or who remove the jelly layer and slice and eat the egg. These practices probably rest on its supposed aphrodisiac quality as the shape of the fungus has always caught people's imagination.

Notes: *Impudicus* means 'shameless'.

Mutinus caninus   Dog Phallus or Dog Stinkhorn

The white oval then cylindrical egg ruptures at the apex and a tall, fragile, finger-shaped receptacle emerges, 8–12 cm long and 1–1.5 cm thick. The top 1–1.5 cm of the hollow, spongy, pitted creamy to orange shaft is covered with the fertile olive-green, glutinous, unpleasant-smelling spore mass, the gleba. The tip which is perforated appears bright orange-red after removal of the spore mass by insects. Mature fruit bodies soon collapse onto the ground.

Spore mass: Yellowish-green and glutinous.

Distribution: *M. caninus* is widespread but uncommon. It grows in deciduous and coniferous woods rich in humus, often around old stumps, among leaves and needles and in sawdust, either singly, or more often gregariously, sometimes in large colonies. July to October.

Possible confusion: *M. ravenelii* is very similar in shape and colour, though the *receptaculum* is much redder and the gleba smells more strongly of rotting flesh. The fungus was probably imported into Europe from North America and is not known in Britain. It was first seen in Berlin in 1942. It grows in glasshouses, gardens and parks. *M. elegans* is larger, its tip much narrower than the stem, and the spores are larger.

Edibility: Inedible.

Notes: *M. caninus* is grouped with the *Gasteromycetes*, the class to which the puff-balls also belong. The genus *Mutinus* is represented by four species in Europe, some of which appear only sporadically. They are saprophytes, living in soil or on rotting wood. *Caninus* means 'pertaining to the dog'.

Anthurus archeri

This fungus develops from a so-called 'witches egg', slightly sunk into the ground. This egg has a whitish-pink, brown-flecked outer surface (peridium). If it is cut through, a gelatinous layer and the whitish-pink embryonic **fruit body** can be seen. When the egg is ruptured the fruit body is seen to consist of four to seven star-shaped arms borne on a short cylindrical stalk and a volva. The arms are porous and fragile, growing to about (10)12 cm and pointed at the tips. The red or reddish-orange surface is covered by a dark, greenish layer of mucilage, the gleba, which has an intense smell of rotting flesh which attracts flies and other insects. As with *Phallus impudicus* (Stinkhorn) and *M. caninus* (Dog Stinkhorn), the glutinous spore mass is removed by insects and the spores are carried away either on, or in their bodies so spreading the fungus.

Spore mass: Grey-green and glutinous.
Distribution: Originally native to Australia, was first found in Europe in about 1914 in the Vosges and has since been spreading rapidly. At present it can be found in any area including northern Spain, Belgium, Lower Saxony as far as the north edge of the Harz mountains, through Czechoslovakia as far as Styria and into Italy. It is well established in southern England. It prefers deciduous and mixed woodland with slightly acid soils, but it can also be found in pine forests and away from woodland in damp meadows. July to September.
Possible confusion: In the tropics and subtropics a similar species *Aseroe rubra* grows. However, this fungus is only known in glasshouses in Europe.
Edibility: Inedible.

Clathrus ruber   Basket Fungus or Latticework Fungus

From the so-called 'witches egg' there emerges in the course of development, which takes only a few hours, a roundish, red, mesh-like **fruit body** with a diameter and height of 5–10 cm. On the inside of the fragile arms is the glutinous dark green spore mass, the gleba. Insects are attracted by the smell of rotting flesh and quickly consume the gluten and with it the spores, and in doing so spread the spores which stick to their bodies. At the base of the fruit body is the remnant of the egg or volva. In old specimens the 'basket' finally breaks apart and disintegrates.
Spore mass: Greenish and glutinous.
Distribution: Rare in southern England, especially in the Isle of Wight, often in gardens. This fungus, very rare in central Europe where it only appears sporadically, but much commoner in the Mediterranean, grows in woods, vineyards and meadows,

chiefly in damper spots. It is found between summer and autumn.
Possible confusion: The colour and smell, and the manner of growth (egg), could lead to its being confused with *Anthurus archeri*, but the latter expands like a star or starfish from the start, so real confusion can be ruled out.
Edibility: It goes without saying that one ought not to eat this beautiful fungus. It should also be spared because of its rarity. Every collector and photographer with a feeling for nature will admire this flower-like fungus and preserve it.
Notes: The genus *Clathrus* is represented in southern and central Europe by this one species. *Clathrus* means 'bars' and *ruber* means 'red'.

265

Pseudohydnum gelatinosum   Jelly Tongue

The **fruit bodies** have a semicircular or shell-shaped form. They reach 5–8 cm across and 1–1.5 cm thick. The upper surface is covered with velvety hairs. It is milky-white or slightly grey, though occasionally violet-brown, dark brown or even velvet-black specimens are found. The underside of the fruit body is thickly covered with pyramidal spines, 2–4 mm long. These spines are whitish or bluish, a light grey-blue colour predominating. The fruit bodies are attached laterally to wood although sometimes they have a short, thick **stem**. The flesh is watery and jelly-like, and even after drying it remains cartilaginous. Its vague colouration depends on the colour of the surface.

Spore print: Whitish.

Distribution: Although widespread but rare in Britain, it is found all over the temperate zone of the northern hemisphere.

Fruit bodies are found from September to November, growing on old, rotten coniferous wood. It favours tree stumps, though sometimes grows on rotting wood on the forest floor. It grows gregariously, often forming intricate colonies.

Possible confusion: The features of this fungus allow an unambiguous identification on the spot: the jelly-like flesh, the teeth or spines on the underside, and the ice-like colour. The genus *Pseudohydnum* consists of just this one species.

Edibility: The Jelly Tongue is edible.

Notes: The spines on the underside increase in the spore-producing surface. *Gelatinosus* means 'slippery'.

Tremiscus helvelloides   Jelly Trumpet

Young **fruit bodies** of the Jelly Trumpet have a spatula or tongue-shaped form; older specimens are shaped like a funnel. A striking feature is that the fruit body always has a deep split on one side. The form is very variable. The edge of the fruiting body is undulating and inrolled, often lobed. The upper or inner surface is initially smooth, later somewhat wrinkled. It is yellowish-red to dark orange in colour, eventually becoming a reddish-brown, and has a translucent appearance. Below it runs into a short, flattened **stem**. This is a pale reddish colour, whitish at the base. The fertile spore-producing layer is on the outside of the fruit body, and has a frosty bloom. The fungus reaches 5–10 cm in height and 4–7 cm in width. The **flesh** is less strongly coloured than the surface, and has a gelatinous consistency. In the stem, the flesh is more cartilaginous.

Spore print: White.

Distribution: Rare in Britain but well established in a few sites scattered over the country, associated with conifers. In Europe hardly ever found in the plains: it is a mountain fungus, rare below 350 m. It colonizes open places, the edges of forest paths, old storage areas for timber and similar places. It favours chalky soils.

Possible confusion: The fungus cannot be mistaken because of its strange shape and striking colour. Similar in form are *Otidea leporina* (Hare's Ear) and *Otidea onotica* (Donkey's Ear). They, too, can occur in clusters but are brownish or yellowish in colour and have brittle flesh.

Edibility: Like few others, this fungus can be eaten raw, in salads, for example.

Notes: The genus *Tremiscus* is represented by this single species in Europe.

267

Auricularia auricula-judae (Syn. Hirneola auricula-judae) Jew's Ear

The **fruit body** reaches about 4–10 cm across and is thin-fleshed, tough, jelly-like and flexible. The name comes from the shape, which is reminiscent of an ear. But this 'ear' can also be shell-shaped, or more commonly helmet-shaped, attached directly to the substrate or narrowing into a stem-like base. The colour range is olive-brown, shades of red and violet-grey. The smooth, shiny interior with its raised irregular folds, bears the sporulating layer, while the sterile outside is downy or velvety and greyish. In dry weather the fruit bodies become cartilaginous and shrink considerably, but become jelly-like again when moist conditions return. The jelly-like **flesh** has no particular taste or smell.

Spore print: White.

Distribution: Widespread and very common in Britain especially on elder and is widespread in southern and central Europe,

but is not found north of the fifty-seventh parallel of latitude. In Germany it occurs from the coast up into the Alps to heights of 1,000 m. It grows on elder, but also on other deciduous hosts. Recently, finds on red-berried elder have been reported. The fruit bodies can be found throughout the year, depending on the weather, a first flush occurring in early spring.

Possible confusion: A. mesenterica is conspicuously zoned and very hairy or felted on the upper surface. The underside is also veined or folded, and its flesh gelatinous. The species is common in Britain especially on stumps of elm.

Edibility: The Jew's Ear is a good edible species.

Notes: Auricula-judae means Jew's Ear. Judas Iscariot is said to have hanged himself from an elder.

Fuligo septica Flowers of Tan

The slime fungi, to which Flowers of Tan belongs, have caused taxonomists a problem but currently they are inclined to regard them as a separate division within the plant kingdom, alongside the other divisions, such as the true fungi (to which all other species in this volume belong), the mosses, ferns and seed-bearing plants. The reason for this is the strange biology of slime moulds. They occur in two quite different forms. In the vegetative state they consist of a simple slime or plasmodium with many cell-nuclei; many individual cells are joined together. These groups of cells are mobile, they shorten at one end and 'creep' at the other. This is termed 'amoeboid motion', because among single-celled animals, the amoeba moves in this way. Such a naked cell group is, of course, dependent on an environment with high humidity. This is why slime fungi are quite common in our forests,

even if we do not always notice them. One only becomes aware of these 'fungi' when they form fruiting bodies. The plasmodial groups move towards the light, come to rest, and form variously shaped fruit bodies which are very brittle and fragile with an outer egg shell-like surface. In this phase they can withstand dry conditions. Within the fruit body, which is often minute, spores are formed. Today the number of known slime fungi is estimated at 500. One species which is striking because of its vivid yellow plasmodium is Flowers of Tan. It is found on rotten wood on the forest floor, but also on rotting leaves or on lawns. It is occasional. Young **fruit bodies** are yellow and slimy while older ones have a yellowish-white skin and a blackish spore mass. June to October.

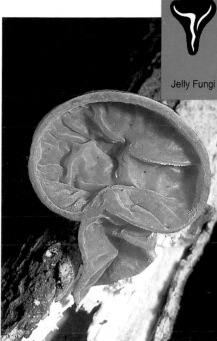

Cup and Morels

Morchella conica

The **fruit body** can reach 20(25) cm in height. The cap, accounting for ½ to ⅔ of the length of the fungus, is an elongated, pointed cone. The edge of the cap which is marked by a furrow, has a diameter 2–8 cm. Pronounced ridges run parallel from top to bottom and are joined by weaker cross-ridges so that the surface resembles a honeycomb. The colour varies between grey-brown and olive-brown, the ribs turning darker or even black in old specimens. The hollow **stem** is, in comparison with the cap, either long or short, sometimes thickened at the base and sometimes with longitudinal grooves. It is whitish or pale ochre with rusty patches and a mealy surface. The **flesh** is elastic, odourless, and mild in flavour.

Spore powder: Whitish.

Distribution: *M. conica* is occasional but widespread, growing in woodland, around burned patches, or near ash trees. It appears from February to the end of May, depending on weather conditions, and in some years it occurs in large number.

Possible confusion: Some experts distinguish several species, other authorities regard these simply as forms of *M. conica*. For the layman, the differences are hardly perceptible. The fungus is very variable in form and size, according to habitat and age, though the substrate may also play a role. *M. elata* is scarcely distinguishable: the join between stem and cap and the colour and arrangement of the ribs are said to be different. The author, however, has found these features on *M. conica* growing in the same place and often joined at the base of the stem.

Edibility: All these morels are edible and good.

Notes: *Conica* means 'cone-shaped'.

Morchella esculenta   Common Morel

The **fruit body** of this morel can be 10–20(30) cm tall. The almost round **cap**, only seldom elongated, is about ½ or ⅔ the length of the stem and can reach a diameter of 4–8(10) cm. The entire head is formed of deep, honeycomb-like pits, the so-called alveoli. The colour varies from a pale ochre to a light brownish-yellow. The caps are always hollow, as are the lighter but similar coloured stems, which can reach diameters of 2–4 cm. Towards the base the stem thickens obviously, displaying a fine mealy or granular surface covered with wrinkles.

Spore powder: Yellowish-white.

Distribution: The Common Morel is widespread but occasional under hedges, on grassy woodland margins, under ash trees, near burned areas, on poor and rich soils alike. It grows singly or gregariously from April to May.

Possible confusion: The Common Morel, too, is very variable. Some authorities divide it into several species and varieties, but variations in colour and form can often be found in one and the same collection. The substrate and habitat appear to play a major role in this variation.

Edibility: All morels are prized edible mushrooms.

Notes: The morels can be divided into three groups: the ridged *conica* group, the honeycombed *esculenta* group, and the half-free, *mitrophora* group. The last represented by *Mitrophora semilibera*, has a relatively tall stem surmounted by a small cap with a free margin. The morels are *ascomycetes*, forming their spores inside cylindrical asci, which line the pits of the cap. *Esculenta* means 'edible'.

Gyromitra esculenta **False Morel**

From above, the whole **fruit body** looks like a brain with its many lobes and convolutions. It can reach a height of 6–12 cm and a breadth of 5–15(20) cm. Closer examination, however, reveals a **cap** and stem. The cap is chestnut-brown to reddish-brown, with more and more blackish patches as it matures. The **stem** is generally short, wrinkled and grooved, thicker at the base and more or less hollow. The surface which has a fine mealy coating, is white to reddish brown. The cap sometimes almost envelops it, so that to observe it the fungus must be twisted out of the ground or cut away just above ground level. The **flesh** is very fragile with no particular smell or taste.

Spore powder: Whitish.

Distribution: The False Morel is found in coniferous woods, especially under pines, but also around roots and trunks or on cleared areas and tips with chippings and sawdust. It generally appears from March or April to May. It is quite rare.

Possible confusion: *G. infula* is slightly similar. It does not appear until autumn. Not so the very rare *G. gigas*, which also grows early in the year, and which needs a microscopic examination for positive identification.

Edibility: It is considered poisonous and has caused deaths. It is possible that the mechanism of poisoning is similar to that which operates in the case of *Paxillus involutus* (Roll Rim) (page 180).

Notes: *Esculenta* means 'edible'. This species name must be retained for taxonomic reasons, although the fungus is very poisonous when raw.

Helvella crispa **Common White Helvella**

The fragile **fruit body** is divided into cap and stem. The **cap**, 2–5 cm across, is made up of several saddle-shaped, irregular, curled and undulating lobes. The edges are turned down and not attached to the stem. The upper surface (fertile layer) is whitish or dirty ochre, later vaguely brownish and smooth. The underside is more or less the same colour and slightly downy or finely hairy. The **stem**, 1–4 cm thick and up to about 10 cm long, is cylindrical, sometimes slightly thicker at the base. Its whitish surface has prominent longitudinal ribs giving a fanciful resemblance to a miniature stick of celery. The **flesh** is fragile.

Spore powder: Whitish.

Distribution: Widespread, growing from August to November singly or gregariously in deciduous and mixed woodland. It favours woodland margins or roadside verges in grass and underneath bushes.

Possible confusion: Common White Helvella grows about the same time and in similar situations as *H. lacunosa*, and the latter can be recognized by its grey-brown or nearly black colour. Common White Helvella never has grey or black shades.

Edibility: This fungus is edible, but with reservations. Raw, it is probably just as poisonous as *Gyromitra esculenta* (False Morel), and it can only be eaten if cooked.

Notes: The large genus *Helvella* is distinguished by smooth spores with a large oil droplet, and more research is needed to help define the species. *Crispus* means 'curled'.

Otidea onotica   Donkey's Ear

The **fruit body** can be up to about 8(10) cm tall and 6 cm across. The form really can be very reminiscent of donkey's ears, the edges of the erect fruit bodies remaining more or less inrolled. The fertile inside is smooth, while the outside is slightly mealy and, lower down, rather wrinkled. The fungus is an attractive yellow-ochre colour outside and a reddish-pink inside. The **flesh** is whitish, thin and fragile, without smell or taste.

Spore powder: Whitish.

Distribution: The Donkey's Ear is not common. It is found occasionally on the ground in deciduous and coniferous woods, in quite dense clusters in summer and autumn.

Possible confusion: Can be confused with other species of its genus. For instance, it resembles the yellow *O. concinna* – the external colour difference is the best diagnostic feature, and this is best appreciated when the two fungi are side by side and can be compared directly. This fungus grows in deciduous woods on mossy ground under beeches, and it is considerably smaller. *O. cochleata* is more yellowish-brown to dark brown and also has more of a cup shape. Many of these *Otidea* species can only be distinguished with certainty with the aid of a microscope. It is necessary to study the whole group quite carefully to avoid mistakes.

Edibility: In southern climes people do not hesitate to pick and cook the Donkey's Ear. It is best left in the interest of conservation.

Notes: The genus *Otidea* comprises eleven species which are difficult to tell apart. Definite identification is in most cases impossible without studying the microscopic features. *Onotica* means 'like a donkey's ear'.

Otidea leporina   Hare's Ear

When fully grown, the **fruit bodies** can reach about 5 cm high and 3 cm across, though generally considerably smaller. The shape is slightly reminiscent of a hare's ear, though there are specimens with a more cup-shaped appearance. Generally one finds broad, irregular sac-like fruit bodies open on one side and with edges that are turned inwards or downwards. Towards the base they taper more and more, having a short stem-like portion which is smooth or slightly wrinkled. The inside, or fertile layer, is rust-yellow to rust-brown, the outside yellowish-brown or ochre and finely scurfy. The **flesh** is wax-like and brittle, rust-yellow to cinnamon-brown, with no particular smell or taste.

Spore powder: White.

Distribution: The Hare's Ear grows particularly in mountainous coniferous woods, on acid soils, where it appears among fallen needles and in mossy places. It occurs in small but dense groups, rarely singly, from July until November.

Possible confusion: The Hare's Ear has a series of relatives which are hard to tell apart. *O. onotica* (Donkey's Ear), described above, for example, or *O. abietina*, a rare fungus occurring in mountainous coniferous forests. It is generally smaller, with the interior orangey-reddish-brown and the outside paler. *O. alutacea* grows in deciduous woodland. It is not obviously ear-shaped. It is a dark clay colour or a dirty grey-brown, the outside paler. The rare *O. cochleata* grows on moss-covered forest floors, having an inrolled and notched edge. Some cup fungi also resemble the Hare's Ear at times.

Edibility: Though it is edible, it should be spared because it is so rare.

Notes: *Leporina* means 'pertaining to the hare'.

Leotia lubrica Jelly Babies

The **fruit bodies** are clearly divided into cap and stem, 3–8 cm high overall. The gelatinous **caps**, 1–2 cm across, are yellow, greenish-yellow or olive-brown, flattened with irregular lobes, the uneven surface having a slight umbo or a depression, the folded edge rolled under and inwards. The surface is slimy and slippery on top, smooth underneath. The fertile layer is on the upper surface of the cap. The **stem** is 2–6 cm long and 3–5 mm thick, lemon or golden-yellow, later cinnamon-brown, rough and granular, round or flattened, sometimes with longitudinal grooves solid at first, then hollow and filled with mucilage, mostly expanding into the cap. The gelatinous **flesh** is yellowish-white, smells slightly mouldy and has very little taste.

Spore powder: Yellowish-white.

Distribution: This rather uncommon and unmistakable fungus appears from July to October, gregariously, often in large clusters, on sodden, clayey patches in almost all types of woodland, preferring moist mixed woodland with beeches. Jelly Babies are widespread in Europe and are common from the coast to the alpine valleys, where they occur to a height of about 1,500 m. Only in fairly dry areas is it less common.

Possible confusion: Can be confused with *Cudonia circinans*, which, however, has a yellowish cap which is not jelly-like. Confusion with the black *L. atrovirens* is impossible because of the colour differences.

Edibility: Edible, with a rather insipid flavour.

Notes: Like the morels, it is an *ascomycete*. *Lubrica* means 'greasy, slippery'.

Tuber melanosporum Perigord Truffle

The **fruit bodies** of this sought-after edible fungus are spherical or irregularly rounded, and very variable in size, generally 2–9 cm across. The surface is covered with black four or six-sided pyramidal warts. The exterior is initially reddish-brown, later black. The flesh (the gleba) is greyish or reddish-beige in young fruit bodies, turning soot-black with maturity. In cross-section whitish or rust-coloured veins or many-branched ramifications cause the inside to look marbled. The smell of this truffle is very strongly aromatic.

Spore mass: Blackish.

Distribution: This fungus grows underground, in symbiosis with deciduous trees, principally oaks, on chalky soils, in the Mediterranean and in southern and central France. It has not been reported north of the Alps. The fruit bodies can be found from mid-November to mid-March.

Possible confusion: This fungus can be confused with other, similar truffles. *T. aestivum* (Summer Truffle), also edible, grows in humus on chalky soils under various deciduous tree species, less commonly under pines and junipers. It is covered with quite large pyramidal warts and grows from August to December.

Edibility: A highly-prized edible fungus, also known as 'the black diamond of the table'.

Notes: The numerous species of truffle are all *ascomycetes* and generally subterranean, growing at depths from a few centimetres to half a metre. The spores are released as the fruit body decomposes. The fungi generally have a very intense aroma, which is detected especially by wild pigs, which dig them up for food and so contribute to the spread of the fungus.

276

Aleuria aurantia Orange-peel Fungus

When mature, the **fruit bodies** reach 2–10 cm across. When young they are more or less hemispherical, then cup-shaped with an irregular naked edge; when old they become irregularly expanded, and flattened with undulating lobes. The fertile layer on the inside is yellowish-orange or a glowing orange-red, while outside, it is paler with a white, mealy frosting which is especially noticeable when the fruit body dries. Cup fungi are generally stemless, seated on the ground and attached at the centre. The wax-like **flesh** is thin and very fragile, without any particular smell or taste.

Spore powder: White.

Distribution: Widespread and fairly common from July to October. It usually grows gregariously, or forms veritable swarms along sandy woodland paths, on fallow land and in cleared areas. Generally it prefers bare clayey, sandy soils with a silica content, inside and outside woods.

Possible confusion: The size, the colour and the habitat make it easy to recognize this striking cup fungus. There is, admittedly, a whole series of smaller cup fungi with similar colours, but hardly any of them grow larger than 2 cm in diameter. In addition they all have either a fairly hairy edge, or darker zones near the edge, which does not apply to the Orange-peel Fungus.

Edibility: Here the opinions of gourmets differ. The Orange-peel Fungus is edible, and can be used in mushroom salad if enough of them are available.

Notes: *Aurantia* means 'orange-coloured'.

Sarcoscypha coccinea Scarlet Elf Cup

Initially chalice-shaped then cup-shaped, the **fruit body** has a diameter between 1 and 7 cm. The fertile surface is a glowing vermilion-orange colour while the sterile outer layer is pink or vaguely ochre, with very fine whitish down or tufts of hairs. If one carefully removes a specimen, it is found to have a small, short, or sometimes very long, **stem** so that the fungus may then resemble a champagne glass. The **flesh** is wax-like and tough without any particular taste or smell.

Spore powder: Whitish.

Distribution: Not uncommon in south-west England but uncommon in the east. It is found in almost all European countries, but even there it is not common. It grows in damp places on dead deciduous branches, which are often covered in moss, generally when the snow is thawing, singly and in groups during early spring.

Possible confusion: The genus *Sarcoscypha* is at present being studied by taxonomists with a view to defining the taxa. The species described above is most probably a composite species, including taxa which are said to differ both on a microscopic level and in their choice of substrate. One form is evidently rigidly dependent on lime trees, another on alders, sycamores, willows and elms. The inexperienced collector could also confuse other cup fungi with this species.

Edibility: Edible, but worth conserving.

Notes: The family *Sarcoscyphaceae* in Europe comprises seven *genera* with barely a dozen species, all of them rare. *Coccinea* means 'scarlet'.

Collecting Mushrooms

Fungi fulfil important ecological functions, not only in natural cycles but also for the many symbiotic relationships in the plant kingdom. Fungi complete much of their life cycle in the soil or in wood, but the visible fruit bodies ensure that fungi survive by the formation of spores.

Do not collect anything that looks edible, take only as many edible mushrooms as you need for a meal. If one pays heed to recent reports of contamination of wild fungi by heavy metals, massive and continued consumption of mushrooms should be avoided even in areas far from roads and industry. Spare very rare fungi, even if they are edible, but also remember that inedible and poisonous species are worthy of conservation. Direct observation in the field and the experience of specialists both in Britain and on the continent show that many mushroom collectors behave irresponsibly. In Europe the large number of cases of poisoning in recent years, many of which ended in fatalities, lend weight to this fact.

Those who collect mushrooms hastily or carelessly, or do not or cannot identify what is found accurately, run a very grave risk! The most important piece of equipment is the right sort of container. A plastic carrier bag is no good at all since the moisture given off by the fungi cannot evaporate properly. In an impermeable bag even at ordinary summer and autumn temperatures, there is a build up of heat and moisture which accelerates the process of decomposition of the fungus considerably, and which may not at first even be visible.

Another unavoidable disadvantage of the plastic bag is that its unsupported floppy nature jumbles the fungi together as they are transported. The mushrooms, especially those at the bottom of the pile, will quickly become damaged and bruised by being jolted and shaken and having the weight of other mushrooms on top of them. This, combined with the rise in temperature, will quickly reduce the mushrooms to a pulp. Eating such poorly-handled and partly decaying mushrooms can have serious consequences for your health, with much the same consequences as food poisoning caused by eating meat or fish in poor condition. A woven basket is ideal and fulfils all the requirements of a container for collecting mushrooms, – it lets the air through and does not squash the fungi. Punnets, such as those in which fruit are sold, can be used to separate the species or unknown mushrooms in the basket.

Bearing in mind the ecological functions of fungi in natural cycles, do not collect over-ripe, old or maggoty specimens. Ceps and other fungi which look perfect on the outside sometimes conceal a considerable amount of insect larvae inside! So, cut the mushroom through where you find it and avoid unnecessary waste at home.

Since no one depends on mushrooms as their only food source, only perfect specimens should find their way into the collection basket. As a nature-lover, you should refrain from picking, or digging out very young mushrooms of particularly sought-after species such as Chanterelles or Ceps. Anyone who does so is contributing to the reduction in numbers of our fungal flora. If you are only interested in edible mushrooms, remember this principle: only pick fungi which can be identified beyond all doubt! The collector of edible mushrooms, once he has definitely identified what he has found, should cut the mushroom with a short, sharp knife close to the ground. The widely-held belief that the base of a mushroom which has been cut off, rots in the ground and damages the mycelium is not true. For millions of years fruit bodies that were not picked or were eaten by animals have been rotting or decaying naturally, without affecting the continued existence of the species concerned. Breakdown of organic matter by rot and decay is a necessary natural process which does not have an effect on living organisms.

For precise identification of unknown species it is advisable to take home a few fungi in various stages of development including both young and well-formed specimens. If possible, also show them to an expert. Some collectors pick all the fungi in an area intending to identify them at home and then, if appropriate, to put them to good use. This is not recommended.

Unknown fruit bodies that you wish to take away for identification purposes should be removed very carefully along with the base of the stem by taking hold of the fruit body and carefully removing it with a knife. Do not handle the fungi unnecessarily. Important identifying features, such as nuances of colour and the form of the stem or the cap, are easily destroyed and become very hard to recognize after rough handling. Containers of aluminium foil or small cartons with lids are useful for separating unknown fungi from others collected in the basket.

Identification of fungi can pose intractable problems. The layman often thinks he can identify a fruit body simply from a photograph in his book. He pays scant or no attention at all to the introductory texts and species descriptions alongside the photographs. This approach is a game of chance which could have an unpleasant ending! Study the features of the species you think you have found in the book and compare them with the fungus in front of you. Within a genus there are often several species which are very similar. You then need to use all the information in the book as an aid to identification, without forgetting to refer to information on habitat.

Many species differ from one another in their choice of habitat, so conscientious identification begins on the spot where the fungus was found. On the other hand, there may be less time for identification in the field, or may be more literature or expert advice available at home. For this reason it is advisable to take along a paper and pencil. Nowadays there are also handy dictation machines which make note-taking easier. The most important thing to note is where and on what material the fungus is growing; this is called the substrate, and may be earth, decaying leaves, detritus of fallen needles under conifers, dead or living wood, animal droppings, other remains of plants or even parts of dead animals. In addition, you should note in what sort of woodland the specimen is growing, under what species of tree (the fungus and tree could have a mycorrhizal association), and what species of shrub is growing nearby. The surroundings need looking at as well – is the habitat dry or moist?

As well as examining the site of the fungus, one should also find out about the general soil type in the area – is it acid (low in chalk) or alkaline (lime-rich)? These concepts are familiar to the gardener and farmer, and they are expressed in the pH value of the soil. To the advanced fungus collector, and certainly to the specialist who is not just seeking edible mushrooms, knowledge of the type of soil is useful in making a definite identification of a species. Many species are specifically acid-lovers or lime-lovers. An example of a lime-loving fungus is *Suillus aeruginascens*, which forms mycorrhizal associations with larch trees. *Tylopilus felleus*, on the other hand, is found on soils low in chalk and nutrients, on acid soils in many types of woodland. On limestone rocks one usually finds alkaline soils, on sandstone and silica bases one finds acid soils. The soil of high moorland is acid, as is the surface soil in pure coniferous woodland.

A whole series of woodland plants give us information about the soil type, and are known as indicator-plants. Daphne, liverwort and coltsfoot are indicative of chalk, while wood sorrel, bilberry and many heathers point to acid soils.

As a serious fungi collector you should also know the most important native tree species, especially those which form symbiotic relationships with edible mushrooms.

Table Value

Sometimes one finds the same species described in different books as edible or inedible. People's tastes differ. Some consider the smell or taste of a mushroom pleasant and describe it as such, while others find it objectionable. The more or less marked mealy smell and taste of *Calocybe gambosa* is an example.

It is also disconcerting for the collector who suddenly finds a species which has generally been considered edible (even a commercial species), declared to be poisonous or very poisonous in a book on fungi. The investigation of unexplained causes of death and the research associated with this has led to a new understanding and to quite astounding changes in defining the edibility or otherwise of fungi. This happened in the case of *Paxillus involutus*. If contradictory claims are found in two books, look carefully at the year of publication, for the older literature may be less accurate.

Certain species of mushroom disagree with some people and not with others. The Honey Fungus, for instance, which is often used as an edible fungus, can cause diarrhoea in people with a sensitive digestive system.

Mushroom Poisoning

At the first sign of mushroom poisoning, a doctor should be called.

It can take fifteen minutes, forty-eight hours or several days from consumption to the first appearance of symptoms of poisoning. There is no patent cure which can be applied to all cases of mushroom poisoning and no antidote that one can take. Vomiting can only help if the mushrooms are still in the stomach.

For the doctor to be able to give effective treatment, it is vital to identify the poisonous mushroom involved. Waste from preparation, left-overs, even dried mushrooms, can be placed before an expert.

Exercise consideration when collecting mushrooms. In many nature reserves it is forbidden to wander away from the marked paths. Plantations and agricultural ground, which might be damaged if walked on, should be avoided. For example, hay fields from May onwards. If people behave responsibly, woods and meadows will remain open to all. If in doubt, a polite enquiry can prevent trouble later. Nature lovers should also be considerate towards wild animals. Their habitat is subject to many pressures and is growing smaller by the day, and collecting can disturb their feeding, resting or nesting. No doubt mushroom collectors represent yet another disturbance to the routine of deer, for instance. It is in the interests of people who enjoy the outdoors to exercise consideration and not disturb the wildlife of woodlands.

Picture Credits

Bibliography

Bon, M. *The Mushrooms and Toadstools of Britain and North-Western Europe* (Hodder and Stoughton, 1987). ·

Dähncke, R. M. & Dähncke S.M. *700 Pilze in Farbfotos* (A. T. Verlag, 1980).

Kibby, G. *Mushrooms and Toadstools, a Field Guide* (OUP 1979).

Kühner, R. & Romagnesi, H. *Flore Analytique des Champignons Supérieurs* (Masson, 1953).

Lange, M. & Bayard Hora, F. *Collins Guide to Mushrooms and Toadstools* (Collins, 1978).

Moser, M. *Keys to Agarics and Boleti* (Roger Phillips, 1983).

Nilsson, S. & Persson, O. *Fungi of Northern Europe: 1. Larger Fungi (excluding gill-fungi); 2. Gill-fungi,* edited by D. N. Pegler & B. Spooner (Penguin Books Ltd., 1978).

Pacioni, G. *The Macdonald Encyclopedia of Mushrooms and Toadstools* (Macdonald, 1985).

Phillips, R. *Mushrooms and other Fungi of Great Britain and Europe* (Pan, 1981).

Rayner, R. *Mushrooms and Toadstools* (Hamlyn, 1979).

Reid, D. *Mushrooms and Toadstools* (Kingfisher, 1980).

Soothill, E. & Fairhurst, A. *A New Field Guide to Fungi* (Michael Joseph, 1978).

Index